P9-BHT-242

I NOVISSIMI

A Blue Guitar Book
Edited by Luigi Ballerini
and Paul Vangelisti

I NOVISSIMI

Poetry for the Sixties

[I Novissimi. Poesie per gli anni '60]

EDITED AND WITH A NEW PREFACE TO
THE AMERICAN EDITION BY
ALFREDO GIULIANI

Prose and Notes Translated by David Jacobson
Poetry Translated by Luigi Ballerini, Bradley Dick,
Michael Moore, Stephen Sartarelli, and Paul Vangelisti

SUN & MOON

MOON

CLASSICS

55

SUN & MOON PRESS, LOS ANGELES
1995

Sun & Moon Press
A Program of The Contemporary Arts Educational Project, Inc.
a nonprofit corporation
6026 Wilshire Boulevard, Los Angeles, California 90036

This edition first published in paperback in 1995 by Sun & Moon Press
10 9 8 7 6 5 4 3 2 1
FIRST ENGLISH LANGUAGE EDITION
Published orginally as *I Novissimi. Poesie per gli anni '60*
©1961 by Rusconi e Paolazzi Editore
Reprinted by permission of Giulio Einaudi Editore (Torino)
English langauge translation ©1995 by Luigi Ballerini and Paul Vangelisti
Preface to the American Edition (1992) ©1995 by Alfredo Giuliani
Biographical material ©1995 by Sun & Moon Press
All rights reserved

This book was made possible, in part, through an operational grant from the
Andrew W. Mellon Foundation, through a translation grant from
the Ministero degli Affari Esteri (Italy), and through contributions to
The Contemporary Arts Educational Project, Inc.,
a nonprofit corporation

Cover: based on the original cover art
Design: Katie Messborn
Typography: Guy Bennett

LIBRARY OF CONGRESS CATALOGING IN PUBLICATION DATA

I Novissimi
Poetry for the Sixties
p. cm — (Sun & Moon Classics: 55)
ISBN: 1-55713-137-6
I. Title. II. Series.
811'.54—dc20

Printed in the United States of America on acid-free paper.

Without limiting the rights under copyright reserved here, no part of
this publication may be reproduced, stored in or introduced into
a retrieval system, or transmitted, in any form or by any means
(electronic, mechanical, photocopying, recording or otherwise),
without the prior written permission of both the copyright owner
and the above publisher of the book.

EDOARDO SANGUINETI

NANNI BALESTRINI

ANTONIO PORTA

Behind the Poetry

Biographies

PREFACE TO THE AMERICAN EDITION

(1992)

Invention is the task of criticism. Saint-Beuve said it first and Alberto Savinio repeated it in our own century. This book, conceived more than 30 years ago, surely was the result of a period of frustration, research and exciting discovery, begun at least a decade earlier. But the result was not obvious. Those were effervescent years, 'critical' and creative years, difficult to recount. In the tradition of the Italian 20th centrury, poetry could flaunt its strength, rich in personality and style polished to perfection. At the end of World War II, all expected a revolution in poetic style, a renewal of its discourse. On the other hand, lyric poetry as a genre was losing the supremacy it had achieved between the wars. Some wished that the form of poetic discourse would become "populist," this giving rise to many misunderstandings. The sophisticated analogies, confessional tone, symbolistic ambiguities of the recently bygone era no longer had any grip on reality. Few, however, were able to realize that the historical depletion of the great poetry blossomed between the two wars meant the end of a particular language, the end of its active function. The new language had to create its own canons. Something was stirring, but at the time this anthology was being conceived an explicit tendency towards a new poetics did not exist.

A group of poets had not rallied around the project of a new style. Nor did I ever have the intention to put one together. I simply had indentified the formative nucleus shared by certain authors, extremely different one from the other, who had arrived at their own programmatic ideas independent of each other. I called that nucleus: *schizo-morphic vision*. This means: to intensify the expression of discontinuity in the imaginative process, to employ a ruptured syntax and weave dissonant propositions within a completely semanticized metric texture. It means: to give a rhythm to heterogeneous lexicons, to the short circuiting of events, to the perpetually disturbed nexuses of reality. Naturally this was the critical invention that enabled me to put together five authors as disparate as we were; and that enabled me to write my best poems *after* the anthology appeared. The *schizomorphic vision* was not an expedient, was not a gimmick. It was the only serious way to tie method and madness into a single knot. The only psychological, psychiatrical, philosophical, historical way possible. And poetically appropriate. I have always been, and still am, willing to support both the schizomorphic method and vision with an inexhaustible repetoire of arguments. But it is also logically inevitable that I have outgrown this book. That I have often *moved* forward, back, sideways, up and down. Thus I feel somewhat peculiar having to introduce *I Novissimi* to readers of English decades after its first appearance.

Today the book is an archeological find, a mechanism rich in interesting contraptions, with a period design, to be exhibited in the museum of contemporary poetry. But then, when first presented to Italian readers, it exuded vitality and provoked almost unanimously rabid reactions and incredulous sneers on the part of the reviewers. Come on, gentlemen, didn't the avantgarde do all of this in the teens and twenties? Whom do you think you are kidding? One of the few favorable critics was, as might be expected, Luciano Anceschi, who could happily write: now, at last, postwar poetry is over. (It was 1961.) I must say the most intelligent, competent and serene review, came out three years later in the *Times Literary Supplement* (September 3). The anonymous reviewer affirmed, among other things: "Although their *stil nuovo* is far from *dolce*, they seem to be working in a spirit that resembles Cavalcanti's or Dante's own, refashioning the poetic vernacular."

INTRODUCTION TO THE FIRST EDITION
(1961)

The aim of "true contemporary poetry," remarked Leopardi in 1829, "is to increase vitality"; and, having made this unsettling observation, he added that in times like his own poetry was rarely capable of such a feat. Being neither classicists nor crepuscular poets, we have a linguistic concept of vitality that we shall attempt to explain. Undoubtedly in every age poetry cannot be "true" unless it is "contemporary"; and if we ask ourselves, contemporary with what?, we meet with a single response: with our sense of reality, or rather with the language that reality speaks within us by its irreconcilable signs. The said *increase* comes from an opening, a shock, which puts within our grasp an occurrence in which we may find ourselves once more.

Such is the background, and, if you will, the state of mind that generated the idea of the present collection. The somewhat apocalyptic title we have given ourselves is the handiwork of Sanguineti, who, in answer to a recent survey about poetry spoke, precisely, of the "latest possible innovation historically available."[1] I think one should interpret "innovation" above all as a deliberate departure from those rather hackneyed and often weightily didactic modes that perpetuate the so-called Novecento while pretending to overturn it through the mechanism of "contents." What much of recent poetry finally offers us is nothing but a form of neo-crepuscularism, a relapse into the 'hostile reality' one tries to flee by adopting hortatory and weak-willed rationalism, sociology and even, if you will, Carducci's poetic legacy. To my mind this is a matter of a mistaken attitude in a dubious operation. I have been careful to isolate a series of poetic intentions that, while they may differ greatly from one another, still share certain essential traits; far from being merely programmatic, they are verifiable in the texts. None of us is set on proving a point, or making "exposés" in any sense: each of us has cultivated, without pieties, his own capacity for contact with the linguistic forms of reality. It is my assumption that our vocation to know will be evident, legible in what we write, and not presumed in what we proclaim we want to write. We think that in speaking of ourselves or of other things or of nothing (*de dreit nien*) poetry must open up a passage: in mirroring reality, it must answer our need to go "through the looking-glass." It seems that of the poets assembled here only Pagliarani has chosen to deal with the problem of literary "realism"; yet he has done so by always *tackling* that lived reality, never assuming it to be a content sufficient in itself to make a new poetry. The rest of us have made a theoretical ques-

1 In *Fiera letteraria,* July 3, 1960.

tion of truth, of structural renewal, not a "compulsary realism."

The question of renewal goes back to the beginnings of the post-war period, when it dawned on us that the glamorous language we had inherited from our "modern" tradition was, like Dora Markus' ivory mouse, an amulet. Of course, it would be unfair to forget that any language, insofar as it is life-sustaining, valiantly fulfills its own apotropaic function. But poetry expresses in its whole being a way of thinking and feeling. Why are we so concerned with diction, syntax, meter, and so on? Because if we grant that, in its "contemporaneity," poetry acts directly on the reader's vitality, then what matters most is its linguistic efficacy. What poetry *does* is precisely its "content": if, let's say, it induces sighs or boredom, its truth is ultimately the reader's sigh or tedium. And in periods of crisis the *modus operandi* coincides almost totally with *meaning*.

When I first read Luciano Anceschi's anthology, *Lirici nuovi*, much of the poetry in it excited me so, I could only relate it to the Rimbaud I had stormily read in my high school years, and which had stayed in my memory in a sort of splendid tropical isolation. These "new" poets were ideally suited to please twenty-year-olds: precious, airy, anti-rhetorical, bashfully pathetic, they seemed to live a mysterious, intense private life in a wholly emblematic, sensitive world. Perhaps it was by virtue of these very qualities that in almost no time their language was shackling all our impulses, and falling short of what was becoming our *experience*. The subject came up a hundred times in the debates of those years, and hardly bears repetition. You would have to have perceived the "modern" tradition falling rapidly behind to understand the distress, and finally the decisiveness, of our emergence as contemporaries. With the end of stylistic 'prosperity,' which began (it helps to recall) in the time of *art nouveau*, being contemporary has become harder and harder, and, in many ways, more exciting. And it is no accident that the critic of the *Lirici nuovi* was almost the only one of his generation to recognize and support—with disinterested, penetrating attention to phenomena—the advent of the "novissimi." His was a gradual revolution, a supple game of absorption and anticipation, from the series "Oggetto e simbolo" to the founding of the journal "Il Verri" and its subsequent development in the direction shown by the liveliest new trends.

Between the "new" and the "newest" there is no continuity but rupture. The coherence comes in having progressed beyond the by-now arid exercise of a "style," to a more impersonal and extensive "writing"—the famous "experimentalism." Everything has changed in a matter of a few years: vocabulary, syntax, verse form, compositional structure. The *tone* has changed; today the perspective implicit in the very act of writing poetry is different from what it was yesterday. Whereas it looked as though the possibilities of "speaking in verse" had shrunk, we have broadened them, indeed making use of that "facility" of which some of us have at times been accused. It is certainly true that if the only rite our culture still practices is "tearing off the mask," we have gone further in the unmasking, challenging the silence that, together with the chatter, inevitably follows the decay of a language, exasperating the senselessness, refusing to be oppressed by imposed meanings, telling with affection and glee stories, thoughts, trifling anecdotes, from this schizophrenic age.

Since all language tends today to become a commodity, one cannot take for granted a single word or grammatical form or syntagm. The harshness and sobriety, the analytical fury, the irreverent jolts, the unexpected use of discourse, "prose,"—in short, all that one expects not to find in other poems and one finds in our poems, should also be considered from this vantage point. On the one hand, the passion of "speaking in verse" jars with today's enveloping consumption and the commercial exploitation to which language is subjected; on the other hand, it jars with its literary code, which maintains the inertia of things, and institutes *the abuse of the habitual* (the fictitious "that's how it is") in a vision of human relations. Thus, before looking to abstract ideology, to cultural intention, we look to the concrete semantics of poetry, mindful that it is after all an art, a *vis mitologica*: for the ideologists, on the contrary, poetry is only a pretext and as such disposed to be either Circe or the sow, depending on the purpose it must serve. For us it is quite obvious that an erroneous stance toward the problems of language is not easily explained by the havoc society wreaks. Historically, there always exists a correct position, even if, for the very reason that it is "correct," it may lead to an "experimental" fate. Here it will again be obvious how unlikely is the return of the neo-crepusculars to the redundant, descriptive ways of the nineteenth century; how futile, in the long run, the solution of those cranks who take their

stacked decks and jack-in-the-box play *in all seriousness*—
and one realizes there was nothing to them but pedantic
gesture, or a somewhat callow craving for exhibitionism.
But having said all this we must add that we also do not
share the neurotic, indiscriminate fear some poets show
toward common contemporary language. There are
forms of this mechanical esperanto of the imagination
which, despite the class manipulation they are subject to,
cannot in themselves be considered negative or positive,
but only factual: they are part of the material, the "heter-
onomous semanticity,"[2] the times give the writer. The
techniques of mass culture entail a mental decomposition
that must be taken into account by anyone recomposing
meanings of experience. It is archaic to aspire to a *contem-
plative* diction which claims to maintain, if not the value
and possibility of contemplation, its unreal syntax. Equally
outmoded is *argumentational* language which in Italian was
one of Leopardi's great inventions. Hence the "schizo-
morphic" vision by which contemporary poetry gains a
grip on itself and present-day life (and which is typified by
discontinuity of the imaginative process, *asyntactism*,[3] the
violent treatment of signs) need not justify itself as "avant-
garde" in the programmatic, marginal sense usually given
to this notion. If anything, we should be at the "center"—
and here I agree with Sanguineti[4]—of a precariousness

2 Cf. Galvano Della Volpe, *Critique of Taste*, New Left Books, 1978.

3 Gillo Dorfles has happily derived this characteristic from his own ex-
perience of contemporary art (cf. *Il divenire delle arti*, Turin, 1959, pp.
232–238).

4 Edoardo Sanguineti, "Concerning *Il Verri*," *I problemi di Ulisse*, 38, 1960.
panying the poems.

which neither exalts us irrationally nor embarrases us with what we are.

This language acquisition is of value to us only in relation to that *activity* which, as we have said, we feel coincides with "content." A writer may be rhetorically up to date, and yet reduce, rather than increase, our vitality; and rather than communicate an experience, he may use his cleverness to involve us in some private metaphor. Often the differences between an "open" and a "closed" writer seem to work to the detriment of the former. In fact the "open" writer learns from things and has no desire to teach; he does not give the impression of possessing a truth but of searching for one, and of dimly contradicting himself. He has no wish to capture benevolence or rouse admiration, since he tends to leave the initiative to the rapport that will be created in the encounter of two semantic dispositions, that of the text, and that of the reader. Of what, then, does the effect of *vitalization* in a poem seem to imply, providing that one has the patience to use it correctly? A poem is vital when it forces us beyond its own inevitable limits, that is, when the things that have inspired its words induce in us the sense of other things and other words, prompting our intervention; one ought to profit from a poem as one would from some rather extraordinary encounter.

I would like to call attention in particular to two aspects of our poems: a genuine "reduction of the I" as producer of meaning, and a corresponding versification, free of hedonism, released from that pseudo-ritual ambition that marks now-debased syllabic versification and its modern camouflages. The problem of metrics, which cannot be evaded by any form of approximation, is discussed in an essay at the end of the volume.[5] As for the reduction of the I, this is something we must be very clear about. Here too, above all, the trumped-up polemic over "content" is thoroughly unenlightening. All too often, in those poems supposedly furthest removed from 'intimism,' the I is stubbornly, proudly hidden behind a presumed objectivity. As ever, appearances are deceiving. In reality—and this explains why we give importance to a certain metrical orientation—the *tone* not only makes music out of the discourse, but determines its operation, its meaning. Thus the reduction of the I depends more on linguistic imagination than on ideological choice.

Clearly, there is more than one mode of "openness." Like Pagliarani and Antonio Porta, one can be totally "narrative": in which case the events in the poem are presented with the same polyvalence they have in life. You can open a text by imitating the ridiculous or threatening ambiguity of daily chatter, as does Balestrini (who has no desire to narrate anything); or as I do, by giving thoughts the value of gestures and figures amid the ghostly figments of things. One can also open in the manner of Sanguineti, exacerbating repressed energy by a grotesquely rational analysis, continually interchanging historical and psychological terms.

Obviously, the inclination to make thoughts and the objects of experience speak is an individual act, the act of me the writer, who has no wish to conceal my subjectiv-

5 Specific observations will also be found in the commentaries accompanying the poems.

ity. The "reduction of the I" is my last historical possibility for expressing myself subjectively—and this is a further interpretation of what we were saying at the outset about the title "novissimi." Now, however, on the side of the object, which can still be penetrated and honestly articulated, a poetry is created which, in the "quality of the times," seeks unity of vision and thus the recuperation of that very I methodically 'reduced' but a moment ago. The dialectic of alienation, if you will. It is in this crux that the problem of tradition truly emerges: our task is to treat common language with the same intensity as if it were the poetic language of tradition, and to have the latter be measured against contemporary life. Here we glimpse a vague possibility of overcoming the spurious antinomy between so-called monolinguism, which degenerates into classicist restoration, and plurilinguism or that "mixture of styles", which winds up in a sort of expressionistic Arcadia—dangers none of us would dream of avoiding at the expense of ordinary language. What is glimpsed, in other words, is the chance to regain, if only in feelings and attitudes, a proportion between the I, the world, and society, between a non-conventional disorder semantically necessary to us and the historical background with its highly compromised forms. So, to give an example, it would be hoped that a truly contemporary reader would return to Dante via Sanguineti, or would understand the *Scapigliati* and *Verismo* writers through Pagliarani. Old and ancient forms are never sequestered, and may be rediscovered in the process of innovation, reanimated by it, and not some hypothetical continuity or polemically archaeological revival. The case of Elio Pagliarani is highly

acter (perhaps a poet who resembles Pagliarani) or a "chorus," as he often does in his *Ragazza Carla*: note in particular those recitatives that continually break up the popular-ballad-like movement and dangle above whatever vestige of lyricism he has let himself indirectly extract.

In the small world of stifled, gray dramas he gives us, banality almost always ceases to be banal thanks to the truth of the writing. The poor Carla, alternately dim and lively, is a very, very *petite* bourgeoise with a small destiny in a large commercial-industrial city. If this girl appears to us as a historical product, a being conditioned as much by her own feelings as by her social standing in a subordinate class that is bound to be exploited and frustrated, it is not because she is the pretext of some thesis, but because Pagliarani has sketched her in her context with objective coherence: never, for instance, is her burgeoning vitality in doubt, that germ of freedom which always seeks to flower in the adolescent, and which always merges into the necessity of living. Nor is the world of the Pratéks, the "bosses" who in turn answer to other "super-bosses," eternal or dialectical: it is mechanical, infinitely blind, a bit comical, and in it each person plays his nasty part. It is undeniably awful that young lives should have to resign themselves to so wretched a fate; yet you are led to refuse this condition by the perception of the horizon that stretches beyond this particular tale. To see the figures of this small world caught in the syntactical clumsiness of the situation, or sticking out in certain harsh "spoken" discursive stopgags, is to come into direct contact with what we mean by a poem's "concrete semantics." Pagliarani has made good use of his Mayakovsky and

Brecht, even his Eliot, as well as a demystified Pound, and the Sandburg of "Chicago." He has drawn no more than cues and suggestions in the construction of a language adequate to the thing that has to be said, and almost all the rest from life experience: the poetics, the notions, vocabulary, characters and modes of discourse. Nothing more "Po Valley," in effect, than Pagliarani's almost vernacular structure, the popular background that seems to bring out a traditional revolutionary-conservative current that is typically Emilian.

When I spoke some pages back of a "schizomorphic vision," I was referring to a common but by no means univocal linguistic canon. In Pagliarani, for example, we are dealing with a fragmentation of reportorial elements, a dissociation of the outer world that is certainly reflected in the unresolved contradiction of personal impulses barely capable of internal hierarchy and maturation. His characters, however, are never undermined to the point that they exist below a historical, naturalistic level of existence. In my poems—if I can explain their intent—the disorder of life, neither evaded nor put in parentheses, but rather presupposed in each discourse, is not assumed as an index of a semantic attitude, nor existentially *taken for granted*. Schizomorphism becomes a logic of correct thinking, because things matter less than the consciousness that forms them in penetrating their structure. The theme is the objectified life in its moments of crisis: life cleansed of its obviousness, not of its tragic implications. What strikes me as paradigmatic is the need to closely pair discourse and symbol. Discourse thus tends to manifest itself in the form of non-conceptual, "gestural" thoughts, not pre-ordained, nor expanding the already-thought. I don't want to express myself, but rather the experience "my self" undergoes in reflecting and also *withstanding* reflection, determining itself *over and above* historical determination. Experience is not the result, it is the biography of consciousness. In other words, I suppose that the aspiration of my poems is to allow thoughts to emerge visibly, like things, not as discursive topics. The hope that they may have been at least partially successful in this attempt prompted me to include them in this collection. From the point of view of writing, I think my procedure has been to reconstruct for myself a language which, without being intimistic, would allow me to articulate an inner world. In this sense I have placed much importance on verse, making it at once more substantial and more flexible than the kind "modern" poetry has bequeathed us. Perhaps this explains why that moment in our tradition which in recent years I have felt closest to encompasses *stilnovo* and Dante's *rime petrose*. A language that is not "intellectual," yet has been thought, and thought dramatically.

To limit the semantic area in order to exert an absolute control over it, and to limit it not according to the dictates of a school but according to a choice of "field": this is a goal to which many other intentions should be sacrificed—intentions apparently more communicative and more accessible to the sluggish suggestiveness to which many readers of poetry would like to yield. Not that I want to give the impression of condemning the contrary strategy: the expansion of the semantic area. Within a discrete area one can achieve strong lexical and syntactic enrichment. These two processes differ, though not

lage materials are metamorphosized into a genuine Italo-humanistic cursus of unsuspected rhetorical energy.

Since his first, remarkable poems, which appeared four years ago in the journal *Il Verri*, Nanni Balestrini showed a strong penchant for drawing upon not so much literature but all sorts of *printed paper*. Like expired tickets, devalued banknotes, old ads, and dead newspaper headlines as in Kurt Schwitters' collages, the already-written words Balestrini 'withdraws' from the transient everyday world are scraps of reality insignificant in themselves, destined to vanish in the wheels of consumerism. Salvaged, surprised in their unexpected freedom and capacity for survival, they are *montaged* into the most amazing and orderly disorder imaginable. Balestrini's clownish streak has become increasingly evident in that, by absurd syntactic strategies, he mixes these bits of used-up words with involuntary fragments of common conversation ("tangles, repetitions, broken and twisted phrases, adjectives and preposterous images"). Whenever he can, he inserts learned or erudite details, perhaps the passage of a classical writer, utterly stripped of contextual value. This playful strategy, ventured deliberately *against* habitual, rigid, and grammatical modes of thought, recalls, beneath its elegant, carefree features, the anxious elusiveness of an F. Scott Fitzgerald; it would be erroneous for anyone to consider this a private matter, pleasant at times but essentially incommunicable and gratuitous. On the other hand, considering the turns his dangerous linguistic adulterations take, unmistakably comico-lyrical in tone, one must conclude that Balestrini's apparent gratuitousness has a precise revolutionary significance. The *asyntacticness* of his

34

poems is a spur that goads discourse to embrace the promptings of chance; it is a highly sensitive and inventive form of responsiveness to the most structural elements of language. One can even stress, in Adornian fashion, the "organized emptiness of meaning" of these poems and read them as a repudiation of existing society. The crucial thing to stress is the artistic element that justifies the process. Here, to be sure, there is no symbol or allegory, but rather the disposition to destroy any germ of narrative or concept; and yet the non-meaning becomes oddly semantic in the same way that Humpty Dumpty celebrates every non-birthday in Wonderland.

Balestrini's ideal is to write poems without a single word, or a single metaphor, of his own: poems that can be used by the reader in so far as he discovers that potential meanings tend to infinity. Strictly speaking, no image or figure recurs in Balestrini: his only true metaphor is in his structural "depagination," in his lyrico-parodistic recourse to what neurologists call "qualitative alterations" of language: paraphasias (as in "meaningless phrases"), semantic deficit (inability to keep up the thread of conversation)—except that in him these data are by no means assumed as abnormal. Even if the inconsistency, the physiognomic instability of everyday language borders on the pathological condition of *Standverlust* ("loss of standing"), for Balestrini this characteristic is simply a natural property of the raw materials he has found as his point of departure. The poet's aim is to create something unprecedented, unheard-of by the use of what has been most taken for granted and neglected. What most fascinates Balestrini about the broken rhythm of everyday speech and commonplace words lies entirely in their temporal sense: for what is said "is said for all time, and can be corrected only by subsequent additions, that is, by a continuation in time." This perpetual uncertainty and temporal suspension of utterance is also the central intensity that Balestrini's poems *communicate* to the reader.

The stress of Antonio Porta's poems falls essentially on physical events and on their extraneousness to the gaze of anyone who seeks to penetrate them: extraneousness, yet a deep bond as well, which fully engages man's very presence. If for Balestrini words are in themselves *facts* (so that animating them is already a vital prospect), for Porta it is facts as such, stripped of any verbal dress, that set themselves up as self-sufficient language. It is this violent linguistic *poverty* that makes his very first poems interesting, juvenilia though they may be in many respects. They display a nervous pithiness, a logical yet vivid economy, an attempt at absolute veracity. From the outset Porta apparently yields himself entirely to troubled, dogged *looking* at the traumatic phenomena of 'current events,' and his problem would seem to be finding adequate plastic expression for the eye's precipitous synthesis. One has the impression that, highly conscious of the stinginess of his means, Porta wants to shake up the page, thus choosing a system of syncopated, brute facts out of which to construct a physiological grammar, an elementary synoptic table of what really goes on in the world. A first reading might fail to reveal the spring that sets this system in motion: the metaphysical anguish, the "Manzonian" duplicity of this restless Catholic, of this unseemly bourgeois who, instead of turning his eyes from "evil" stares it down, aware he will never manage to explain it fully: if it is a social product, the cruel, accidental fate of nature remains for him unresolved; if evil is human destiny, the possibility, relative yet demonstrable, of historical redemption still calls for an explanation. Porta thus expresses a situation more subjective than his *language of events* would have one believe; and again, contrary to Balestrini, who in his own extremely subjective manner is highly impersonal, Porta confesses himself, removing himself and making a most secret commitment to shed raking light on characters and objects. The exact narrative attitude of this poet is evidenced by the somber "functionality" with which he tries to exact energy and insight from parts of speech: the absence of a period that convention decrees, the persistence of arresting commas in an obsessive atonal fabric, an incongruous syntactic perspective that creates condensation, are all devices that confirm the *objective* tension words are subjected to in order for them to be camouflaged as facts. In his most recent poems Porta's early trust in the univocity of occurrence seems strongly eroded—his trust, that is, in evil as violent, unmotivated insurgence. The events of his early poems were spatialized into time in a sort of well-configured vortex, which the gaze had only to seize and cleanly model. Yet gradually as that gaze came to penetrate the infinitesimal time of events, the temporal plane began to split: the poetic quest is no longer a summary dialectic between *here* and *beyond*, but an undefinable movement of the *before* and *after* and vice versa, an interlacing of incidents and objects that no longer obey the immediate categories of knowledge. The gaze has learned (and I apologize for those cases of *explicatio non petita*) are mere experiment: will the reader be stimulated by these brief paraphrases, specifications of facts, and scattered stylistic remarks? Will he be tempted to devise other commentaries?

Alfredo Giuliani
(translated by David Jacobson)

INTRODUCTION TO THE SECOND (1965)
EDITION OF *I NOVISSIMI*

guage in conferring on it some diachronically achieved "form," but rather in estranging it from its semantic properties, tearing away at its syntactic fabric, decomposing its harmony, and reconstructing it in violently synchronic provisional arrangements. We can quite briefly and summarily say that to understand contemporary poetry it is best not to refer to the memory of past poems, but rather to the physiognomy of the contemporary world. This does not mean that the poet has made a clean slate of tradition: it is the reverential reader who wrongly associates tradition with the idea of duty.

Today these notions have become commonplaces, yet four or five years ago Italian literary criticism was all but unanimous in supporting a regressive and purely "local" phenomenon such as Neo-Crepuscularism, and the disciples of such a pious-minded tendency were carrying out a provincial ideological terrorism against those who had chosen other paths and were trying out other itineraries. The Neo-Crepuscular writer was obsessed by the desire to be in the Opposition yet remain within History, and wanted poetry delicate and internal, to take an outward, "popular" turn; he was dogged, stifling, and verbose. Projecting his emotional conflicts and his subdued if not depressed mythologies onto a largely journalistic problematic, mounting his lyricism on the support of subjects taken from the culture's raw "current events," he would seize on the most spurious forms of sociology and journalism, and almost invariably end up (with the exception of a few authentic moments of rage) on the dreary, plangent note of autobiography. What he did however excel at was describing the suburban landscape in which he lived, the winters of his own heart, the buses he would board in the morning, the *mamma* who dusts off his desk for him; whereas he was more reticent and modest about his actual economic and sexual experiences (about which he might really have had something to say). His poetics, linked to the conventional notion of "content" as a sum of thoughts, visions, and feelings of intrinsic value, beyond the pale of poetry, and which may become "poetical" merely by being set down metrically, were old hat, patriotic, and particularly ineffectual: to combat the so-called Novecento, (or rather the small Italian portion of the whole modern tradition), he had set out to revisit our humble nineteenth-century tombs; from Tommaseo on to Pascoli, democratizing D'Annunzio and 'philologizing' Saba, arriving at Gramsci and a monstrous blend of botched nationalism and a fanciful socialism. Official criticism was draining the value of this period in the vogue of social elegiacs, and allowed at most for the emergence of certain facile, post-Montalian epigrammatic tricks. There was a sordid confusion in the air, no small amount of bad faith, and a maddening, wrongful waste of intelligence.

Which is why the present book was created and why we provided so many accessories, tools, and instructions for its use. It was a gesture of impatience, yet a well-considered one, prompted by a long series of grievances, experiments, reflections, discoveries, and polemics—as harsh as they were sincere—against opposing tendencies. On the eve of the 1960s we were convinced that another poetry had just barely come into maturity, that it was "breaking" with the period before it and that it would "come into its own" over the next few years. The poems we as-

Though all five of us have put this book behind us, it has continued to lead a life of its own and may be about to find that wider reception we had hoped for at the outset. So today, when its new publisher has asked me for a brief update, I'm at once pleased and embarrassed. I should not be the one to point out the shock effects *I Novissimi* created among the Italian literary regime, and it also strikes me as premature to be looking backward.

Just as, four years ago, I said that we had no intention of justifying ourselves as "avant-garde," in the hackneyed sense that term has acquired, but rather that we felt we were "at the center" of precarious circumstances, so today we can, rather, look around and try to define the condition of the writer in an unending quarrel or contestation with the reality of language, or rather with himself and society's institutions.

Today poetry is less a privileged domain than ever before: the forms of prose which interest us have the same problems of structure and handling of material and, when they're successful, the same intensity we are wont to attribute to poetry. But this occurs inasmuch as prose has ceased by now to enjoy its assumed prerogative of discursiveness, while poetry in turn has sharpened its capacity for contact, which was once limited by the bias toward rhythm, rhyme, poetic diction, and so on. A prose that takes on poetry's stylistic responsibilities is by no means a "poetic prose," nor is a poetry freed from falsely poetic rules by any means a "prosaic poetry." Differences remain, no doubt, between the two, but not differences in nature: rather, in their destination and their use; the sorts of differences that may exist between neighboring products of the same material culture. Since poetry is an object that is more compact, more "visible" as a whole, than a prose work (just as a sculpture is more compact and visible than a house), less open to observation but more conspicuous at its sore spots, it is practically a "sample," a more certifiable test by which to assay the degree of energy of a given linguistic culture (all culture is linguistic, but there exists a deliberate culture of language coinciding with the one the structuralists call the "poetic function" of the message) and this remains true even if, as Roman Jakobson rightly points out, "the linguistic analysis of poetry cannot be limited to its poetic function" (Roman Jakobson, *Essais de linguistique générale,* Les Editions de minuit, Paris, 1963). It is necessary, then, that a "contemporary" poetry exist and that the idea that sustains it be on a level, if not with the future, at least with the present.

Though the seeds of language grow out of "nature," and a linguistic explosion can manifest itself at the level of "natural" communication, the controlled and tested, directly experienced energy of language is produced through certain devices built by technicians: the source is purely "artificial." When a given notion of poetry is entered into at the level of common sense, it is easy to see that this is a matter of popularizing, in however deformed and degraded a form, the technical sense on whose level it has primarily been conceived. The petty bourgeois notion of poetry—as it is still expressed by my fellow countrymen: "quant si poet," or a phrase like "what a poet," for someone who is dreamy, overly tender, foolish—precisely translates the romantic-crepuscular idea of poetry in common-

48

of dreams and the expression of psychosis, the juxaposi-
tion of the elements of different logics, the language-chal-
lenge, the non-finite: all this coincides with an anthropo-
logical attitude that precise historical conditions have
roused to create an *epoch-making* literary language it will
now be impossible to turn back from. A choked or muffled
apparition, demented, mocking rite, knowing discourse,
incorporeal pantomime and reckless game, the new po-
etry is gauged by the *degradation of meanings* and by the
physiognomic instability of the verbal world we are im-
mersed in, yet is also to be gauged by itself, by its own
inventive capability. The shadow—says Jung—"represents
that which man can never bring to a head, that which
therefore remains in a constant state of emotion that can
never be touched on" (*Contribution to the Psychological Study
of the Figure of the "Trickster"* in *The Divine Trickster* by P.
Radin, C.G. Jung and K. Kerényi). Poetry being less a form
of knowledge than a mode of contact, its relations with
the shadow are probably a "coming to a head," however
provisional and ambiguous, of that reality which the sea-
horse, the "visceral brain" linked with the ideational life
and the emotional processes, is ceaselessly filming. In the
same book from which I have quoted Jung, there is a pref-
ace by Karl Kerényi, dated 1964, in which, referring to
Cervantes and to Don Quixote's relation to the chivalric
romances, he ventures to define the romance and the
mythological tale as an "enlargement of existence," a
growth and enrichment that is not at all cognitive but
rather, imaginative. I had presented the same idea at the
start of this book to justify the function of poetry in gen-
eral and, in particular, to determine the purpose of a truly

every modern poet is forced to put the foundations of communication in parentheses, in a sort of linguistic *epochè,* has found that this postulate of "methodical doubt" had begun to appear in poetry roughly with Mallarmé. It would be more correct to trace the discovery of the "modern" method to Rimbaud, as is clear from his theoretical texts (his letters) and his poems. Yet it is true that with Mallarmé the phenomenon takes on obsessive qualities. In *Un coup de Dés* (1897) we already encounter suppression of words and of contextual links for phrases, the intersection of planes of discourse, the actual abandonment of a line's "tempo" and even of traditional typographical spacing. Mallarmé is already theorizing the intervention of chance in the poetic process, the structure of probability, and the "project" in place of inspiration. What developed in Mallarmé's theory was a mode of poetic thinking that Apollinaire would express some years later when he said: "our intelligence must adapt itself to understanding in a synthetic-ideographic way, and not discursively." What emerged so forcefully out of all the avant-garde movements of the early twentieth century—futurism, cubofuturism, imagism, vorticism, dada—was a methodical blend of ideogrammatic language and collage-language. To this the surrealists added the technique of free association. These methods have not exhausted their function. On the one hand, they arose with the "modern" world: cultural evolution from the mid-nineteenth century to the present day is, substantially, the fruit of major methodological discoveries; it was the analytic methods elaborated by the social sciences, economics, psychology, physics, linguistics, sociology, that set off the explosion of those

naming us, evidently out of discretion, did the honor of crediting us with responsibility for having formulated "the significant horizon" of a new period in poetry (Luciano Anceschi, "Orizzonte della poesia," *Il Verri,* n. 1, 1962), to succeed the one that came into maturity between the two world wars. In what precisely lay the book's power of intervention, its capacity to cause change? Probably in the fact that its act of rupture demonstrated an equal interest in reconstruction. With all the negative premises we were making our own, and all the contradictions and immaturities our poems contained, we were displaying a shared positive trait. Because it is not enough to believe, as Adorno does, that the current task of art "is to introduce chaos into order" (*Minima moralia*). Even in the subtle elaborations of his student Metzger (who, in reference to the composer Cage, noted, at the start of a lecture: "whereas the dodecaphonic composers were devoted to problems of organization, Cage was engaged in problems of disorganization") there is the awareness that disorganization, "chaos," is a structural problem. And all our concerns and "technical" idiosyncracies showed a particular type of "engagement" too often shirked in Italy's postwar culture. The fact that we did not propose an "ideological" poetry was a carefully calculated move: by showing that poetry cannot be created by thinking about poetry as anything but technique, we left all routes open to ideology, or, as Sanguineti would say, to language-ideology. And precisely on this point, which strikes some people as a sore one, but strikes me as an obvious one, it must be added that we did not even propose a univocal "poetics." Poetry must be delivered up naked to language, not redressed in ideology; and, whatever his political and socio-logical interests, the poet must above all study the influences, the signs, the wounds that this language wields over him. This said, each of us had, and has continued to develop his own idea of the "structural" (and NOT content-related) functions of ideology. For my part, I simply view it as part of building material.

We are moving to the limits of an inexorable contradiction not so much between "naturalism" and "avant-garde" as between the rationales for either. The rationale for naturalism is a "plain," smoothly fluent vision of the relations occurring between life and literature. Life lives, literature "represents": you either live or write. But the moment naturalism passes into expressionism, a more uncertain operation has already been performed on that "living" life. It is the moment in which one becomes aware that representing is a useless action, inasmuch as life already independently writes itself, precisely in its living: "One must look at the world to be able to represent it: only, in so looking at it, one comes to notice that it has, to some extent, already represented itself: already the soldier, ahead of the poet, has spoken of the battle, and the sailor of the sea, and the new mother of her childbirth" (C.E. Gadda, "Belle lettere e contributi delle tecniche," *I viaggi, la morte*, 1958).

Expressionistic naturalism can easily resolve its problem, sometimes by minutely adopting ("documenting itself" in a more philological manner, if you will, but in the same way as earlier naturalism) the linguistic particulars of individual "techniques"; sometimes by recomposing "for itself" the scattered expressive material into a new whole. Here it may seem to approach the neo-avant-garde modes practiced, as it were, by contemporary poetry. But there is a substantial difference. Structuring single moments of language is not necessarily the same thing as integrating them. The primacy of structure, of linguistic invention, over individual materials or moments of language is for us a binding axiom; and structure must be exhibited in its heteronomy vis-a-vis real appearance (which the naturalist, on the other hand, always wants somehow to "reproduce"); so that, by the same token, the real can only be found in poetry as the object of that process that is language. The primacy of structure, more than depending on any stylistic product, depends on a choice by virtue of which the historicist dialectic, the transcendence of memory, the arguments of images, elegy and satire give way to an antilogy, a counter-argument, to the emergence of the present, to the violation of images, to tragedy and farce. If to live is already "to represent," i.e. to write, biologically to carve memorial signs, creating poetry means forcing life to rewrite itself, to scramble and reassemble memorial signs in unprecedented connections, to push it to free itself from the fetishes of representations into visions that "traverse," without stopping and "forming" in either one or the other, the language of life and the language of art.

In other words: the primacy of structure, its putting itself in place of representation, means that poetry, rather than offering itself whole as a metaphor of the real, is constituted as another pole of the linguistic world we all write in living.

At this point I think I may have said enough, and what's

worse, have done so fragmentarily, about the theory of the literary process that we in fact first put forward four years ago with the volume *I Novissimi*. Having brought us into the midst of the advanced movements shaking up literature in other countries, and having allowed for new developments which have convinced each of us that the moment had come for confronting other literary genres (the novel, the drama), the operation has freed from isolation some "fellow travellers" who found in it corroboration and stimulation. It has also brought us organically closer to the language of music and painting. The future will tell us, and the readers will sense, whether this is due to mere chance, or necessity, or some ambiguous merit of the times.

Alfredo Giuliani

ELIO PAGLIARANI

Translated by Luigi Ballerini and Paul Vangelisti

NARCISSUS PSEUDONARCISSUS

E un po' come dire che c'è poco da bruciare, oramai,
lo zeppelin è sgonfiato, il fusto è nudo
che fa spavento
                    io ho avuto tutti i numeri per finir male,
l'amore vizioso, l'ingegno e più l'ambizione pudica
e al momento opportuno un buco nei pantaloni
che ci passano due dita
                    allora bruceremo pali di ferro
il nostro paese aggiornato, la draga la gru l'idroscalo.

Ma se:
            ho lottato con vigliaccheria e tenacia
            pasto per pasto, e non intendo mollare

            non so come risponde la corteccia
            ma intendo seguitare

L'A. celebra con molta autoironia le indistinte e scomposte ambizioni
dell'adolescenza. Il *Narcissus pseudonarcissus* è chiamato volgarmente
« narciso poetico ».
Il richiamo allo zeppelin è volutamente démodé; il dirigibile a cui è
sgonfiato il pallone di tela resta un nudo e goffo scheletro di ferri. Bru-
ceremo dunque il ferro e aggiorneremo il paesaggio con gli « oggetti »

NARCISSUS PSEUDONARCISSUS

It's somehow like saying there's not much left to burn, by now,
the blimp's deflated, the skeleton so bare
it's frightening
             I had what it takes to turn out badly,
wicked love, talent plus a modest ambition
and if need be a hole in my pants
to slip two fingers through
               and so we shall burn iron posts
our up-to-date country, the dredge the crane the seaplane
    [harbor

But if:
        cowardly and unyielding I struggled
        meal after meal, and I will not let go

        I have no idea how the cortex responds
        but I plan to go on

With great self-irony the author celebrates the indistinct, unseemly
ambitions of adolescence. *Narcissus pseudonarcissus* is commonly called
"poetic narcissus."
The reference to the zeppelin is deliberately old-fashioned; the diri-
gible whose canvas balloon has deflated remains a bare, hulking, iron
skeleton. So let us then put our irons in the fire and update the land-

il mio bagaglio non è pesante
la mia schiena non è ingombrante
tengo un tessuto connettivo che permette
alcune metamorfosi

dopo la pioggia con i rospi in mezzo alle strade
ho fede che mi potrai trovare.

Oh, la nostra razza è la più tenace, sia lode al suo fattore,
l'uomo è l'unico animale che sverna ai poli e
        [all'equatore
signore di tutte le latitudini che s'accostuma a tutte
        [le abitudini,
così ho violenta fiducia
non importa come lo dico—ah l'infinita gamma dei toni
che uguaglia solo il numero delle anime sensibili delle
        [puzze della terra
ho violenta fiducia, non importa, che tu mi trovi
        [in mezzo alla furiana
e dopo, quando le rotaie dei tram stanno per aria.

---

ferrigni: sono, tuttavia, è bene notarlo, oggetti che implicano
movimento di approdi, atterraggi, trasporti.
La « corteccia » è, ovviamente quella cerebrale. Nell'affermare la pro-
pria possibilità di metamorfosi, l'A. ricorre a un costrutto idiomatico
di stampo meridionale (« tengo » per *ho)* che dà l'idea del trasformismo
morale cui appunto sono socialmente soggette le popolazioni del sud.

        my baggage is not heavy
        my back is not too bulky
        I got connective tissue that permits
        some metamorphosis

        after the rain with toads in the streets
        I trust you will find me.

O, we are the race most tenacious, praised be its creator,
man's the only animal to winter at pole and equator
lord of all latitudes accustomed to all habits,
thus my confidence is fierce
no matter how I say it—ah the endless range of tones
equal only to throngs of sensitive souls to earth's stenches
my confidence is fierce, no matter what, you can find me
        [in the storm
and later, when the trolley tracks are up in the air.

---

scape with steely "objects": yet those, we would do well to note, are
objects that imply movements of approach, landings, transport.
The "cortex" is obviously that of the brain. In asserting his own possi-
bility of metamorphosis the author has recourse to a southern idiom-
atic construction ("I got" for *I have*), which conveys the idea of the moral
"transformism" that the southern population is socially subjected to.

No? È successo un caso, un incidente?, a te gloria,
        [se a te non ti tocca
io, tanto, ho consegnato un biglietto—c'è scritto
        [che non rinuncio:
a me amen, la volta che mi tocca.

La lode alle capacità di adattamento e di resistenza, proprie all'uomo,
comporta un atteggiamento polemico verso la *sensibilità* (e qui è
soprattutto la sensibilità del lettore, abituato alla poesia raffinata): i
« toni » possibili dell'esperienza sono infiniti, cosí l'A. accosta violenza
e fiducia e si assume un certo disimpegno stilistico (« non importa come
lo dico ») che è la rudezza necessaria a sopportare coscientemente il
bagaglio sulla schiena.
E se capita un accidente? Beato te, chiunque tu sia, se ti salvi dalla
« furiana »; intanto i poeti non rinunciano al proprio lavoro.

No? What happened, an accident? Glory be to you, if
        [your turn hasn't come
I anyway delivered a note—it says I don't give up:
amen to me, the time my turn will come.

The praise of powers of adaptation and resistance typical of mankind
bears with it a polemical attitude toward *sensitivity* (and here it is pri-
marily the sensitivity of the reader accustomed to the refinements of
poetry): the possible "tones" of experience are endless, so that the au-
thor combines violence with trust and assumes a certain stylistic casu-
alness ("no matter how I say it")—the very coarseness he needs if he is
consciously to shoulder his baggage.

And if an accident occurs? Lucky you, whoever you are, if you manage
to escape the "storm;" meanwhile the poets don't give up their work.

I GOLIARDI DELLE SERALI

I goliardi delle serali in questa nebbia
hanno voglia di scherzare: non è ancora mezzanotte
e sono appena usciti da scuola
                    « Le cose nuove e belle
che ho appreso quest'anno » è l'ultimo tema da fare,
ma loro non si danno pensiero, vogliono sempre scherzare.

Perché il vigile non interviene, che cosa ci sta a fare?

È vero però che le voci son fioche e diverse, querule
        [anche nel riso,
o gravi, o incerte, in formazione e in trasformazione,
disparate, discordi, in stridente contrasto accomunate
senza ragione senza necessità senza giustificazione,
ma come pel buio e il neon è la nebbia che abbraccia
        [affratella assorbe inghiotte
e fa il minestrone,
            e loro ci sguazzano dentro, sguaiati e contenti
— io attesto il miglior portamento dei due allievi sergenti,

Tutt'altro che « goliardi » (studenti, cioè, spensierati e pagati) questi
allievi delle serali; alcuni giovani, altri già invecchiati, e tutti con strani
mestieri. E stanchi del lavoro fatto durante il giorno, ma ugualmente
capaci di puerili schiamazzi (fastidio ai benpensanti) proprio come son
bravi a fare gli studenti veri. Ma questi—nel « minestrone » di nebbia
buio e neon—sono ancora più veri.

THE GOLIARDS OF NIGHT SCHOOL

The goliards of night school in this fog
feel like joking: it's not yet midnight
and they got out of class just now

                              "The new and lovely things
I learned this year" is the last essay to hand in,
but they don't think about it, they just want to joke.

Why doesn't the constable step in, what's he waiting for?

It's true though the voices are hoarse and varied, peevish
        [even in laughter,
or serious, or uncertain, in the making or mutation,
disparate, discordant, in shrill contrast, come together
without reason without necessity without justification,
but as with darkness and neon it's the fog that embraces
        [fraternizes absorbs swallows
and makes the stew,

                    and they wallow in it, crude and happy
—I attest to the best behavior of the two sergeant cadets,

These night-school students are anything but "goliards" (i.e., carefree
and sponsored students). Some are young, others have grown older,
and by day all have odd trades. Worn out from their jobs, but as ca-
pable of childish horseplay (to the displeasure of right-minded people)
as they are of being real students. Yet these—in the "stew" of the fog,
darkness, and neon—are even more real.

il calvo in ispecie, che se capisce poco ha una forza di volontà
militare, e forse ha già perso il filobus.

Quanta pienezza di vita e ricchezza di esperienze!
  di giorno il lavoro, la scuola di sera, di notte schiamazzi
(chi sa due lingue vive due vite)
    di giorno il lavoro la scuola di sera,—non tutti la notte però
        [fanno i compiti
e non imparano le poesie a memoria, di notte preferiscono
        [fare schiamazzi,
nascondere il righello a una compagna
                            e non fanno i compiti
—ma non c'è nessuno che bigi la scuola
                                    sono avari
tutti avari di già, e sanno che costa denari denari.

the bald one especially, who's hard to understand has a military
willpower, and may have already missed his bus.

What fullness of life and richness of experience!
  work by day, classes in the evening, rowdy at night
(who knows two languages lives two lives)
  work by day classes in the evening,—at night though not all
      [do their homework
and learn poems by heart, at night they prefer to get rowdy,
hiding a girl's ruler
                    and they don't do their homework
  —but no one cuts classes
                              they are greedy
all of them greedy, they know it costs money.

DOMENICA

Una volta per settimana
li prenderemo di petto,
andiamo al cinematografo.

La domenica al cinema Cantù
si può far collezione di gente: è
sempre quella di cui canta al Gerolamo il balletto
la Sposa del Sole, così bella che gli stessi saggi smagati
sanno soltanto destinarla in alto, al sole dei pagani
—ma onestamente il sole non invitto (Milano!)
la rimanda al nembo
il nembo al vento il vento alla montagna

         —il nembo m'oscura
          il raggio non dura
         —il vento m'assalta
          la nube si sfalda
         —il monte mi spezza
          la furia dimezza

Il cinema Cantù a Milano, è un locale del centro, di infimo ordine e bassissimo prezzo.

Il balletto *La Sposa del Sole,* rappresentato al teatro Gerolamo dalle marionette dei Colla ancora qualche anno fa, è uno spettacolo fin de siècle tipo Excelsior. Eccone la trama: chi è degno di sposare la « Sposa del Sole », così bella e sublime? Soltanto il Sole, ovviamente; ma l'onesto

SUNDAY

We'll face them
once per week,
and go to the movies.

Sunday at the Cinema Cantù
you make a collection of people: it's
always that of which the Bride of the Sun sings in the show
at the Gerolamo, she's so beautiful that even wise
    [dismayed men
can only place her on high, give her to the pagan sun
—honestly a sun not undefeated (Milano!)
sends her back to the nimbus
the nimbus to the wind the wind to the mountain
                —the nimbus shades me
                  the ray fails me
                —the winds attacks
                  my cloud cracks
                —the mountain shatters me
                  the fury scatters me

The Cantù is a movie house, of the lowest order, in the center of Milan,
offering cut-rate prices.

The ballet *The Sun's Bride*, still performed at the Gerolamo Theatre by
the Colla marionettes only a few years ago, is a fin de siècle piece in the
style of "Excelsior." The plot is as follows: who is worthy to marry the
"Sun's Bride," so beautiful and sublime? Obviously only the Sun; but

La montagna può partorire con facilità
basta un ometto che sappia aprire i fianchi
bravo a brillare la mina, un minatore
(Oh San Gottardo, oh Moncenisio, oh Ottocento)

A un minatore gloria!, e il circolo di ferro si rinchiude.

Sarà meglio ch'io m'appoggi a questo vecchio
altro male forse non ha, quella ragazza è spuria
con il busto di ferro

Io non so come fare a ritrovarli—

Io non so quale innesto se non hanno—

Ma quanta gente perdio che non reclama

(sì, sono buono e bravo
eccomi le natiche nude
eccomi tolte le mutande
Dottore, eccomi pronto)

molta felicità.

Sole dice: la Nube è più forte di me; a sua volta la Nube dice: il Vento
è più forte di me; e il Vento dice: la Montagna infrange la mia forza; la
Montagna dice: il Minatore è più forte di me; dunque il Minatore è il
più forte di tutti: è l'unico degno sposo della « Sposa del Sole ». Eppure
il minatore è uno di quelli che bazzicano il cinema Cantù.

The mountain may happily give birth
long as some little man can open her flanks
smooth at setting off the mine, a miner
(Oh San Gottardo, oh Moncenisio, oh 19th Century)

Glory be to the miner! and the iron circle seals up.

Better that I rely on this old man
other evil he may not have, the girl's a fake
with that metal corset

     I don't know how to find them again—

     I don't know which graft if they don't have—

     And so many people damn it do not

(yes, I'm nice and sweet
here's my naked buttocks
here's my underwear
Doctor, I'm ready)

     claim much happiness.

---

the good, honest Sun says: the Cloud is stronger than I am; the Cloud in turn says: the Wind is stronger than I am; and the Wind says: the Mountain outstrips my powers; the Mountain says: the Miner is stronger than I am; thus, the Miner is the strongest one of all: he alone is worthy of "the Sun's Bride." And yet the miner is a regular at the Cantù Cinema.

POÈME ANTIPOÈME

Io non prendo le cose come vengono, tu non eri
in programma, Mamsell, le mie figure
di donna portano altri segni distintivi:
nessuna mai, e baciata con più ardore
che avesse una volta uno dei tanti
tuoi profumi di guerra e di vacanza.
                                    È meglio
guardarti il profilo in lontananza
e non con gli occhi d'ora, ma a memoria
per esempio sullo scoglio, distesa in fronte al mare
morbida, palpitante. Ma lo sai
che mi viene in mente perfino Rita da Cascia, protettrice
degli impossibili? che il tuo riso allo squillo di un telefono
non mi si spegne più? Oh, basta
sii lusingata e scrollane le spalle al tuo ritorno
da te, dove non sto, né so, né posso o voglio, dove non sarei
io se mi fossi.

Scappa Mamsell, che il mio amore non ti uguagli
          le mie pallide figure
Se io ti prendo anch'io ti sono vita
          certo, ma con mani pesanti
Scappa Mamsell, l'amore fa più ricchi
solo i poveri:
          nemmeno io lo sono.

POÈME ANTIPOÈME

I never take things as they come, you weren't
in my plans, Mamsell, my figure
of a woman has other distinguishing marks:
none ever, and kissed with greater passion
had any of your many wartime
and holiday perfumes.
                    Better
to look at your profile from afar
and not with today's eyes, but from memory
for instance on the rocks, lying before the sea
tender, throbbing. Do you know that I
even think of Rita da Cascia, patron saint
of impossibilities? that your laughter at the phone ringing
cannot be turned off anymore? Enough
be flattered and shrug your shoulders going back
to your place, where I'm not, nor know, nor can nor wish, where I
wouldn't be myself if I were.

Run away, Mamsell, that my love may not compare you
            to my colorless figures
If I take you I will also be life for you
            surely, though with heavy hands
Run away, Mamsell, only the poor get rich
with love:

            nor am I one of those.

Quando scrivere è vizio. [Perché non sempre
scrivere è vizio: può costare all'Austria
più di una battaglia perduta.] Perché
se c'è da spremere una verità

> la Chiesa lo sa
> che la verità
> è trina

si tratta di righe inutili: / se veramente ci fosse volontà
che la giovane estranea se ne vada / o « scappi », che fa
    [più effetto
l'unica è non parlarle / o urlarle dietro le notti
che sudi e diventi viscido.

(Oppure c'è un altro sistema « t'amo » / dille, insisti che
    [l'ami molto
se proprio hai deciso di perderla / vedrai come se ne va
    [placata.)
Se invece è una finta e si vuole / che pensi « come è
    [generoso (o orgoglioso)
lui e il suo cuore, aspetta che in risposta / io lo
    [sorprenda buttandogli
tutti i miei arti al collo » / si tratta di meschinità.
E anche più dell'idea del raggiro / è meschina la scelta
    [prepubere
del mezzo.
        Quindi si chieda impudicizia alla cronaca
dicendo da che mondo è mondo
massime sulle donne
e altre banalità.

When writing is a vice. [Because it isn't
always a vice: it may cost Austria
more than a battle lost.] Because
if there's a truth to squeeze out

> the Church knows
> that truth
> is triune

it's a matter of useless lines:/if there were truly a desire for
the strange young woman to leave/or "run away,"
        [which makes a stronger impression
the only thing is not speak to her/or yell at her at night
when you break out in a sweat and become slimy.

(Another way would be "I love you"/tell her, insist you
        [love her very much if
you've really decided to lose her/you'll see how she
        [leaves pacified.)
If instead you're faking and you want her/to think
        ["how generous (or proud)
he is and his heart, he expects in reply/that I'd surprise
        [him and throw
all my limbs around his neck"/it's a matter of shabbiness.
And even more than the idea of the con/ the prepubescent
        [choice of means
is shabby.
            So let's ask the news for immodesty
saying from time immemorial
maxims about women
and other platitudes.

(E lei, Mamsell, non ha da dire niente?
è data assente? non c'è una verità di lei?
Certo: risulta—ma s'è già detto, almeno nel commento—
che se ne è andata naturalmente.

O è già in secca nel banco del pallore?)

(And she, Mamsell, has nothing to say?
is she reported absent? isn't there any truth about her?
Surely: there's evidence—but it's been said already at least
        [in the commentary—
that she left naturally.

Or is she already aground on the bar of pallor?)

Da LA RAGAZZA CARLA

> *Un amico psichiatra mi riferisce di una*
> *giovane impiegata tanto poco allenata*
> *alle domeniche cittadine che, spesso, il*
> *sabato, si prende un sonnifero, oppor-*
> *tunamente dosato, che la faccia dor-*
> *mire fino al lunedì. Ha un senso*
> *dedicare a quella ragazza questa*
> Ragazza Carla?

I.   1

Di là dal ponte della ferrovia
una trasversa di viale Ripamonti
c'è la casa di Carla, di sua madre, e di Angelo e Nerina

Il ponte sta lì buono e sotto passano
treni carri vagoni frenatori e mandrie dei macelli
e sopra passa il tram, la filovia di fianco, la gente che cammina
i camion della frutta di Romagna.

> Chi c'è nato vicino a questi posti
> non gli passa neppure per la mente
> come è utile averci un'abitudine

Il racconto è ambientato a Milano nell'immediato dopoguerra. La
ragazza Carla è la figlia minore della vedova Dondi; la figlia maggiore,
Nerina, è sposata da poco e vive in casa col marito Angelo. La ragazza
Carla è in fase di fuga di fronte alla vita e sta subendo gli eventi in due
direzioni: quella sessuale (i rapporti della sorella col marito, il solito
« letto che cigola », ecc.) e quella economico-sociale (va alle serali di

THE GIRL CARLA

A psychiatrist friend tells me of a
young secretary whose distaste for city
weekends is such she takes enough
sleeping pills to stay asleep until Mon-
day morning. Does it make any sense
to dedicate this Girl Carla *to that girl?*

I.   1

On the other side of the railroad bridge
a street off Viale Ripamonti
is Carla's house, her mother's, Angelo's and Nerina's

The bridge just sits there and underneath pass
trains cars wagons brakemen and cattle for the slaughterhouse
and above the tramway and the trolley bus alongside, people
       [walking
the fruit trucks from Romagna.

              Who's born around there
              it never crosses their minds
              how useful a habit can be

The story takes place in Milan, just after the War. Carla is the younger
daughter of the widow Dondi; Mrs. Dondi's older daughter, Nerina,
has recently married, and lives at home with her husband Angelo. Carla
is at a stage where she flees life, and is going through two different
kinds of experiences: sexual (her sister's relationship to her husband,
the usual "creaking bed," etc.) and socio-economic (typing class at night

Le abitudini si fanno con la pelle
così tutti ce l'hanno se hanno pelle.

Ma c'è il momento che l'abitudine non tiene
chissà che cosa insiste nel circuito
                    o fa contatto
                              o prende la tangente
allora la burrasca
                    periferica, di terra,
il ponte se lo copre e spazza e qualcheduno
può cascar sotto
e i film che Carla non li può soffrire
un film di Jean Gabin può dire il vero
è forse il fischio e nebbia o il disperato
stridere di ferrame o il tuo cuore sorpreso, spaventato
il cuore impreparato, per esempio, a due mani
che piombano sul petto

                    Solo pudore non è che la fa andare
                    fuggitiva nei boschi di cemento
                    o il contagio spinoso della mano.

---

dattilografia, deve trovarsi un impiego). Ora è messa a prova la sua
scarsa capacità di diventare adulta, di adeguarsi coscientemente alla
vita, alla città che grava oggettiva sulle vicende individuali. I suoi
rapporti con l'uomo rischiano di mutarsi in repulsione, la sua con-
dizione sociale di restare accettazione supina.
L'A. fa uso di un verso « epico » sul quale hanno influito diverse

Habits grow with the skin
so everyone who has skin has them.

But there comes the time when habits don't hold
who knows what insists on the circuit
                           what makes contact
                                      who takes a cut
then a ground squall
                           on the outskirts,
covers the bridge and sweeps across it and someone
might fall below
and the movies that Carla cannot stand them
a Jean Gabin movie can speak the truth
it's the whistle maybe and the fog or the desperate
screech of iron or startled heart, a heart
frightened and unprepared, for instance, for two hands
that swoop on your breast

                    Modesty alone is not what drives her
                    a fugitive in cement forests
                    or the thorny infection of the hand.

---

school, since she needs work). She is being tested now in her meager
ability to enter adulthood, to adjust consciously to life, to the city as it
weighs objectively on private lives. Her relationship to men risks turn-
ing into repulsion, her social condition risks remaining passive accep-
tance.

The author uses an "epic" verse-line influenced by such diverse poets

È dalla fine estate che va a scuola
>*Guida tecnica per l'uso razionale*
>*della macchina*

>>la serale
di faccia alla Bocconi, ma già più
>*Metodo principe*
>*per l'apprendimento*
>*della dattilografia con tutte dieci*
>*le dita*

non capisce se è un gran bene, come pareva in casa,
spendere quelle due mila lire al mese
>*Vantaggi dell'autentico*
>*utilità fisiologica, risultato*
>*duraturo, corretta scrittura*
>*velocità resistenza*

PIANO DIDATTICO PARAGRAFO PRIMO

La scuola d'una volta, il suo grembiule
tutto di seta vera, una maestra molto bella
i problemi coi mattoni e le case, e già dicevano la guerra
Mussolini la Francia l'Inghilterra.

---

esperienze: un filone Eliot-Pound-Maiakowski-Brecht. È un verso a
fisarmonica, che si restringe e si allunga a seconda delle necessità, ora
espressionistiche ora veristiche, del racconto. Struttura metrica di fondo
atonale che l'A. adopera costantemente anche nelle poesie più brevi.
Il poemetto è diviso in tre parti. La prima ha un movimento circolare:
l'episodio iniziale è, cronologicamente, l'ultimo e ad esso riconduce la

7

Since the end of summer she's been going to school
   Handbook for the Smart Use
   of the Typewriter

        nightschool
across the street from the Bocconi, but she no longer
    World's Finest Method
    for Learning
    Typing with All
    Ten Fingers
understands the big advantage, as it seemed at home,
spending those two thousand monthly
     Benefits of the Authentic
     Physiological Practicality, Lasting
     Results, Precision Writing
     Speed Endurance

     LESSON PLAN PARAGRAPH ONE

The old time school, her pinafore
all real silk, a very pretty teacher
problems with bricks and houses and already talk of war
Mussolini France England.

---

as Eliot, Pound, Mayakovsky, and Brecht. It is an accordian-like line,
which can squeeze in or stretch out as needed, depending on the story's
demands, sometimes expressionistic, sometimes naturalistic. The au-
thor uses a basically atonal metrical structure constantly, even in the
shortest poems.

The poem is in three parts. In the first, which has a circular movement,

Qui di gente un campionario : sei uomini e diciotto
donne, più le due che fanno scuola

> *Nella parte centrale del carrello, solidale ad esso*
> *ecco il rullo*

C'è poca luce e il gesso va negli occhi

> *Nel battere a macchina le dita*
> *devono percuotere decisamente*
> *i tasti e lasciarli liberi, immediatamente*

Come ridono queste ragazze e quell'uomo anziano che fa steno
e non sa, non sa tener la penna in mano

> *Ciascun esercizio deve continuarsi*
> *sino ad ottenere almeno*
> *tre ripetizioni consecutive*
> *senza errore alcuno e perfettamente*
> *incolonnate*

O quella povera zoppina, la più svelta
a macchina

> *Quando il dispositivo per l'inversione*
> *automatica del movimento del nastro, o per difetto*
> *di lubrificazione o per mancanza*
> *del gancio*
>
> > *non funziona*

O Maria Pia Zurlini ch'era nata
ricca e ha già trent'anni e disperati
sorrisini

---

sezione finale. Una sera sul ponte, il compagno Piero, che ha preso
l'abitudine di ricondurre la Carla a casa dopo la scuola, le mette
decisamente le mani addosso; e lei fugge sgomenta. Le sezioni succes-
sive sono un *flash-back*; nella 7 è presentata la scuola e i pezzi in corsivo
son tratti da un popolarissimo manuale di dattilografia.

Here a sampler of people: six men eighteen
women, plus the two in charge

>   *In the heart of the carriage, integral to it*
>   *the roller*

There's little light and chalk dust finds the eyes

>   *When typing the fingers*
>   *must strike the keys decisively*
>   *and leave then immediately free*

How the girls laugh and the old man learning short hand
who cannot hold a pen in his hand

>   *Each exercise must continue*
>   *until reaching three*
>   *consecutive repetitions*
>   *without error and perfectly*
>   *columned*

O that poor girl with the limp, the fastest
typist

>   *When the device for the automatic*
>   *reversal of the ribbon, either from insufficient*
>   *lubrification or failure*
>   *in the catch*
>   *does not function*

O Maria Pia Zurlini born
to wealth and already thirty with her
desperate little smiles

---

the initial episode is chronologically the last, with the final section
leading back to it. One evening on the bridge Piero, who regularly
walks Carla home after school, puts his hands on her; she flees in hor-
ror. The next sections are a flash-back; I,7 depicts the school, and the
italicized lines are taken from a standard typing manual.

l'inversione
si può provocare in vari modi:
colle mani

9

Ma quei due
hanno avuto poche sere per parlare
la prima fu d'impaccio
                    la seconda
che risero ragazzi per un tale
che parlava da solo d'una bomba
                              e un altro poco
altro che bomba, all'incrocio di via Meda
la circolare lo piglia sotto se non era svelto
il tranviere
              urli, sfoghi pittoreschi e qualcheduno
              pronto a far capannello, al raduno
              scappano i cani, si tormenta il pizzetto
              il bravo ometto ebete e la dentiera.

Dialogo che possiamo immaginare, un vestito sciupato
[troppo in fretta

Nella sez. 9 c'è la goffa e timida amicizia della Carla con Piero, la cronaca dei loro ritorni a casa. Il parco Ravizza a Milano è situato vicino all'Università Bocconi; un Giuseppe Ravizza fu l'ideatore della macchina da scrivere (ma i ragazzi non lo sanno).
Tacito narra che i Germani provavano la resistenza naturale dei bambini gettandoli d'inverno nei fiumi.

the reversal
can be carried out in various ways:
by hand

9

But those two
have had few nights to talk
the first was awkward
                    the second
kids laughed about some guy
who was talking to himself about a bomb

                                    and the next minute
forget the bomb, at the corner of Via Meda
the circle-line runs him over if the driver
wasn't quick

                yells, picturesque outbursts and somebody
                ready to form a crowd, at the rally
                the dogs get loose, the good little dimwit
                fusses with his goatee and dentures.

A dialogue only to be imagined, a suit ruined in too
    [big a hurry

Section I,9 presents Carla's shy, awkward friendship with Piero, and chronicles their walks home from school. Milan's Ravizza Park is located near Bocconi University; it so happens that Giuseppe Ravizza designed the typewriter (but the two young people don't know that). Tacitus tells how the Germanic tribes tested the natural resilience of their babies by throwing them into rivers in winter.

e tira e molla—barba ometto bomba, che ridere che piangere
dialogo che possiamo immaginare, uno così voleva riparare
una bicicletta scassata e aveva fretta

                            fino al portone di Carla

persuasi della colpa originale.

                  La terza

un istinto battagliero
                  li condusse a passare per il parco
e fu peggio, che un silenzio
gli cadde addosso e Carla aveva freddo
e Piero zitto e lei anche nel parco di dicembre

                  Chi sarà questo Ravizza?
chiese Piero, e pentito si nascose
le mani in tasca, che gli davan noia.
Poi uscirono, che zone luminose, allora
qui a Milano,
            a Carla assorta e lieve
Piero prese a dire:
                Marcia,
                    quest'anno,
                         il campionato,
      [che è un piacere.

            Certa gente si sveglia in quei momenti
            ridendo a un sonno buono, equilibrarsi
            sopra il trolley, amare un'infermiera per baciarla
            è troppo facile. Chi abita nel cielo e quanto paga
            d'affitto? Ecco le lune

and pulling and letting go—beard little man bomb,
        [what laughing what crying
a dialogue only to be imagined, so that one wanted to fix
a wrecked bicycle and was in a hurry

                        all the way to Carla's door
swayed by original sin.

                    The third
a battle instinct
                led them through the park
and things got worse, a silence
came over him and Carla was cold
and Piero quiet and she too in the park in December

                    Who's this Ravizza?
asked Piero, and embarassed he hid
his hands in his pockets, that bothered him.
Then they came out, what luminous corners, here
in Milano,
            to Carla absorbed and gentle
Piero decided to say:
                    The soccer season's

                            just fine

                                    this year,

    [a real treat.

            Some people wake in those moments
            smiling at a good sleep, to balance
            on a trolley, to love a nurse to kiss her
            that's too easy. Who lives in heaven and how much
                    [rent

di Giove sopra i fili del telefono, il viale
sarà tutto magnolie e i giardinieri
avranno un gran lavoro.

Pallavolo, se fosse un altro gioco sportivo, con la gente
O palla prigioniera?

Ecco ti rendo
i due sciocchi ragazzi che si trovano
a casa tutto fatto, il piatto pronto.
Non ti dico risparmiali
Colpisci, vita ferro città pedagogia
I Germani di Tacito nel fiume
li buttano nel fiume appena nati
la gente che s'incontra alle serali.

does he pay? There the moons
of Jupiter above the telephone wires, the street
will be all magnolias and the gardeners
will have a lot to do.

Volleyball, might it be another sport, with people
Or dodge ball?

Here I return
the two silly kids who find everything
ready at home, the plate full.
I don't ask you spare them
Strike, iron life city pedagogy
The Germans in Tacitus toss them
into the river barely born into the river
the people you meet at night shool.

II.   I

Carla Dondi fu Ambrogio di anni
diciassette primo impiego stenodattilo
all'ombra del Duomo

    Sollecitudine e amore, amore ci vuole al lavoro
    sia svelta, sorrida e impari le lingue
    le lingue qui dentro le lingue oggigiorno
    capisce dove si trova? TRANSOCEAN LIMITED
    qui tutto il mondo...
                  è certo che sarà orgogliosa.

    Signorina, noi siamo abbonati
    alle Pulizie Generali, due volte
    la settimana, ma il Signor Praték è molto
    esigente—amore al lavoro è amore all'ambiente—così
    nello sgabuzzino lei trova la scopa e il piumino
    sarà sua prima cura la mattina.

    UFFICIO A UFFICIO B UFFICIO C.

Perché non mangi? Adesso che lavori ne hai bisogno
              adesso che lavori ne hai diritto
                     molto di più.

Carla ha l'impiego: alla *Transocean Limited Import Export Company;*
padrone un certo Praték. Nella sezione II: il curioso pensiero sulla civiltà
che s'è trasferita al nord, per via del freddo che forza la gente a muoversi
e a lavorare, è un modo comico di esprimere la « morale locale ».

II.   I

Carla Dondi born of the late Ambrose seventeen
years of age first job shorthand typist
in the shadow of the Duomo

> Solicitude and love, love's needed at work
> be quick, smile and learn languages
> languages here languages nowadays
> understand where you are? TRANSOCEAN LIMITED
> here the whole world...

>> it's certain she'll be proud.

> Miss, we are clients
> of General Sanitation, two times
> a week, but Mr. Praték is very
> particular—love of work is love of workplace—so
> in the closet you will find the broom and duster
> it will be your first duty in the morning.

OFFICE A OFFICE B OFFICE C.

Why don't you eat? Now that you're working you need it
        Now that you're working you are much
                more entitled.

Carla has found work: at the *Transocean Limited Import Export Company*;
the boss is a certain Praték. In section II: the curious notion that civili-
zation has been driven northward by the cold which forces people to
move about and labor is a comical way of expressing a "local belief."

S'è lavata nel bagno e poi nel letto
s'è accarezzata tutta quella sera.

   Non le mancava niente, c'era tutta
   come la sera prima—pure con le mani e la bocca
   si cerca si tocca si strofina, ha una voglia
   di piangere di compatirsi
         ma senza fantasia
   come può immaginare di commuoversi?

   Tira il collo all'indietro ed ecco tutto.

  2

All'ombra del Duomo, di un fianco del Duomo
i segni colorati dei semafori le polveri idriz elettriche
mobili sulle facciate del vecchio casermone d'angolo
fra l'infelice corso Vittorio Emanuele e Camposanto,
Santa Radegonda, Odeon bar cinema e teatro
un casermone sinistrato e cadente che sarà la Rinascente
cento targhe d'ottone come quella
TRANSOCEAN LIMITED IMPORT EXPORT COMPANY
le nove di mattina al 3 febbraio.

   La civiltà si è trasferita al nord
   come è nata nel sud, per via del clima,
   quante energie distilla alla mattina
   il tempo di febbraio, qui in città?

She had a hot bath and then in bed
she carressed herself all over that night.
     Nothing was missing, it was all
     like the night before—even with the hands and the mouth
     she searched she touched she rubbed, she has an urge
     to cry to pity herself
                         but without fantasy
     how can she imagine to be moved?

     She cranes her neck back and that's all.

          2

In the shadow of the Duomo, on one side of the Duomo
the signals' flashings colors the electric fizzing granules
moving on the face of the large tenements on the corner
between the unhappy Corso Vittorio Emanuele and
     [Camposanto,
Santa Radegonda, Odeon bar cinema and theater
a huge shelled and crumbling tenement that will be the
     [Rinascente
hundred brass nameplates like that one
TRANSOCEAN LIMITED IMPORT EXPORT COMPANY
nine in the morning February 3rd.

     Civilization has moved north
     born as it was in the south, for the climate,
     how much energy does February weather distill
     in the morning, here in the city?

Carla spiuma i mobili
Aldo Lavagnino coi codici traduce telegrammi night letters
una signora bianca ha cominciato i calcoli
sulla calcolatrice svedese

      Sono momenti belli: c'è silenzio
      e il ritmo d'un polmone, se guardi dai cristalli
      quella gente che marcia al suo lavoro
      diritta interessata necessaria
      che ha tanto fiato caldo nella bocca
      quando dice buongiorno
                       è questa che decide
      e son dei loro
            non c'è altro da dire.

E questo cielo contemporaneo
in alto, tira su la schiena, in alto ma non tanto
questo cielo colore di lamiera

      sulla piazza a Sesto a Cinisello alla Bovisa
      sopra tutti i tranvieri ai capolinea

non prolunga all'infinito
i fianchi le guglie i grattacieli i capannoni Pirelli
coperti di lamiera?

I telegrammi « night letters » viaggiano la notte a una tariffa ridotta; le società commerciali li fanno in codice.

Carla dusts the furniture
Aldo Lavagnino with the codes translates telegrams
        [night letters
a lady in white has begun computing
on the Swedish adding machine

> These are beautiful moments: there's silence
> and the lung's rhythm, if you look out the windows
> the people who march to their work
> straight ahead interested necessary
> with so much hot breath in their mouths
> when they say goodmorning
>   they are who decide
> and it's all up to them
>   nothing else to say.

And this contemporary sky
on high, straightens your back, on high but not too much
this sky the color of tin

> on the piazza at Sesto at Cinisello at the Bovisa
> over all the conductors at the end of the line

doesn't it infinitely prolong
the columns the steeples the skyscrapers the Pirelli
        [warehouses
covered with tin?

"Night letter" telegrams are sent at night at a lower cost; commercial
companies transmit them in code.

È nostro questo cielo d'acciaio che non finge
Eden e non concede smarrimenti,
è nostro ed è morale il cielo
che non promette scampo dalla terra,
proprio perché sulla terra non c'è
scampo da noi nella vita.

3

Negli uffici s'imparan molte cose
    ecco la vera scuola della vita
alcune s'hanno da imparare in fretta
    perché vogliono dire saper vivere
la prima entrare nella manica a Praték
       che ce l'ha stretta

    A Praték gli vanno bene i soldi
e un impiegato mai, perché la fine
    del mese i soldi l'impiegato pochi o tanti
li porta via, e lui li guarda coi suoi occhi
    acquosi, i soldi, e non gli pare giusto
    A Praték gli van bene anche le donne
e Lidia che era furba lo sapeva
e l'ha passato mica male, il tempo, sullo sgabello della
  [macchina
con le sue cosce grasse

It's ours this steely sky that does not pretend
Eden and does not allow lapsing,
it's ours and moral the sky
that does not promise escape from the earth,
just because on earth there is no
escape from us in life.

3

As a clerk you learn many things
                  here's the real school of life
some things you've got to learn them fast
                  because that means you know how to live
the first to get on Praték's good side
                                which is very tight indeed

                  Praték likes money just fine
but never an employee, because at the end
                  of the month the money little or a lot the
      [employee
takes it home, and he watches it with his watery
                              eyes, the money, and it doesn't seem
      [right to him
                  Praték likes women just fine too
and Lidia who was smart knew it
and she didn't spend it badly, her time on the stool at the
      [typewriter
with her thick thighs

Ma la moglie coi soldi che è gelosa
vigila sulla serenità delle fanciulle,
Monsieur Praték—in fondo, io sono un filosofo—
         non per niente è stato anche in galera
rispetta gli istituti: Lidia parte
entra Carla: può servire che si sappia:
col dottor Pozzi basta un po' di striscio,
fargli mettere la firma in molti posti.

    4

Monsieur Goldstein un mite segretario tradito dal cognome
ha chiesto gli anni a Aldo Lavagnino
                ventidue
ho un figlio che combatte in Palestina
anch'io di ventidue, ha detto
             questa terra
avrà un pezzo di terra per i nostri
figli?
    Questa terra ha mercati
e sul mercato internazionale delle valute
libere o no, Cogheanu, il suo padrone, tiene una rete fitta:

Il Pozzi nominato nella sez. 3 è evidentemente un socio, in subordine,
di Praték.
Goldstein (sez. 4) è un famoso cognome di banchieri ebrei; il mite e
gentile personaggio è in realtà un trafficante di valute. Il « cancelliere
matto » è il laburista Cripps, inventore in quegli anni della « austerity »
inglese; la sua politica ostacolava un certo tipo di speculazioni sulla
sterlina.

But his wealthy wife who is jealous
watches over the girls' peace of mind,
Monsieur Praték—at bottom, I'm a philosopher—
                no accident he was in jail
he respects institutions: Lidia leaves
enter Carla: it might be useful to know:
with Mr. Pozzi a little rubbing is enough,
to make him put his signature anywhere.

4

Monsieur Goldstein a meek clerk betrayed by his surname
asked Aldo Lavagnino's age
                twenty-two
I have a son fighting in Palestine
also twenty-two, he said
                this earth
will it have a piece of earth for our
sons?
    This earth has markets
and over the international currency market
free or not, Cogheanu, his boss, holds a tight net:

The Pozzi referred to in section II,3 is clearly a lesser partner in Praték's
firm.
Goldstein (section II,4) is a family name of Jewish bankers; the kindly,
mild-mannered character is actually a money-trader. The "mad chan-
cellor" is the English Labor Party MP Cripps, creator of the English
"austerity" of this period—a policy which prevented a certain type of
speculation in sterling.

da un'area all'altra trasferiscono ogni giorno
valute in questo modo:
      Tel Aviv le quinze Avril o Bombay March twenty five
              su blok notes, carta straccia
      Monsieur x veuillez payer à notre Monsieur Ypsilon
      la somme de quatre vingt dix mille neuf cent cinq dollars
              Signé Goldstein o Cogheanu

A Bombay a Tel Aviv a Casablanca un ometto Mister x
per quel foglietto paga le sterline
anzi i dollari dollari, oggi son dollari che vanno

      nell'affare della soda, bell'e concluso in un
          [momento delicato
      in quel momento che la soda sul mercato risentiva
          [del rilancio
      jugoslavo e la Germania era alle porte
      e Praték a Roma aveva già comprato
      con lire d'Italia e alcune scappellate
      al mercato nero delle licenze la licenza
      d'esportazione per ventimila tonnellate
              fu il rapporto dello scambio
      dollaro sterlina—si compra a sterline si vende in dollari
          a Londra c'è cancelliere un matto—
      che buttò a mare l'affare: tremila dollari di spese
      quarantacinquemila non guadagnati quarantotto.

      Angelo un osso buco intero, con patate
      Carla un pezzo col midollo che le piace
      l'altro pezzo Nerina la madre le patate

from one area to another they transfer each day
currency this way:
> Tel Aviv le quinze Avril or Bombay March twenty five
> > on memo pads, foolscap
>
> Monsieur x veuillez payer à notre Monsieur Ypsilon
> la somme de quatre vingt dix mille neuf cent cinq dollars
> > Signed Goldstein or Cogheanu

In Bombay in Tel Aviv in Casablanca a little man Mister x
for that little slip of paper pays British pounds
or better dollars dollars, today it's dollars that count

> in that soda deal, good and done at a delicate
> > [moment
>
> when the soda market felt the Yugoslavian
> comeback and Germany was at the door
> and Praték in Rome had already bought
> with Italian lire and a few compliments
> on the black market for licenses the export
> license for twenty thousand tons
> > it was the exchange rate
>
> dollar pound—you buy in pounds sell in dollars
> > in London there's a mad chancellor—
>
> who blew the whole deal: three thousand dollars expenses
> forty-five thousand not earned forty-eight thousand.

> > Angelo a whole veal shank, with potatoes
> > Carla a piece with the marrow she likes
> > Nerina the other piece mother the potatoes

nessuno sa cosa vuol dire pagamento
contro documenti e perché s'usi
ma la madre orgogliosa guarda Carla

crescere.

6

Per esempio, bisogna sentir come bestemmia
che parole volgari come un uomo solamente
—a Carla nausea e niente voglia di domande—
oggi non mite Aldo

quando la gatta è via i topi ballano

La signora Camilla per calmarlo
non liscia il pelo giusto—con la schiena
che tiene su le spalle, sulla macchina
Carla china la faccia rifugiandosi
nei tasti più veloci

Il « pagamento contro documenti » è un termine commerciale che
designa le modalità di una transazione nella quale il pagamento, anziché
avvenire alla consegna della merce, avviene appunto alla consegna dei
titoli che trasferiscono il diritto di proprietà sulla merce stessa.
La sez. 6 è un « paradigma » delle cose che la Carla non è preparata a
capire. La « signora Camilla » è una dipendente della ditta, la stessa che
nella sez. II fa i conteggi sulla calcolatrice svedese.

none of them knows what it means payment
on receipt of invoice and why it is used
but a proud mother watches Carla

grow.

6

For example, you should hear him swear
such dirty words that only a man
—Carla's disgusted and has no use for questions—
today Aldo's not meek

when the cat's away the mice will play

Mrs. Camilla to calm him
doesn't rub him right—with her back
holding her shoulders, Carla lowers
her head over the typewriter hiding
in the fastest keys

"Payment on receipt of invoice" is a commercial term designating a
transaction in which the payment, rather than falling on consignment
of merchandise, falls on consignment of the titles transferring the prop-
erty right to the merchandise itself.
Section II,6 is a "paradigm" of those things Carla is not prepared to
understand. "Mrs. Camilla" is one of the firm's personnel, the same
person who in section II,2 does figures with the Swedish calculator.

« Ci sono cose che superi soltanto
a letto, incastrato in una donna, e maledetto
il frutto del suo grembo »—Aldo trema
non sa come sfogarsi
A third world war

FONDAMENTO DEL DIRITTO DELLE GENTI, L'ISTITUTO
DELLA GUERRA È ANTICO QUANTO GLI UOMINI: A
    [DIRIMERE
LE CONTROVERSIE FRA GLI STATI, SIA PURE COME
    [ESTREMA RATIO
NULLA DI PIÙ RISOLUTIVO ED EFFICACE DEL RICORSO
A CODESTO, CHE LA DOTTRINA CONFIGURA E LA PRASSI
    [TUTELA
COME SANZIONE DECISIVA CUI SI AFFIDA
IL RIPRISTINO DELLA VIOLATA LEGALITÀ
    [INTERNAZIONALE
—NON C'È DA FARSI ILLUSIONE, NON È TALE LEGGE
    [SENZA SANZIONE—
E LA SCIENZA SPECIFICA, I TRATTATI, DAL GROTIUS AI GIORNI NOSTRI
NE ILLUSTRANO LE RAGIONI E LA FUNZIONE DELLA GUERRA-
    [SANZIONE).

INOLTRE, LA DOTTRINA PIÙ RECENTE, SULLA SCORTA
    [DEGLI ACCADIMENTI

Il passo in maiuscoletto è costruito con il linguaggio dei manuali di
diritto internazionale: è un « corale » che commenta l'ira del giovane
Aldo, costretto a fare da interprete tra il padrone Praték e il super-
padrone, il « turco », che dà per certa la terza guerra mondiale. La ditta
è una succursale italiana di un trust commerciale internazionale.

"Some things get resolved
in bed, stuck in a woman, and damned be
the fruit of her womb"—Aldo trembles
and doesn't know how to let off steam
                    A third world war

CORNERSTONE TO THE RIGHTS OF PEOPLES, THE
      [INSTITUTION
OF WAR IS AS OLD AS HUMANITY: TO RESOLVE
QUARRELS AMONG STATES, BE IT AS LAST RESORT
NOTHING MORE RESOLUTE AND EFFICACIOUS THAN
      [RECOURSE
TO THIS, AS REPRESENTED IN DOCTRINE AND
      [GUARANTEED IN PRACTICE
A DECISIVE SANCTION UPON WHICH RELIES
THE RESTORATION OF VIOLATED INTERNATIONAL LAW
—LET THERE BE NO ILLUSIONS, LAW IS NOT LAW
      [WITHOUT SANCTIONS—
AND SCIENCE SPECIFIES, ALL TREATISES, FROM GROTIUS
      [TO THE PRESENT
ILLUSTRATE THE REASONS FOR AND FUNCTION OF
      [SANCTION-WAR).

FURTHERMORE, THE MOST RECENT DOCTRINE, IN
      [LIGHT OF EVENTS

The passage in block lettering is based on wording from international
law manuals: it is a "chorus" expressing the wrath of young Aldo, who
is forced to serve as interpreter between his boss Praték and the abso-
lute boss, the "Turk," who takes the Third World War as a fact. The
firm is an Italian branch of an international commercial trust.

E DELL'ESPRESSA VOLONTÀ DEI SOGGETTI DI DIRITTO
  [INTERNAZIONALE,
HA ELABORATO UNA NUOVA FIGURA DEFINITA GUERRA-
  [RIVOLUZIONE
MASSIMA PRODUTTRICE, EX NOVO, DI DIRITTO:
  [LADDOVE LA PRIMA
RIPRISTINA, LA SECONDA CREA, MIRABILMENTE
  [INTEGRANDOSI
IL SORGERE DELLA LEGGE E IL SUO PROSEGUIMENTO.

A third world war

is nécessary, né-ces-sa-ry, go on translate my friend
sporgendo il petto in fuori come un rullo e fronte dura
e io certo ho tradotto, che faccio il traduttore,
che ce ne vuole un'altra, un'altra guerra

> Ci sono anche quelli che a sera
> si tolgono un occhio mettendolo accanto
> alla scrittura di Churchill, sul comodino,
> intanto che fumano la sigaretta:
> è un occhio fasullo, di vetro, ma è vera
> l'orbita cava nel volto.
>
> Ma farlo di giorno, in piena luce di sole
> per sgomentare l'amore
> mi vuoi bene così?

I passi in corsivo sono commenti di una voce recitante che esprime la
protesta privata, le ragioni soggettive contro la guerra da poco
trascorsa.

AND WITH THE EXPRESS WISHES OF THE SUBJECTS OF
    [INTERNATIONAL LAW,
HAS EVOLVED A NEW CONCEPT DEFINED AS
    [REVOLUTION-WAR
GREATEST PRODUCER, EX NOVO, OF RIGHTS: WHEREAS
    [THE FIRST
RESTORES, THE SECOND CREATES, ADMIRABLY
    [INTEGRATING
THE RISE OF LAW AND ITS CONTINUANCE.

A third world war

is necessary, ne-ces-sa-ry, go on translate my friend
chest sticking out like a steamroller and a stiff lip
and I have certainly translated, who am a translator,
that we have need of another, another war

> *There are also those who at night*
> *take out their eye putting it next to*
> *the writings of Churchill, on the night stand,*
> *while they smoke a cigarette:*
> *it's a phoney eye, glass, but what's real*
> *is the socket in the face.*

> *But to do this by day, in full sunlight*
> *to scare off love*
> *do you love me this way?*

The passages in italics are commentaries: a reciting voice expresses private protest, an individual reasoning against the war that has recently ended.

ma farlo di giorno smerciandolo
come salvacondotto al tedesco
non sono un uomo intero pertanto
puoi fare a meno di uccidere
me

che la terza guerra mondiale è necessaria
con le mie parole a me
l'ha fatto dire—in un angolo in silenzio
Praték con gli occhi a dire sì e il beota
ridanciano di Biella « Andiamo piano, signori,
non scherziamo ».

      Lui dice pane al pane
      il turco è assai potente
      fare il furbo non gli serve a niente.

Poi, chissà perché, mai fatto prima,
Aldo la segue all'uscita le offre un Campari
Carla adesso rifiuta—ci ha già pensato scendendo—
e invece dice di sì, a Cappellari
si prende il suo aperitivo, se lo mescola
con un po' di vergogna
e in tram le gira la testa

      fortuna che i tram
      fortuna che nei tram di mezzogiorno
      la gente ti preme ti urta ti tocca
      magari ti blocca col gomito
      ma non ti lascia cadere.

but to do this by day peddling it
like safeconduct to a German
I'm not a whole man so
you do not have to kill
me

then the third world war is necessary
in my own words he forced me
to say it—in a corner quietly
Praték saying yes with his eyes and that happy-go-lucky
nitwit from Biella "Easy, gentlemen,
we must be serious."

      He calls a spade a spade
      the Turk is quite powerful
      trying to be cagey won't help him much.

Then, who knows why, never done it before,
Aldo follows her to the door offers a Campari
here Carla refuses—she'd given it a thought on the stairs—
and now says yes, on Cappellari Lane
she sips her aperitif, mixing it
with a little shame
and on the streetcar her head spins

      lucky that the streetcars
      lucky that on the noontime streetcars
      people shove you poke you touch you
      even block you with elbows
      but never let you fall.

No, no, no,—Carla è in fuga negando

    una corsa fra i segnali del centro non si nota
    se non c'è fra i venditori di sigarette
    un meridionale immigrato di fresco
    ancora curioso di facce
                avanti in marcia
    chi ci mette la carica?
                  scapigliata pallidona
    non è vero se non urli, come, paonazzo atrabiliare,
    quel tale per diffondere un giornale

questo no. Ho paura, mamma Dondi ho paura
c'è un ragno, ho schifo mi fa schifo alla gola
io non ci vado più.
Nell'ufficio B non c'era nessuno
mi guardava con gli occhi acquosi
se tu vedessi come gli fa la vena
ha una vena che si muove sul collo
Signorina signorina mi dice
mamma io non ci posso più stare
è venuto vicino che sentivo
sudare, ha una mano

Carla è di nuovo in fuga: stavolta è il padrone che probabilmente ha tentato l'approccio. La parte in corsivo, nella sez. I, è un controcanto dove appaiono le figure dell'inconscio di Carla, le immagini di attrazione-repulsione destate in lei dalla manovra di Praték (l'idea della « mantenuta », della vita peccaminosa, del mistero sadico-sessuale, ecc.).

III.   1

No, no, no,—Carla is on the run denying

>   a sprint through the downtown lights isn't noticed
>   unless there is among the cigarette peddlars
>   a Southerner freshly immigrated
>   still curious about faces
>   forward march
>   who's going to wind her up?
>   disheveled little paleface
>   it's not true unless you scream, like that bilious character
>   turning purple to sell newspapers

not this. I'm afraid, mamma Dondi I'm afraid
there's a spider, it disgusts me I'm disgusted in my throat
I won't go there anymore.
Office B was empty
he looked at me with his watery eyes
if you could see what his vein is like
he has a vein that throbs on his neck
Miss Miss he says to me
mamma I can't stay there anymore
he came so close I could feel
him sweating, the back of his hand

The girl has fled again: this time it is probably her boss who's made
advances toward her. The italicized part, in section III,1, is a counter-
melody featuring the images of Carla's unconscious, models of attrac-
tion/repulsion roused in her by Praték's advances (the idea of the "kept
woman," of a life of sin, of sado-sexual mystery, etc.).

coperta di peli di sopra
io non ci vado più.
Schifo, ho schifo come se avessi
preso la scossa
            ma sono svelta a scappare
io non ci vado più.
                    Sagome dietro la tenda
                    Marlene con il bocchino sottile
                    le sete i profumi i serpenti
                    l'ombra suona un violino di fibre
                    di nervi, sagome colore di sangue
                    blu azzurro viola pervinca, sottili
                    le braccia le cosce
                    enormi, bracciali monili sul cuore
                    nudo, l'amore
                    calvo la belva che urla la vergine santa
                    l'amore che canta chissà
                    dietro la tenda
                    le sagome.
La vedova signora Dondi
forse si sarà spaventata
ma non ha dato tempo a sua figlia
Non ti ha nemmeno toccata
gli chiederemo scusa

Nella sez. 2, seguendo il consiglio della madre, Carla va a trovare la
signora Praték per « riparare » e farsene un'alleata contro eventuali
« rappresaglie » del padrone.
Il collega Aldo, che l'accompagna alla penosa incombenza, per distrarla
le racconta una storiella, involontariamente simbolica: Carla è proprio
come il cavallo da circo, che vuole di più Praték?

is covered with hair
I won't go there anymore.
Disgusting, I'm disgusted as if I had
gotten a shock
               but I'm quick to run
I won't go there anymore.

> *Shapes behind the curtain*
> *Marlene with that slender cigarette holder*
> *the silks the perfumes the serpents*
> *the shadow plays a violin of nerve*
> *fibers, shapes color of blood*
> *blue azure violet periwinkle, the arms*
> *slender, the thighs*
> *enormous, bracelets jewelry on the naked*
> *heart, bald*
> *love the beast that howls the blessed virgin*
> *love that sings who can tell*
> *behind the curtain*
> *the shapes.*

The widow Mrs. Dondi
might have been frightened
but didn't give her daughter a chance.
He didn't even touch you
we'll apologize

In section III,2, following her mother's advice, Carla pays a visit to
Mrs. Praték to "patch things up" and make her an ally against any of
her boss's future "reprisals."
Her colleague Aldo, who accompanies her on this painful errand, tries
to distract her by a brief, unwittingly symbolic, story: Carla is just like
the circus horse: what more does Praték want from her?

fin che non ne trovi un altro
tu non lascerai l'impiego
bisogna mandare dei fiori
alla signora Praték.

2

Domenica con un fascio di fiori
Aldo a fianco occupato di lei « Telefonano in un circo.
Pronto: batto a macchina e parlo francese, non basta?
So andare in bicicletta e dire il credo, non basta
per il circo? Non sentite che nitrisco, che volete di più
da un povero cavallo? »

con un fascio di fiori più pesante
di una sporta di pane e di patate
in visita ai signori Praték.

Ma madama è squisita, dice belli
ai fiori, bravi ai ragazzi, dice che schiocchezze
dice che Aldo è un giovane per bene
che sono proprio una coppia divertente

Quanto alla signora Praték, che conosce le « tentazioni » del marito, si
compiace che i due *stiano bene insieme*: se Aldo la corteggia, la
proteggerà anche dalle mire del padrone.
I versi in corsivo sono un controcanto elegiaco: chissà com'è bello
vivere in solitudine; ma è un po' una parodia, naturalmente.

until you find another
you won't quit your job
we must send flowers
to Mrs. Praték.

2

Sunday with a bunch of flowers
Aldo next to her attending "Someone calls a circus.
Hello: I type and speak French, isn't that enough?
I can ride a bicycle and say the Creed, isn't that enough
for the circus? You can't tell I whinny, what more do you want
from a poor horse?"

with a bunch of flowers heavier
than a bag of bread and potatoes
on their way to visit the Pratéks.

But Madame is exquisite, she says beautiful
to the flowers, nice to the youngsters, says what nonsense
says that Aldo is the right sort
that they are an amusing couple

As for Mrs. Praték, who knows of her husband's "temptations," she is
pleased that these two *get along well*: if Aldo courts her, he will also
protect her from the boss's intentions.
The italicized lines are an elegiac counter-melody: how great it must
be to live in solitude; but the tone naturally is a bit parodic.

forse dice fra i denti almeno questo
le facesse la guardia l'impiegato.

> *Autour des neiges, qu'est-ce qu'il y a?*
> *Colorati licheni, smisurate*
> *impronte, ombre liocorni*
> *laghi cilestri, nuvole bendate,*
> *risa dell'eco a innumeri convalli*
> *la vita esala fiorisce la morte*
> *solitudine imperio libertà.*

5

Quante parole nei comizi e folla
nel marzo quarantotto! Gente fissa
ogni ora del giorno e della notte in piazza Duomo.
Aldo, Angelo, persino la collega dell'ufficio accanto
vestita così bene
dicono che la gente che lavora
deve stare al suo posto
che si sa bene per chi si deve votare.

A Carla per il voto le mancano degli anni
e a lei sembrano molti

La sez. 5 canta la necessità, il cerchio che piano piano si stringe intorno
a Carla (il sesso che bolle a primavera, il lavoro, la vita: bisognerà pure
decidersi a tirare un bilancio provvisorio). Ma Carla tenta ancora di
rifiutarsi alla necessità.
La parte in corsivo commenta espressionisticamente la situazione.

unwittingly she might even mutter
the clerk ought to keep an eye on her

> *Autour des neiges, qu'est-ce qu'il y a?*
> *Colored lichens, immense*
> *footprints, unicorn shadows*
> *cerulean, blindfolded clouds,*
> *the echo's laugh at numberless vales*
> *life exhales death flowers*
> *solitude dominion freedom.*

5

How many speeches at rallies and crowds
in March '48! People stuck
any hour of the day and night in Piazza Duomo.
Aldo, Angelo, their colleague too from the next office
who dresses so well
they say working people
should keep their place
they ought to know for whom to vote.

Carla is some years away from voting
too many she believes

Section III,5 sings of the necessity, the circle that gradually closes in
around Carla (sex seething in springtime, work, life: she'll have to de-
cide to reach some provisional account of herself). Yet once again Carla
tries to go the way of denial.
The italicized part offers an expressionistic commentary on the situation.

Aldo s'arrabbia

> e invece è lui che fa rabbia
> disoccupato quand'è sera, sofferente
> al rifugio che notte gli presenta
> per molti o pochi soldi,
> e se accarezza Carla
> le accarezza le mani, e parla.

Ma il sangue, è vero che ha un ritmo
in certi mesi detti primavera
accelerato? e vale anche per noi, qui sotto il ritmo
della città?

> e quest'interno rigoglio come viene
> tradotto sopra i volti? ma dietro i vetri
> che cosa bolle alla Montecatini
> dov'è la primavera della Banca
> Commerciale?

Aldo s'è messo in testa che la Carla
vada con lui a mangiare, una sera

ma sarà una sera che Carla ha da fare
con tante cose in casa, col bambino
ch'è nato a sua sorella.

Col bambino che è nato e si prende
altro spazio, è più esiguo
l'esiguo margine a fughe

> a un totale parziale o sub-totale
> non è che può mancare molto; sopravvive
> difatti, solo chi impara a vivere.

Aldo gets angry
        instead it's him who gets her mad
        unoccupied at night, restless
        in the shelter night brings him
        for much or little money,
        and if he caresses Carla
        he caresses her hands, and talks.

And blood, is its true rhythm
accelerated during certain months
called spring? and does that go for us as well, here
in this urban rhythm?
        and this internal lushness how does it
        transfer to the faces? behind the windows
        what's cooking at Montecatini
        where is the springtime of Banca
        Commerciale?

Aldo's got it in his head that Carla
will dine with him, some night

and it will be a night Carla must have
lots of work at home, with the baby
newly born to her sister.

With the baby newly born who takes up
another place, it's more meager
the meager margin for escape

        for a partial total or sub-total
        there cannot be much more; he survives
        in fact, only who learns to live.

Necessità necessità verbo dei muti
idillio accanto alla calcolatrice
corsa proficua degli storpi, amore
del badilante sullo sterro, gravità
sul capezzolo dei nati, erba del prigioniero,
lo stesso capriccio del vento nel tuo nome
fa portatore di polline natura.

6

Come quelli che non seppero servirsi nell'assenza
del genitore è un trauma poi se manca
la frutta sulla tavola, nessuna scusa a Carla
la pazienza di Aldo sa concedere.
Tacitamente passa una domenica
che uno gira da solo e l'altra è in casa,
procedendo poi i giorni come al solito

                    come strumento
                    come strumento di tesaurizzazione
                    come strumento di tesaurizzazione
                    [l'oro in Europa

Nella sez. 6 sembra che Carla cominci suo malgrado a sciogliersi.
Passano i giorni monotoni della *Import Export*; Aldo, che s'è visto
rifiutare un invito un po' più impegnativo della solita passeggiata, ha
perduto la pazienza.
Le domeniche si ripetono solitarie. Ma la Carla è spinta fuori di casa (a
proposito: è nato un bambino alla sorella, e Carla diventa, in casa, sem-

Necessity necessity the word of the voiceless
daydream at the adding machine
profitable race for the cripple, love
of the digger in a ditch, sternness
on the newly born's nipple, the prisoner's grass,
the same trick of the wind in your name
nature makes it the carrier of pollen.

6

Like those who couldn't take care of themselves without
their parent it's a trauma then if fruit
is missing from the table, no excuse for Carla
Aldo's patience can allow.
A Sunday goes by silently
one goes out alone the other stays home,
the days then continue as always

> as instrument
> as instrument of capitalization
> as instrument of capitalization
> [European gold

In section III,6 Carla seems to start loosening up despite herself. Dull
days pass by at *Import Export*; Aldo, who is turned down when he sug-
gests something more than the usual walk, has lost his patience.
Sundays are spent in solitude. But Carla is pushed out of her house (by
the way: her sister gives birth, and Carla becomes less and less impor-
tant at home); walking through the city she has a vague sense of being

si arriva a un altro sabato, ma casca
un approccio, o si perde per aria: domenica bis.
Si può dire benissimo « Esco
a prendere una boccata d'aria » ma anche a questo
a non affogare per strada di domenica da soli
ci vuole temperanza ed abitudine.

Carla non lo sapeva che alle piazze
alle case ai palazzi periferici succede
lo stesso che alle scene di teatro: s'innalzano s'allargano
scompaiono, ma non si sa chi tiri i fili o in ogni caso
non si vede: attraversando da un marciapiede all'altro sono bisce
le rotaie, s'attorcigliano ai tacchi delle scarpe
sfilano le calze all'improvviso—come la remora che in altomare
ferma i bastimenti.
Quei bambini sul ponte mentre fanno
una festa dolorosa a un animale c'è il fumo che li assale,
a San Luigi sono i ladri che ci stanno, via Brembo è una fetta
        [di campagna, peggio,
una campagna offesa da detriti, lavori a mezzo, non più
        [verde e non ancora
piattaforma cittadina; meglio il fumo sul ponte che scompare
col merci, via Toscana, piazzale Lodi con un poco
d'alberi e grandi chioschi di benzina, dove fischia un garzone
        [*bela tusa*

---

pre meno importante); camminando per la città quasi comincia a
sentirsi « dattilografa milanese ». Intanto i passi la portano a una mostra
di pittura (un « giro usato » con Aldo) dove scorge il collega « in
confidenza » con un'altra donna. Qui la gelosia arresta, ma lei non lo
sa ancora bene, la sua fuga: la gelosia è un pensiero che la porta nella
direzione della necessità.

Saturday comes again, an advance
falls through, or gets lost in the air: Sunday encore.
You could certainly say "I'm going out
for a breath of air" but for this too
not to drown in the streets alone on Sundays
you need a tolerance and self-control.

Carla did not know the same awaits
piazzas houses suburban buildings
and scenery on stage: they rise open out
disappear, but no one knows who pulls the ropes or anyway
no one sees it: crossing from a sidewalk to another the tracks
are snakes, they twist around the heels of shoes
suddenly slip off the stockings—like the remora stops
ships on the high seas.
Those children on the bridge meanwhile make
a painful fuss over some poor animal smoke assaults them,
San Luigi the thieves hang out there, Via Brembo is a slice of
     [countryside, worse,
a countryside offended by debris, work half-done, no longer
     [green and not yet
flat cityscape; better the smoke on the bridge that disappears
with the freight, Via Toscana, Piazzale Lodi with a few
trees and big gas stations, where an errand boy whistles
     [*bela tusa*

---

a "Milanese typist." Meanwhile her route takes her to an art show (an "habitual route" with Aldo) where she spies her colleague being "intimate" with some other woman. Here her jealousy checks her flight, without her quite realizing it: jealousy is a notion that steers her toward necessity.

e un altro stona *ha fatto più battaglie la mia sottana*
        [—uno stornello di Porta Romana—
ma è un uomo sciupato, che porta
un cane a passeggio.

Due giovani sul serio non permettono
con baci spudorati alcuna sosta
su una panca nella rotonda del piazzale, incalza il giorno
il cammino di Carla: viale Umbria si muove un po' di gente
c'è qualche faccia di ragazza fatta, motociclette in moto
        [della festa.
Un bar, gente che ride fa richiamo, ma non entra così
        [una signorina
a bere un'aranciata: intrusa, ciccolataia, figurina
è fuori l'aria, anche se ansima ormai
la passeggiata per mutarsi in corsa, e sorprende una parola
una parola qualsiasi scappata a sé sola—come i vecchi alla
        [Baggina,
i matti.
        Pure, dopo il silenzio del verziere
—vedessi che fermento domattina—capita che ritrova la città
i negozi coi vetri luminosi, la folla, il salvagente. Come gli altri
        [il camminare di Carla riacquista sicurezza e andamento: è
        [milanese come è periferia
calare per la festa attorno al centro.
                        Un giro usato
la riprende, un comizio l'attarda e fa pressione
uno sguardo per lei, si perde il tempo.

                        L'aria scura dov'è? qui sono luci
vive, abbaglianti, ci sono i quadri colorati dei pittori nelle sale
dove l'ingresso è libero.
128

and another squawks *ha fatto più battaglie la mia sottana*
     [—a stornello from Porta Romana—
but it's a haggard man, who takes
his dog for a walk.

Two youngsters really won't allow
their shameless kisses a moment's pause
on a bench in the piazza's garden, Carla's walk
forces the day: Viale Umbria with a few people stirring
a few faces of grown-up girls, motorcycles in holiday cruise.
A cafe, laughing people entice, but a young lady doesn't go in
     [like that
just to drink an orangeade: intruder, out of it, little doll
fresh air's outside, even if she gasps by now
her stroll about to turn to flight, and a word surprises
a word whatever escaped from her alone—like old people at
     [Baggina,
the insane.
          Yet, after the peacefulness at the farmers' market
—what bustle in the morning—she happens to regain the city
the bright store windows, the crowds, the traffic island. Like
     [others
Carla's walk regains security and steadiness: it's as Milanese as
     [suburban
to flock downtown on holidays.
                         An habitual route
catches up to her, a rally holds her up and a stare
pressures her, time passes.

                    Where is the dark air? here lights are
bright, dazzling, painted pictures by artists hang in the rooms
where admission is free.

Oh la Coscienza che guarda le sue Mani
orribili, vestita solo di Calze nere fino all'Inguine! Pittore
[espressionista ancora ancora
si sbanda la ragazza e vuole uscire
di corsa,
       o è per Aldo, che si effonde
pendendo dalle sue labbra una giovane bionda
e un'enorme signora con le volpi? O questi invece fermano
la nuova fuga di Carla?
       Contegno, fingimento, con la mano
una ravviata ai capelli e poi lo sguardo a confrontare l'altra
in confidenza con Aldo: ancora rossa o bianca per la pallida
vampa Carla avvampa, ma il pensiero più veloce del freno è
[già pensiero
pensato: ha gambe quella lì
con le caviglie grosse, come è grassoccio il viso, poco fine.

7

Nerina ha voglia di ridere, perché ride ogni tanto
adesso, con il figlio, Carla ha la faccia seria mentre provano
allo specchio, mentre Nerina insegna e Carla impara
a mettere il rossetto sulle labbra: ci deve essere in un cassetto
un paio di calze di nylon, finissime
bisogna provarle.

Il brano « Oh la Coscienza che guarda » si riferisce a un dipinto
espressionista e le parole con l'iniziale maiuscola suggeriscono appunto
che il quadro ha qualche ascendenza tedesca.

                              Oh Conscience staring at its horrible
Hands, clad only in black Stockings to the Groin! Expressionist
        [painter alright alright
the girl swerves and wants to get out
in a hurry,
                or is it because of Aldo, who is effusive
a young blonde hanging on his words
and an enormous lady in foxes? Or do they instead halt
Carla's new flight?
                        Composure, feigning, running a hand
through her hair and then a look to size up the other
hanging onto Aldo: still red or white in the pale
flush Carla flushes, but the thought faster than the bit is
        [already a thought
thought: that one has legs
with thick ankles, how chubby her face, not much class.

        7

Nerina feels like laughing, indeed every so often she laughs
now, with her son, Carla's face is serious while they try
at the mirror, while Nerina teaches and Carla learns
to put on lipstick: sure there must be a pair of nylon
stockings in a drawer, very sheer
you have to try them on.

_____

The passage "Oh Conscience staring" refers to an expressionistic paint-
ing, and the words starting with capital letters suggest some German
influence.

Questo lunedì comincia che si sveglia
presto, che indugia svagata nella piazza
prima di entrare in ufficio, che saluta
a testa alta « buongiorno » con l'aggiunta
« a tutti », che sorride cercando Aldo con gli occhi
che gli dice « Bella la ragazza e come
attenta ai tuoi discorsi », che incomincia—forse—il lavoro
    [fresca.

Quanto di morte noi circonda e quanto
tocca mutarne in vita per esistere
è diamante sul vetro, svolgimento
concreto d'uomo in storia che resiste
solo vivo scarnendosi al suo tempo
quando ristagna il ritmo e quando investe
lo stesso corpo umano a mutamento.

Ma non basta comprendere per dare
empito al volto e farsene diritto:
non c'è risoluzione nel conflitto
storia esistenza fuori dell'amare
altri, anche se amore importi amare
lacrime, se precipiti in errore
o bruci in folle o guasti nel convitto
la vivanda, o sradichi dal fitto
pietà di noi e orgoglio con dolore.

Nella sez. conclusiva Carla impara a mettere il rossetto sulle labbra. Il finale in corsivo riassume tutti i commenti e lascia aperta la situazione umana al proprio consumo.

This Monday begins with her waking up
early, lingering absently in the piazza
before stepping in the office, greeting
with head held high, "Good morning" with the added
"everyone," smiling searching for Aldo with eyes
that say to him "Pretty girl and so
attentive to your talk," starting in—maybe—on her work
       [wide awake.

How much death surrounds us and how
much must be turned to life to exist
it's diamond on glass, concrete
development of man in opposing history
only alive unfleshing in his time
when rhythm mires and invests
even the human body with change.

Yet understanding is not enough to give
impetus to the face and make it law:
there is no solution to the conflict
history existence outside of loving
others, even if love means loving
tears, if it falls into error
or burns in neutral or food rots
at banquet, or from the thick yanks pity
for ourselves and painful pride.

In the final section Carla learns to put on lipstick. The italicized finale
recapitulates all the commentaries and leaves the human situation open
to further exploitation.

PROLOGO

Illesi, piaga o errore non badiamo.
Spande il sangue prodigio degli anni.
Azzurri i selciati dell'alba.
Circonclude il tramonto noi che tramontiamo.

Impaziente, paziente sempre il ritmo s'attarda
e conviene al presente fedele. I vuoti
son pieni, realtà fantasma realmente.
Vivere, lungo l'attimo è buona guardia.

Distinzione di fini riconosce uguale,
getta via la paura la cara contraddizione,
del passo incespico fa una danza.
L'offesa ritorce un dolore speciale.

Insaziato groviglio di ciò che non accade,
tenerezze orribili della mediocrità.
Il naufrago è onorato con il suo rottame,
il malcompiuto un flusso storico pervade.

Iniziazione alla ripresa della vita dopo la catastrofe (la guerra, il passaggio rovinoso tra due epoche) e conclusione-riassunto dei temi essenziali a « noi che tramontiamo » in un tempo di lunga minaccia. La violenza della precarietà è resa dallo schizomorfismo dei singoli blocchi che s'incastrano nelle quartine. Il ritmo dissonante del verso risulta dal rapporto dinamico di due accenti principali con un numero vario (da uno a tre) di accenti secondari.

Il nucleo dell'intero discorso è, naturalmente, la « cara contraddizione » protagonista della terza strofa. Nelle due quartine successive è sviluppato il tema della convivenza: tra gli emblemi negativi appare l'imma-

PROLOGUE

Unharmed, no matter if by error or wound.
The prodigy of years brims over with blood.
Blue are the flagstones of dawn.
We the setting are by sunset enclosed.

Impatient, patient the rhythm's always late
to suit the faithful present. Voids
are solids, and reality really a ghost.
To live by the instant would be safe.

Dear contradiction considers any difference
in goals the same, casting off fear,
creating a dance from stumbling steps.
A special pain retaliates for the offence.

Unfulfilled muddle of what will not ensue,
the horrid kindness of mediocrity.
The survivor is honored with his wreckage,
the poorly done, by a historical flow imbued.

Initiation as life resumes after catastrophe (war, the disastrous passage
between two eras) and summary-conclusion of the essential themes
for us "by sunset enclosed" in a time of sustained threat. The shock of
precariousness is rendered by the schizomorphism of single blocks set
into quatrains. The dissonant rhythm of the verse comes from the
dynamic relation between two main stresses and a varied number (from
one to three) of secondary stresses.

The core of the entire discourse is, of course, the "dear contradiction"
dominating the third stanza. The two following quatrains develop the
theme of cohabitation: among the negative emblems there appears

Violenza di pulcinella, disciplina da caporale.
L'avida smorfia è tuttofare e disfare.
Di sorte in sorte la spola s'incanta,
il meglio viene vestito del male.

Come il malato nel giardino dell'ospedale,
nel paese dell'anima va tedioso lo spettro;
confuso dalla brezza e dai colori della nube,
il misero aborre le corsie dell'abissale.

Morire, come vorresti? Fare ponte al passaggio.
Non corteo d'elezione, non pietoso trapasso;
né contesa né approccio aver rinviato,
mancanza supplita con spurio coraggio.

---

gine neutrale della spola del destino. Il singolo è il malato che s'aggira nel giardino dell'ospedale.

La considerazione della morte è connessa con l'idea della vita giusta; « grazia e giustizia » si riferisce con evidente ironia all'omonimo Ministero. Per il valore iniziatico della domanda-risposta con cui s'apre la settima strofa, il miglior commento è forse questo passo di M. Eliade: « Il ne nous incombe pas de décider en quelle mesure les initiations traditionnelles tenaient leurs promesses. L'important est qu'elles proclamaient l'intention, et revendiquaient le pouvoir, de transmuter l'existence humaine. La nostalgie d'une *renovatio* initiatique, qui surgit sporadiquement des tréfonds de l'homme moderne areligieux, nous semble alors hautement significative: elle serait, en somme, l'expression moderne de l'éternelle nostalgie de l'homme de trouver un sens positif à la mort, d'accepter la mort comme un rite de passage à un mode d'être supérieur » *(Naissances mystiques,* Paris 1959).

Violence of Pulcinella, discipline of a corporal.
The greedy smirk is all doing and undoing.
From fate to fate the shuttlecock tangles,
the best is redressed in evil.

Like an invalid in the hospital yard,
a tedious ghost walks in the soul's land;
confused by the breeze and the colored clouds,
a poor man abhors the abysmal ward.

And how would you die? Build a bridge to the passage.
No march of the chosen, no piteous crossing;
postponed no dispute no approach,
want supplanted by spurious courage.

---

the neutral image of the shuttle of fate. The solitary person is the pa-
tient roaming the hospital garden.

The consideration of death is linked with the idea of the just life; "jus-
tice and grace" refers, with obvious irony, to the Ministry of the same
name (ed.note: the equivalent of the u.s. Department of Justice). As to
the initiatory value of the question-answer which begins the seventh
stanza, the best comment may well be this quote from Mircea Eliade:
"It is not for us to decide to what extent traditional initiations kept
their promises. The important thing is that they declared the inten-
tion, and claimed the power, of transforming human life. The nostal-
gia for an initiatory *renovatio*, which rises up sporadically from the
depths of modern a-religious man, thus strikes us as highly significant:
the modern expression, in essence, of man's eternal nostalgia for finding
a positive meaning for death, for accepting death as a rite of passage
toward a higher mode of being" (*Naissances mystiques*, Paris 1959).

Tutto a grazia e giustizia aver innalzato
in continuato fervore e riparazione:
i mostri dell'infanzia, le fioche persone,
nel volo mancino obblighi e colpe rovesciato.

A che servono i grimaldelli la ruggine la chiave,
il crepitio delle cicale nel crogiolo dell'estate?
Esplodono i gonfi propositi nel cuore, il cane latra
alla porta, la luna appende un riflesso alla trave.

C'è un'avventura che si chiama ragione,
margine della misura e dello smisurato.
La prima idea fu l'evento, stupore proclamato
d'essere e tempo nella coniugazione.

Recita un grido, adora un albero di vita,
pensa l'opera immane l'eroe nella desolazione.
Nell'agonia dell'ozio il dio ironico
l'ossessione che agì immune ricompensa.

Il « volo mancino » è una ricognizione nello spazio vietato,
nell'elemento totalmente umano (razionale e irrazionale); secondo
Jung, la sinistra indica il *Selbst*, l'oggettività psichica.
Nella quartina dei « grimaldelli » c'è un contraccolpo esistenziale a quanto
di teoretico e programmatico è detto precedentemente; di conseguenza,
la ragione è affermata quale « avventura ». L'eroe e l'albero di vita
sono archetipi; l'albero simboleggia la forza femminile della natura.
Anche il « dio ironico » è un segnale dello spirito della vita.

In steady fervor and amends having raised
all to justice and grace:
the monsters of childhood, the hazy souls,
in left-handed flight guilt and duty reversed.

What good are the picklocks the wrench the rust,
the crackle of locusts in summer's cauldron?
Swollen intentions snap in the heart, the dog barks
at the door, the moon hangs its reflex on a truss.

There is an adventure called reason,
margin of measure and immeasurable.
The first idea was the event, proclaimed amazement
at being and time in conjugation.

In desolation the hero offers a cry,
worships the tree of life, thinks the immense work.
In slothful agony the ironic god
repays an obsession with immunity.

The "left-handed flight" is a reconnaissance of forbidden space, the
totally human element (rational and irrational); according to Jung, the
left indicates the *Self*, psychic objectivity.

In the quatrain of the "picklocks" there is an existential counterthrust
against earlier programmatic and theoretic statements, so that reason
is now affirmed as an "adventure." The hero and the tree of life are
archetypes; the tree symbolizes nature's feminine power. The "ironic
god" also is a signal of the life-spirit.

Tenebra splende nel delirio aperto,
l'aversi al dare si conforma.
Sotto le palpebre la combustione del tatto.
Vita in morte, che sconcerto.

Molti nomi ha la terra. Pochi suoni
colmano l'ora, traboccano per dire
alla viva quiete moto rivelazione
di semi e figure che sùbito abbandoni.

Parola fu in origine voce dell'assente;
né tu l'ignori che, l'ombra capovolta,
scendi per l'aria ferita dal rompito dei motori
e tumultuare ascolti dal muto frangente.

Enfatica è l'unione del passo e della strada,
o sommessa nella felpa cauta e ansiosa,
o sotto la selce perduta; perduta nella febbre
che solleva i talloni, la voce palpita, richiama.

Nella quartina che comincia « Tenebra splende » si fondono l'esperienza
erotica e la modalità essenziale della conoscenza. Nella dichiarazione
« l'aversi al dare si conforma » è espressa la modalità dell'individuazione.
La frase sulla « parola » è una contaminazione da Freud (« Lo scrivere
fu in origine la voce dell'assente », ved. *Il disagio nella civiltà*): il tema
della comunicazione è qui stravolto e immerso in una figurazione di
traffico cittadino e di folla che riempie le strade. In realtà, la parola è
ambigua, è anche assenza di sé all'altro, è non-comunicazione,
informazione gratuita, silenzio travestito. Anche il silenzio, quale
negazione della necessità di prender la parola, dev'essere sorpassato.

Darkness shines in open frenzy,
having oneself takes the shape of giving.
Beneath the eyelids combustion of touch.
Life in death, what perplexity.

Many names hath the earth. A few sounds slake
the hour and overflow to bespeak
the living quiet movement revelation
of seeds and figures you instantly forsake.

In the beginning word was the voice of absence;
nor with shadow turned do you pretend not
to descend through air wounded by coughing motors
to hear rioting from a reef of silence.

When step meets street the noise shouts
or is softened by cautious troubled felt,
or beneath lost flagstones; lost in the fever
that lifts up heels, a voice trembles, recalls.

The quatrain beginning "Darkness shines" merges erotic experience
and the essential modality of knowledge. The statement "having one-
self takes the shape of giving" expresses the modality of individuation,
ethical and erotic.

The sentence about the "word" alters a statement from Freud: ("Writ-
ing was originally the voice of the absent," cf. *Civilization and Its Dis-
contents*): the theme of communication is upset here, plunged into a
figuration of city traffic and crowds filling the streets. In reality, the
word is ambiguous, being also self-absence for the other, non-commu-
nication, gratuitous information, disguised silence. Even silence, as the
negation of the necessity of beginning to speak, must be gotten beyond.

Viene l'enorme silenzio da sorpassare,
inevidenza assoluta s'accende nei dilegui.
Non sapere dove la svolta conduce
è il modo buono di pensare.

Vagabonda scarabocchia la terra,
chi ha temprato la punta alla mente?
La carta vetrata dei giochi, l'adulto coltello
che sbucciò l'evidenza dal niente.

Nella chiusa si offrono all'iniziato gli strumenti di cui può far uso; la
mente è il soggetto dei primi due versi (non dovrebbero sussistere
dubbi, giacché « scarabocchiare » è soltanto transitivo).

Up looms the huge silence to ring,
absolute lack of evidence lights up in trickles.
Not knowing where the turn may lead
is the best way to think.

Oh earth, you vagabond scribble,
who sharpened the point for the mind?
The toy sandpaper, the adult knife
that peeled the evidence from nil.

The ending offers the initiate tools for this; the mind is the subject of
the first two lines (there should be no lingering doubt about this, since
"scribbling" is only transitive).

RESURREZIONE DOPO LA PIOGGIA

Fu nella calma resurrezione dopo la pioggia
l'asfalto rifletteva tutte le nostre macchie
un lungo addio volò come un acrobata
dalla piazza al monte
e l'attimo sparì di volto in volto
s'accesero i fanali e si levò la buia torre
contro la nostra debolezza
i secoli non ci hanno disfatti.

I GIORNI AGGRAPPATI ALLA CITTA

I giorni aggrappati alla città e diseredati,
la vuota fornace ribrucia scorie morte.
Tortuoso di scatti e abbandoni, il polso feroce
misura l'orologio di sabbia e l'orme ineguali
dell'ansia. Lo scrimolo del mare, oltre di me
nel mio canto si sporge.

Segreto è il lavoro che a farmi l'occhio sereno
nomina il mare distante. Nessun amico può dirmi
menzogne ch'io non conosca, nessuna donna
oltrepassare il suo messaggio di lode o di resa.

                              Io vedo le mie parole,
le mie terre brucate dal silenzio mortale, schierarsi
lungo l'ultima ora del giorno tormentato di vele,
e rievocarmi.

RESURRECTION AFTER THE RAIN

It was in the calm resurrection after the rain
the asphalt reflected all our stains
a long goodbye flew like an acrobat
from the piazza to the mount
and the moment vanished from face to face
the floodlights turned on and the dark tower rose
against our weakness
the centuries have not undone us.

THE DAYS CLINGING TO THE CITY

The days clinging to the city and disinherited,
the empty furnace blasts the dead slag.
Careening through leaps and abandons, my wild pulse
keeps time by the sand-clock, the unsteady footsteps
of anxiety. From without the edges of the sea
invade my song.

Secret is the work that to uncloud my troubled eyes
would name the distant sea. No friend can tell me
lies I do not know, no woman
exceed her message of surrender or praise.

My lands grazed
by deadly silence, I see my words line up
beside the final hour of the day harangued by sails,
and summon me again.

QUANDO VIDI IL SALICE

Quando vidi il salice scuotere le sue tristi piume
nel giardino dell'ospedale, mi ferì una scheggia
dell'ora mormorante per la cascata dei colli
dalla costa lontana; la composta luce
giacque senza palpebre sul confine dell'erba.

E vidi nel ricordo la torre al vento sulla scogliera,
la sua toppa verde e la scacchiera spallidita.
Vidi che tutto è bello e uguale:
ala di pietra spuma di mare inverno...

GRIGIE RADURE S'ACCENDONO

Una banda di ragazzi preda le cavallette
Nei terreni da vendere e pianta fazzoletti
In cima a pertiche, tra i cardi.

Il lavoro è già dietro lo steccato, avanza
Col tonfo delle betoniere, cola con gli asfalti,
Spela il cielo con la sega elettrica;
Al suolo è rasa la muta torre.

Dal mio guscio di rovine saltano note di colomba.

WHEN I SAW THE WILLOW

When I saw the willow shaking its sad feathers
in the hospital garden, I was wounded by a shard
of the hour murmuring through the rolling hills
from a distant shore; the composed light
lay eyes unblinking along the edges of the lawn.

And I saw in my memory the tower in the wind on the cliffs,
its green patch and faded chessboard walls.
I saw everything is beautiful and the same:
wing of stone froth of sea winter…

GREY CLEARINGS LIGHT UP

A gang of boys pillages grasshoppers
On lands for sale and sticks handkerchiefs
To poles amid the thistles.

Work underway behind the fence keeps moving
With the churning of cement-mixers, pouring with asphalt,
Shaving the sky with electric saws;
The silent tower is razed to the ground.

From the shell of my ruins leap notes of a dove.

Lascia un sentore felice la banda in fuga.
Laggiù sulle ville tramonta e grigie radure
S'accendono, il fiume rabbuia, soffia
Un vento che non devasta né punge.
I lumi rossi vegliano ai cantoni del castello.

COMPLEANNO

Sgroviglia gli arruffati pensieri dei trent'anni
mentre imbruna il cielo tra meriggio e inverno,
filano le antenne verso il nord
e s'impolvera l'orecchio.
Angeli viola preludiano in torma ad ogni svolta.
Ecco l'omacchio disarmato
in mezzo al petto del campo;
ecco sul dorso dei colli, in figure di dolore,
ulivi aspri e forti,
a due a due contorti in tenero colloquio.

Poesia quasi interamente onirica in cui sono condensati numerosi temi. L'A. celebra il proprio trentesimo compleanno proiettando l'occasione in un viaggio, forse simbolico. L'orecchio « s'impolvera », oltre al significato letterale, richiama l'immagine dei capelli che imbiancano sulle tempie; l'omacchio è un neologismo per « spaventapasseri » o « spaventacchio ». Nella seconda strofa il viaggio sprofonda bruscamente nel sonno, che si prolunga fino al « risorgere » finale. Alcune immagini—il « vento in forma d'arco », la siepe che « si apre » —derivano dal Libro dei Mutamenti. L'idea dell'orto sacro « rinchiuso

The fleeing gang leaves a happy glow
That sets on the houses below, and grey clearings
Light up, the river darkens, a wind
Blows that neither ravages nor stings.
At castle corners red lights keep watch.

BIRTHDAY

Unravel the tousled thoughts of thirty years
while the sky darkens between noontime and winter,
antennas march northward
and the ear fills with dust.
Hosts of violet angels forebode at every turn.
Behold the unarmed boogey man
in the chest of the field;
behold on hilltops, in figures of sorrow,
bitter strong olive trees
twisted two by two in tender conversation.

An almost completely oneiric poem condensing numerous themes.
The author celebrates his own thirtieth birthday by projecting the oc-
casion into a journey, perhaps a symbolic one. The ear "fills with dust"
in more than a literal sense, recalling the image of hair going white at
the temples; "boogey man" is a neologism for "scarecrow" or
"strawman." In the second stanza the journey plunges abruptly into
sleep, which continues until the final "rising." Certain images—the
"wind bent like a bow," the hedge that "opens wide"—derive from the
Book of Changes. The idea of the sacred garden "locked in an iron cage"

Un soffio e declina la terra,
il cielo volubile si scioglie nell'occhio.
Dove il passato resiste la colpa fa il suo nido,
la lunga notte abbacìna il sangue
e loschi sogni ha il bosco.

Quando il cuore è zoppo e la mano tormenta
la corda d'amore stretta al collo,
l'enigma del soffrire cigola in un pozzo.
Quando dici:—la mente si disfà, la vita
è triste di ciarle—è un vento in forma d'arco
tra luce e pioggia.

Ah il gallo che canta dentro il sonno!
L'orto sacro fu rinchiuso nella ferrea gabbia,
la lingua premuta tra un muro e una moneta.

Sempre dietro le sillabe che il Nemico lacera
Il flagello degli spiriti morti va e viene
e la casa accoglie una luna sconsolata.
Lascia ch'io soffra per te la discesa
del ricco autunno: oltre i ponti
dei miei pensieri torcerò una strada
fino alla più ardua primavera.
Se è tardi per rastrellare la sorte

---

nella ferrea gabbia » è nata dal fatto che E. Pound, nel campo di
concentramento di Pisa, fu appunto segregato in una gabbia d'acciaio;
l'episodio è stato qui assunto in termini leggendari, escluso ogni
riferimento cronachistico: è la condizione del poeta nel mondo
moderno, che ha la lingua « premuta tra un muro e una moneta ».

A gust of wind and the earth wanes,
the fickle sky thaws inside the eye.
Guilt makes its nest where the past still holds,
the long night betrays the blood
and the wood falls into shadowy dreams.

When the heart is lame and the hand torments
love's cord wrapped round the neck,
the enigma of suffering creaks inside a well.
When you say—the mind goes to pieces, life
is sad with prattle—it is wind bent like a bow
between light and rain.

Ah the cock who crows in his sleep!
The holy garden was locked in an iron cage,
the tongue pressed between a wall and a coin.

Behind the syllables the Enemy slashes
the scourge of dead spirits always comes and goes,
and the house welcomes a dejected moon.
Let me suffer the rich Autumn's
descent for you: over bridges
in my thoughts I will wring out a road
to the toughest Spring.

---

comes from the fact that, in the concentration camp at Pisa, Ezra Pound
was indeed kept in a steel cage; here the episode is couched in legend-
ary terms, free of any chronicle-like reference: it is the condition of the
poet in the modern world, his tongue "pressed between a wall and a
coin."

col minuto ingiallito
io verrò con la forza che crea.
Ecco: il tuono declama nelle vene,
la siepe si apre.
Lascia che gli amanti rifiutino al polline la resa
e il lupo indossi la cuffia della nonna:
io verrò per ritagliare lo spazio
di fresche abitudini
e raccontarti il viaggio dell'insetto
nel campo di grano.

Chi ricorda la foglia protesa
al freddo dei cancelli? I lunghi
affardellati occhi dell'anno?
Sempre verrò
per riempire del mio cuore la spina vuota
e per risorgere.

If it is late to go sifting through fate
with the yellowed minute,
I will come with the creating force.
Behold: the thunder declaims in my veins,
the hedge opens wide.
Let the lovers not succumb to pollen
and the wolf don grandmother's cap:
I will come to cut out the space
of fresh habits
and tell you about the insect's trip
through the wheat-field.

Who remembers the leaf hanging
on the cold of the gates? The long
bundled eyes of the year?
Always will I come
to fill with my heart the empty thorn
and to rise again.

PREDILEZIONI

I   Accordo è la passione della mia ignoranza,
questo mondo lambito dai canili, sesso d'un sogno,
veramente s'umilia in periferie ricciute e rosa,
puerilmente si macchia per capire l'ospitalità.

I torti sono tortosi, ma il nudo movimento
tenta di vivere la sua esistenza, il mimato dolore
è il sollievo che parla. Pure, il cuore si ghiaccia,
sùbito è tempo per la rivoluzione delle pene.

L'anno licantropo ha dodici lune soltanto. La mia viltà
per la bellezza è incredibile, ho bisogno dell'orma.
Perché fortuna e danno rapiscono la fiamma e
nella grigia ossea dignità non c'è che eleganza.

Il verso di questo gruppetto di poesie ha generalmente quattro tempi, un'andatura discorsiva e piuttosto rapida. Lo schema della prima si può disegnare nel modo seguente: ai tempi dell'infanzia ignorante vivevo in periferie favolose, dove in realtà era il vero centro, l'origine dell'esperienza. I canili fanno parte dell'affettuosa e derelitta scena urbana del sogno, insieme con l'erotica ospitalità che è proprio dell'infanzia scoprire in cose e persone. Nell'età adulta la situazione perdura, ma i suoi termini sono dissociati e occorre una volontà precisa per ricongiungerli: da un lato c'è la verificazione di uno stato di estraniamento, dall'altro l'urgenza di rompere « subito » le convenienze con un atto di denudamento, di smascheramento. Le dodici lune, le occasioni del licantropo, significano l'incalzare del tempo, la rarità e insieme il bisogno periodico di sperimentare intensamente l'accordo, il dissonante unisono con la vita.

La seconda poesia è ispirata dal contrasto tra impulso vitale e spirito di conoscenza. La terza è un epigramma sadico-giocoso, un notturno dove i termini della poesia precedente sono rovesciati e mescolati.

PREDILECTIONS

I   Agreement is the passion of my ignorance,
this world, licked by kennels, sex of a dream,
truly humbled in curly pink suburbs,
soils itself like a child to grasp hospitality.

The wrong are wrongful, but the naked movement
tries to live its life, imitated pain
is relief that speaks. Yet the heart turns to ice,
it's time for punishment's revolt.

The werewolf year has only twelve moons. My cowardice
before beauty is incredible, I need distress.
Because fortune and damage kidnap the flame and
all I find in bony grey dignity is elegance.

The verse in this small group of poems generally has four beats, a
discursive and rather quick pace. The first poem might be sketched as
follows: in the days of ignorant childhood I lived in fabulous outskirts,
which were in fact the true center, the origin of experience. The ken-
nels are part of the dream's tender, forlorn urban setting, together with
the erotic hospitality which children typically find in things and people.
The situation continues into one's adult years, but the terms grow
dissociated, and require a precise act of will to link them together again:
on the one hand, there is the examination of a state of estrangement,
on the other, the urgency of "suddenly" breaching decorum by dis-
robing and unmasking. The twelve moons, the werewolf's opportu-
nities, signify the pressing on of time, the rarity but also the periodic
need to keenly experience harmony, discordant unison with life.
The second poem is inspired by the contrast between vital impulse
and the spirit of knowledge. The third is a sado-burlesque epigram, a
nocturne in which the terms of the preceding poem are reversed and
scrambled.

II   Non c'è rimedio al disordine d'aprile,
scossa di paradiso dei cieli che spurgano
e rovesciano l'inverno nei fossi, dei vènti
che s'irradiano asciutti di colpo.

Non c'è rimedio a quei nostri disguidi,
al lezzo delle rose, notturne per la mente
e per l'aria gelose. Amore sempre fiorisce
prima del conoscere, in un buio tremore.

E il rammarico non apre questa porta chiusa,
fa misera la lotta, tradisce solitudine.
L'odore disfatto in scirocco soffoca le sere;
e non c'è onore, né calma, né tregua.

III   Prendi il nero del silenzio, tanto parlare
disinvoglia la nuca, in sé pupilla, palato
di cane, oppure pensa le notti che risbuca
nel gelo il firmamento dei gatti, amore.

Prendi l'alito dell'ansimo nero, così dolce
in punta di lingua, fumo di mosto s'arrotola
sulla fronte, mescola l'osceno e l'assurdo,
cambia di posto, e sia come non detto, amore.

Prendi il volo nero, valica l'altra tua vita,
Voltano il fianco i terrori, non gridano più,
un sorso d'alba che nausea, è splendido ora
questo barbaglio stanco, mucosa fiorita, amore.

II   There is no cure for the riots of April,
quaking in the heavens in the sky's upheaval
and purging of winter into ditches, in winds
that sweep out and suddenly go dry.

There is no cure for our bad directions,
for the stench of roses, nocturnal to the mind
and jealous to the air. Love always blooms
before you're aware, with a tremor in the dark.

And regret won't open this bolted door,
it sours the fight, strips solitude bare.
The smell becomes scirocco and strangles the night;
and there is no honor, no calm, no truce.

III   Take the black of silence, such talking
dissuades the eye behind the neck, palate
of dog, or else think the nights the firmament
of cats popping out of the cold, my love.

Take the breath of black panting, so sweet
on the tip of your tongue, musty smoke curling up
on your brow, mixing the obscene and absurd,
changing place, and is as you say, my love.

Take the black flight, your other life crosses over,
the terrors turn their backs, no longer shout,
a sip of dawn, how nauseating, so splendid now
this flowering mucous, this tired flashing, my love.

IL VECCHIO

ad Antonio Porta

Spenta l'imminenza, l'ombra che sale riconosce.
Il più terribile fuoco è adolescenza sui vetri,
caldo getto dei rami nella stanza sognata di fresco.
Il farnetico sciala di queste minuzie invase.

Barcolla nella ruota che invecchia l'aria,
velocemente, i polsi lenti incespicano
nel passo della gru, lo scampanio scivola
sulla volta dei carpini in fondo al parco.

I nani intagliati nella pietra più bizzarri
non sono del cane buono figlio dell'uomo.
Il padrone è triste, tira al bersaglio, stecca,
rigano le biglie invisibili il prato che abbaia.

I movimenti e i pensieri del vecchio barcollano. Non c'è più storia,
non c'è più anticipazione, indizio di rinnovamento (l'imminenza, la
tensione verso la realtà, è «spenta»). L'unica presenza viva è quella del
cane, creatura che l'uomo ha inventato; ma la paura del vecchio investe
anche il cane nella grottesca riflessione finale. La forma nitida della
poesia contrasta lo scompaginamento interiore del personaggio.

THE OLD MAN

to Antonio Porta

Its threat extinguished, the rising shadow knows.
The most dreadful fire is adolescence on windows,
hot spray of branches in a room desired of fresh.
He squanders the madness of invaded trifles.

He staggers on the wheel that ages the air,
quickly, his slow pulse stumbles
in the steps of the crane, the tinkling of bells glides
through the hornbeam vault in the park.

The dwarfs carved from stone are no more
bizzare than the good dog son of man.
The master is sad, lines it up and scratches,
invisible billiards stripe the barking meadow.

The movements and thoughts of the doddering old man. There is no
more history, no more anticipation, signs of renewal (imminence, the
straining toward reality, is "extinguished"). The only living presence is
the dog, a creature man has invented; but the old man's fear affects
even the dog in the final grotesque reflection. The poem's clear-cut
form contrasts with the character's inner disorder.

Frenesia degli usignoli! Nessuno sa compatire,
e tu vaneggi, minacci, la misura sùbito colma.
Siamo davvero pazzi di paura. Se il cielo esagera,
sottrai la gabbia alla plumbea alleanza.

Cicli s'annientano contro una ragione ostile.
Evadi, pensa la luna che si strofina il dorso
ai ruscelli primaverili. In Cina, sai, i cani,
è quasi l'ora di cena, sì, li frollano vivi.

The frenzy of nightingales! None can sympathize,
and you rage, threaten, your cup instantly full.
We are truly wild with fear. If the sky exaggerates,
remove the cage from the leaden alliance.

Cycles clash and die against hostile reason.
Escape, thinks the moon rubbing its back
on the brooks of spring. In China, you know, the dogs,
yes, it's almost suppertime, they age them alive.

PROSA

a Nanni Balestrini

Bisogna avvertirli Les essuie-mains ne doivent servir qu'à
    [s'essuyer
les mains Non sputate sul pavimento Uscita, son tutti uguali,
    [falsissimo,
se ne sentono tante, fenomeno facile da spiegare, lascia un'idea
    [(nitrito)
di esaltata padronanza, ma sai che poi svanisce, è bene o male?,
    [la flussione
particolarmente intensa delle regole elementari, la prescrizione
    [è contenuta
nel prodotto (è un nitrito, potrebbe essere), se ne sta ai
    [giardini a leggere
l'Ordine Pubblico o Il Cavallo. Inutile lamentarsi. Avrà la
    [pensione,
Les théories déductives sont des systèmes hypothètiques...
    [Il pleut... Cette
proposition est vraie ou fausse suivant le temps qu'il fait.
    [La figura siede
dolcemente astratta presso la fontana. E tu? me lo ripeto
    [sempre.

Questo brano narrativo è un monologo in cui il verso lungo e atonale esprime l'abbandonarsi semantico del personaggio alla propria situazione (con l'automatica presenza di fatti importanti e di altri irrilevanti); il verso 'continuo' ha anche funzione di legamento tra contenuti « interni » e contenuti « esterni », per cui pensieri e proiezioni si amalgamano con cose e figure in un perpetuo rovesciamento. È il riflusso dell'esperienza in un momento di stanchezza convulsa, gremito di incertezza e di fallimento.

PROSE

to Nanni Balestrini

They should be warned Les essuie-mains ne doivent servir
     [qu'à s'essuyer
les mains Don't spit on the floor Exit, they're all the same,
     [so phony,
they've heard it all, a phenomenon easy to explain, it gives an
     [idea (whinnying)
of exalted ownership, but you know it vanishes, is it good or bad?,
     [the particularly
intense fluxion of elementary rules, the prescription is contained
inside the product (it's a whinnying, could be) he's in the gardens
     [reading
the Ordine Pubblico or Il Cavallo. No use complaining. He'll have
     [his pension,
Les théories déductives sont des systèmes hypothètiques...
     [Il pleut... Cette
proposition est vraie ou fausse suivant le temps qu'il fait.
     [The figure sits down
next to the fountain sweetly abstract. And you? I keep telling
     [myself.

This narrative fragment is a monologue whose long atonal line ex-
presses the character's semantic abandonment to his own situation
(with the automatic presence of some important and some irrelevant
facts); the "continuous" line also serves to connect "internal" and "ex-
ternal" contents, through which thought and projections are amal-
gamated with things and images in a perpetual reversal. It is the ebb-
ing of experience in a moment of feverish exhaustion, full of uncer-
tainty and failure.

PENURIA E FERVORE

E questa è la nostra penuria nel fervore.
Le lacrime sommerse non sanno giacere
sotto la pioggia come le righe nere
del mio taccuino, come i brividi che scrivo
col calamo delle ossa.

Sappiamo il segreto che tristemente spiega
la vita dell'eroe, come vediamo la luna
concitare gli squarci sereni.
Fortuna se la notte profonda il dolore
e lo restituisce al vento che langue
dietro la porta.

Esulta la biografia dell'errore, una domanda
che non sai formulare umilia l'ansia.
Ogni giorno che l'arte invecchia
e ci gonfia l'anima di vesciche,
spirano i sempreverdi nel grigio lustrale,
le vie c'incontrano con un pudore di fiamma.

Nella prima parte (strofe 1–3) si tratta esplicitamente della condizione
attuale dello scrittore e dell'arte; nella seconda è invece espresso il *climax* dei nostri sentimenti. I due temi, fusi nel verso iniziale che ritorna
al principio dell'ultima strofa, si intrecciano. La lunatica apparizione
dell'eroe ha riferimento in una nota allusivamente personale apposta
da Kierkegaard a un passo di *Timore e tremore* in cui si parla della natura
di Faust.

PENURY AND FERVOR

This is our penury in fervor;
hidden tears will not lie
in the rain like my notebook's
black lines, like the tremors I write
with the quill in my bones.

We know the secret sadly explained
by the hero's life, like seeing the moon
excite a peaceful gash.
Lucky if the night deepens pain
and returns it to the wind simpering
behind the door.

An error's biography exults, a question
you cannot phrase humbles distress.
Each day art ages
and swells the spirit with bladders,
evergreens die in lustral gray,
roads meet us with the pudor of flames.

In the first part (stanzas 1–3) the explicit topic is that of the present
condition of the writer and his art; the second expresses instead the
climax of our feelings. The two themes blended in the first line, return-
ing at the beginning of the last stanza, intertwine. The hero's weird
apparition is mentioned in an allusively personal note of Kierkegaard's
in his *Fear and Trembling* in which he discusses Faust's nature.

Fanno domestici i cancelli i passeri ignari
di svolare e immaginarsi nella tenerezza
più nostra, alle orecchie dell'asino giunge
il canto dei serafini, la pecora sul greppo
bruca la dolcezza precaria dell'erba.
Bella incertezza dell'orizzonte.

Lenta minaccia, altera resistenza, la speranza
di sé consuma la passione del rovescio.
Il gigante si nasconde nel pollice del guanto.
Toccami nell'estasi, a questo tepore d'inverno
chi non sacrifica la primavera?

Questa è la nostra penuria nel fervore.
Grazie! diciamo, senza celare impeto e tormento,
quando l'anima è colma fino all'indifferenza,
se tentiamo di amare tutta la verità,
se una promessa sorvola i baratri
che abbiamo tra le braccia.

Nella figura dell'asino, le cui orecchie attingono i suoni celesti, è rappresentata teriomorficamente un'attitudine dello spirito. Il gigante sembra esprimere la nefasta astuzia umana, la potenza della simulazione.

Sparrows tamed by gates innocent
of flying or imagining themselves in a tenderness
more ours, a donkey's ear senses
the seraphim's song, a sheep in the manger
grazes on the precarious sweetness of grass.
Beautiful uncertainty of the horizon.

Slow threat, haughty resistance, hope
alone consumes the passion to reverse.
The giant hides in the thumb of a glove.
Touch me in ecstasy, who wouldn't sacrifice spring
to this tepid winter?

This is the penury in our fervor.
Thanks! we say, loathe to conceal impetus and torment,
when the spirit is filled to indifference,
if we try to love the whole truth,
if a promise flies over the chasms
between our arms.

The image of the donkey, whose ears capture heavenly sounds, is a
theriomorphic representation of an inclination of the spirit. The giant
seems to express the nefarious human cunning, the power of simula-
tion.

CHI GUARDA PER ESSERE GUARDATO

Chi guarda per essere guardato vede
un viso cieco. Le mura s'affrettano
a scantonare dove il gatto vomita e
divora senza vergogna. Ma non sanno

le mie nazioni, i cortili, in vetta
alle cuspidi lo stormire che le ali
fanno delle serrature per aprire, o
quando di narcisi giù sulle quattro

candele mattutine grondano i cerei
ghiacci. Versiamo pure i cari debiti
nella cassa comune, e come tutto si
finisce per amare della sofferenza.

Lo « stormire » che apre in alto le « serrature » è, archetipicamente, lo
spirito del vento. Esso affronta le tenebre della morte, come lo sguardo
veridico gli aspetti oscuri della realtà. Lo sgocciolio delle candele
funerarie rovescia e rimpiccolisce l'immagine verticale delle cuspidi.
La « cassa comune » simboleggia la vita e la morte. Ogni unità tiene in
sé una duplicità: lo sguardo intero è quello della *doppia vista*, per i fatti
e per le essenze. La stretta connessione di tutti i temi è espressa
formalmente dal fatto che tutti i versi sono legati dall'enjambement.

WHOEVER LOOKS TO BE LOOKED AT

Whoever looks to be looked at sees
a blind face. The walls hurry
to cut corners where the cat shamelessly
vomits and devours. But they don't know

my nations, the courtyards, at the peak
on spires the rustling wings
make to open locks, or
when down on the narcissus' four

morning candles the wax ices
are dripping. We even deposit our dear debts
in a joint account, and how you end up
loving all in your pain.

The "rustling" that opens the high "locks" is, archetypically, the spirit
of the wind. It faces the shadows of death, as a truthful look does the
dark aspects of reality. The dripping of funeral candles overturns and
diminishes the vertical image of the spires. The "joint account" sym-
bolizes life and death. Each unity contains a duality: the whole gaze is
that of *double vision*, for facts and for essences. The strict connection of
all the themes is formally expressed by the fact that the lines are all
linked in enjambment.

Chi dagli occhi ripiega le ali, tra
non molto dovrà strisciare; e almeno
calpestare scheletri di brina, noia,
descrivere in memorie le dune eoliche

che accumulano i fianchi sottovento,
non le ceneri sciolte fotografare.
Guardano le cuspidi la spuma: urla,
abbranca i garretti del mare. Il

sapore del gatto, quando le ombre
sul batticuore passarono la fiamma
ossidrica. E ricordati di gettare
una fronda di polvere sullo spettro

dell'aria umida. Poi esplodono i fori,
la chiave sventra l'azzurra lapide.

Al « fotografare le ceneri sciolte » (= macabro lavorio sulle cronache
della morte) è contrapposta l'attività volta a fugare la noia: la ricerca
intellettuale (simboleggiata dagli studi geologici sulle arenarie eoliche)
e l'attività bramosamente cieca (« calpestare scheletri di brina »).
Assurde operazioni involute nell'inconscio; mentre appare l'inconscio
stesso, il mare, elemento eternamente mobile di fronte alla stabilità
provvisoria delle cuspidi.
Il ritorno di fiamma dell'apparecchio funebre, con l'immagine della
saldatura della cassa, e il sapore del gatto (= sapore di morte) sono
esorcizzati con la « fronda di polvere », con un nulla.
L'esplosione finale suggerisce il prevalere della distruzione sui riti
umani. Ma la distruzione è una « chiave » che si gira nella toppa della
morte.

Whoever folds back the wings from their eyes will
have to grovel before long; and at least
trample skeletons of frost, boredom,
to describe in memories the aeolian dunes

that hips gather downwind,
not to photograph the melted ash.
Spires look at the froth: it shouts,
clutching the sea's ankles. The

taste of cat, when shadows
on the heart-beat went through the oxyhydrogen
flame. And remember to throw
a garland of dust at the specter

of muggy air. Then the holes explode,
the key disembowels the blue tombstone.

"To photograph the melted ash" (= macabre belaboring of the
chronicles of death) is contrasted with the activity of routing ennui:
intellectual investigation (symbolized by geological studies of Aeolian
sandstone) and zealously blind activity ("trample skeletons of frost").
Absurd intricate workings of the unconscious; while the unconscious
itself appears as the sea, the eternally mobile element in comparison
to the provisionally stable spires.
The backfire of the funeral equipment, together with the image of the
welding of the box and the taste of cat (= taste of death) are exorcised
by the "garland of dust," by a nullity.
The final explosion suggests that destruction prevails over human rites.
But destruction is a "key" turning in death's keyhole.

È DOPO

all'amico musico Franco Evangelisti

I latrati, che vogliono dire? nella bruma,
non abbiamo intenzione, è l'insorgenza
del caso, quella vecchia infingarda sa
la cosa, ha cessato di essere privata, la
tua paura legge col cavo dell'occhio, la
tua paraforia intende nel cerebro vuoto.
Ma io-qui-ora, dolorosa sospensione, so
che non basta, non ammetto la conclusione,
non indulgo, è lo stesso, la noncuranza
si corruga. Con gli anni tutto diviene
simbolico, capire è un sentito dire, poesia
nient'altro che paralogia dei soliti discorsi.

Il tema della poesia—la coesistenza dell'essere-qui-ora e dell'essere-già-oltre—è psicologico e culturale e allude alla situazione storica. La psiche ha un duplice volto (guarda indietro e in avanti), così la cultura è tradizione e anticipazione.

I latrati simboleggiano gli istinti, le premonizioni, ciò che si stenta a decifrare. La bruma è l'indeterminato, l'indistinto, la distanza della coscienza dall'inconscio; quest'ultimo è impersonato dalla vecchia che « sa » e « intende » la condizione dell'io. La vecchia simboleggia anche il mondo storico.

Secondo l'esperienza junghiana « la psiche non è affatto una nostra intenzione »; l'uso di questo termine nel contesto si riferisce a tale oggettività psichica e storica. La « noncuranza si corruga » è detto con evidente richiamo figurativo alla fronte che s'increspa. La noncuranza, scelta difensiva dell'alienato che così controlla la propria affettività disgregata, è alternativa alla paraforia (= discorso delirante). Gli ultimi tre versi della prima strofa compendiano ironicamente la situazione.

IT'S AFTER

to the composer Franco Evangelisti

What's this barking supposed to mean? in the mist,
we have no intention, it's the surging
of fate, that sluggish old dame knows
something, she's stopped being private, she
reads your fear with her eye-socket,
understands your paraphoria in her empty cerebrum.
But me-here-now, sorrowful suspension, I know
it's not enough, I cannot accept the conclusion,
I do not indulge, it's the same, neglect
knits its brows. Over the years all becomes
symbolic, understanding is hearsay, poetry
no more than paralogia of the same old story.

The poem's theme—the coexistence of being-here-now and being-al-
ready-beyond—is psychological and cultural and hints at the historical
situation. The psyche is two-faced (it looks behind and forward), thus
culture is tradition and anticipation.

The barks symbolize the instincts, premonitions—whatever one la-
bors to decipher. The mist is the indeterminate, the indistinct, the dis-
tance of consciousness from the unconscious; the latter is personified
by the old woman who "knows" and "understands" the ego's condi-
tion. The old woman also symbolizes the historical world.

According to Jungian experience "the psyche is by no means our own
intention"; the use of this term in this context relates to just such psy-
chic and historical objectivity. "neglect knits its brow" clearly refers to
the figure of the furrowed forehead. Neglect, the defensive choice of
the 'mentally alienated' person who thus controls his own disintegrat-
ing affectivity, is an alternative to paraphoria (= delirious speech). The
last three lines of the first stanza ironically sum up the situation.

I latrati la vecchia non sono irrelati, ma
non c'è congiunzione, o almeno è sclerotica,
sebbene, volendo, con gli anni il passo
diviene più valgo, possa, l'affanno è al valico,
cuore e cura ridurre la tua sintassi.
Altra logica. E possa nello sterco secco
di naturali arabeschi verdi striati di bianco
e di ocra esaudire quel po' di puerile bramosia
estetica che in te resta come l'eco del flauto.
Frena, ti prego, la tua pietà per i frenetici
aspetti, ascolta i latrati senza pensare
ai cani, coprile la faccia con un giornale.

Le premonizioni e l'inerzia della vecchia vita, l'attualità degli istinti e il
fondo oscuro dell'inconscio, sono congiunti da un tessuto comune,
che è disseccato, sclerotico. Il valgismo dei piedi rappresenta
l'invecchiamento. Il periodare nei primi cinque versi della seconda strofa
è volutamente affannoso e ansima negli incisi; quando si giunge a
«l'affanno è al valico» finisce la serie paratattica degli incisi e si apre
una possibilità di discorso più disteso e coerente sul mondo vissuto.
Coerenza che si ottiene mediante un inevitabile adattamento: la
«sintassi» (cioè l'ordine, la razionalità) potrà in qualche modo «ridurre»
a proporzioni controllabili l'affettività (cuore) e la passionalità
indagatrice (cura, nel duplice senso terapeutico e di preoccupazione
esistenziale). La sclerosi continua, tuttavia, a dominare il discorso. Essa
consente un simulacro di percezione estetica. La seconda strofa termina
con alcuni consigli pratici.

The barking the old dame are not unrelated, but
there is none but a sclerotic conjunction,
although, if you wish, your stride gets bow-legged
over the years, anxiety sits on the threshold,
your syntax may reduce heart and care.
Different logic. And in the dried dung
of natural green arabesques streaked with white
and ochre can it fulfill that tad of puerile aesthetic
craving that sits in you like the echo of a flute.
Please curb your pity for the frenzied
parts, listen to the barking without thinking
of the dogs, cover her face with a newspaper.

The premonitions and the inertia of the old life, the currency of the
instincts and the obscure depths of the unconscious, share a common
fabric, one which is parched, sclerotic. The valgus condition of the
feet represents aging. The sentence construction of the first five lines
of the second stanza is deliberately laborious, gasping in its parenthe-
ses; with "anxiety sits on the threshold" the parataxes of the paren-
thetic phrases ends, and there opens up a possibility for more relaxed,
coherent discourse about the world of experience. A coherence gained
by inevitable compromise: the "syntax" (i.e., order, rationality) can in
some way "reduce" affectivity (heart) and investigative passion (care,
in the dual sense of therapy and existential concern) to manageable
proportions. And yet the sclerosis continues to dominate the discourse.
It allows for a simulacrum of aesthetic perception. The second stanza
ends with some practical advice.

Eh, il cielo impallidì, venne lo scroscio,
la musica è quella dei condotti di scarico,
la pioggia non spegne il camino, a ben vedere
la cosa, riparo nubi asfissiate dal fulmine
fogne meccanismi premonitori, è tautologica.
Il mastodonte troppo altamente adattato sparì
quando variò l'ambiente; e nella pioggia o bruma
possa andare e venire dentro di te ogni altro
(reciprocamente) giacché, utopia è più vera
della nostalgia, la vecchia governa i latrati.
Stormire, da dove verso che cosa, la fine stipata
dei simulacri fa soffrire, ma già è dopo, è dopo.

Lo scroscio, il maltempo, è un simbolo di sovvertimento e, se si vuole,
di purificazione; la spugnosa organizzazione sociale assorbe, al riparo,
la tempesta. Il tutto è tautologico: la tempesta fa funzionare il
parafulmine e questo neutralizza gli effetti della prima. L'accenno al
mastodonte (il borghese, o meglio il simbolo dell'adattamento alla
società borghese e di questa a se medesima) richiama l'idea della
catastrofe che muta l'ambiente vitale, idea che agisce ora come uto-
pia, pre-figurazione.
Nelle difficoltà della conoscenza e nelle avversità sociali, il compito è
di resistere alle seduzioni dell'orrido nella tensione verso l'essere-già-
oltre. Il discorso stretto della poesia è configurato dalla forma
colloquiale e gremita e dall'uso dell'enjambement. Il verso è atonale,
la sua struttura non dipende dagli accenti ritmici ma dagli sviluppi
armonici di una « serie » semantica.

Eh, the sky grew pale, the downpour came,
it's the music of gutters,
the rain won't put out the fireplace, at second
glance, shelter clouds asphixiated by lightning
sewers warning devices, it's tautological.
The overly adapted mastodon vanished
when the environment changed: and in the rain or mist
every other (mutually) can come and go
inside you since, utopia is truer
than nostalgia, the old dame rules the barking.
Swarming, from where toward what, the end crammed
with simulacra makes you suffer, but already it's after, it's after.

The shower, the bad weather, is a symbol of subversion and, if you like, of purification; the sponge-like social organization protectively absorbs the storm. It is all tautological: the storm makes the lightning rod work, and the latter neutralizes the effects of the former. The allusion to the mastodon (the bourgeois, or rather the symbol of adaptation to bourgeois society and of this society to itself) recalls the idea of the catastrophe that alters the vital environment, an idea which now functions as a utopia, a pre-figuration.

In the travail of knowledge and in social adversities, the task is one of resisting the seductions of horror as one strains toward being-already-beyond. Poetry's strict discourse is characterized by a thick colloquial cast and enjambment. The verse is atonal, its structure dependent not on rhythmic accents but rather on the harmonic developments of a semantic "series."

Da LABORINTUS

composte terre in strutturali complessioni sono Palus
    [Putredinis
riposta tenue Ellie e tu mio corpo tu infatti tenue Ellie eri
    [il mio corpo
immaginoso quasi conclusione di una estatica dialettica
    [spirituale
noi che riceviamo la qualità dai tempi
        tu e tu mio spazioso corpo
di flogisto che ti alzi e ti materializzi nell'idea del nuoto
sistematica costruzione in ferro filamentoso lamentoso
lacuna lievitata in compagnia di una tenace tematica
composta terra delle distensioni dialogiche insistenze
    [intemperanti

Il poema si apre con la descrizione di un paesaggio mentale in disfacimento, una cartografia metafisica lunare al cui centro è la « Palus Putredinis ». La *palude* è psicologicamente l'archetipo di una situazione; quando Renée, la giovane schizofrenica curata dalla signora Sechehaye, trova il primo contatto con la Mamma (impersonata simbolicamente dalla psicanalista) sente di essere racchiusa nel corpo di lei come in un mondo di terra e di acqua che chiama *palude*. L'accostamento immediato del personaggio femminile Ellie al *nomen loci* è molto significativo. Lo stesso A. spiega: Ellie è il mio corpo, è tutto il mondo, è il 'totius orbis thesaurus', predicabile all'infinito. Ellie è l'*Anima* nel senso di Jung, è la stessa Palus, la 'lividissima mater' della sez. 26. L'immagine della madre, con le sue implicazioni cosmologiche e antropologiche, è un simbolo polivalente dell'unità e del desiderio di abolire gli opposti. La Palus-Ellie è il termine di riferimento di questa

from LABORINTUS

I

compound soils in structural complexes are Palus Putredinis
hidden soft Ellie and you my body you in fact soft Ellie were my
fanciful body almost a conclusion of ecstatic spiritual
dialectics we who receive our quality from the times
                  you and you my spacious body
of phlogiston that rises and materializes in the idea of
      [swimming
systematic construction in wirey whining iron
leavened lacuna in the company of a tenacious thematic
compound soil of dialogical distensions intemperate
      [insistences

The poem opens with the description of a decomposing mental land-
scape, a metaphysical lunar cartography with the "Palus Putredinis"
at its center. Psychologically the *swamp* is the archetype of a situation;
when Renée, the young schizophrenic treated by Mme. Sechehaye
makes her first contact with Mother (symbolically personified by the
psychoanalyst) she feels shut up in her body as in a world of earth and
water she calls *swamp*. The proximity of the female character Ellie to
the *nomen loci* is highly significant. The author explains: "Ellie is my
body, it is the whole world, it is 'totius orbis thesaurus,' endlessly predi-
cated. Ellie is *Anima* in the Jungian sense, the Palus itself, 'lividissima
mater' of section 26.
The image of the mother, with its cosmological and anthropological
implications, is a polyvalent symbol of unity and the desire to do away
with opposites. The Ellie-Palus is the reference point of this descent

le condizioni esterne è evidente esistono realmente queste
    [condizioni
esistevano prima di noi ed esisteranno dopo di noi qui è il
    [dibattimento
liberazioni frequenza e forza e agitazione potenziata e altro
aliquot lineae desiderantur
        dove dormi cuore ritagliato
e incollato e illustrato con documentazioni viscerali dove
    [soprattutto
vedete igienicamente nell'acqua antifermentativa ma fissati
    [adesso
quelli i nani extratemporali i nani insomma o Ellie
nell'aria inquinata
       in un costante cratere anatomico ellittico

---

discesa agli inferi, al caos dell'anima storica (« Ellie tenue corpo di peccaminose escrescenze / che possiamo roteare / e rivolgere e odorare e adorare nel tempo »). La ierofania (e demonologia) sessuale è combinata con l'ideologia: la frase del Foscolo sui poeti (« noi che riceviamo la qualità dai tempi ») e la citazione da Stalin (« le condizioni esterne è evidente esistono realmente ») valgono come iscrizioni sulla porta dell'inferno.

Con il richiamo al « flogisto » si apre il tema alchemico: l'immagine del corpo, vaso della combustione, suggerisce l'idea della matrice tellurica e della trasmutazione della natura mediante il fuoco.

L'avventura faustiana si ripropone nel clima dei rapporti tra psicologia e alchimia indagati da Jung. Come la psicologia del profondo, l'alchimia è un *regressus ad uterum*: l'impresa volta all'unione dell'inunibile non è che l'opera di integrazione della coscienza con l'inconscio. Jung tratta i simboli alchemici quale materia psichica di impronta collettiva; così desunti dall'A. essi vengono posti in un altro circolo: la ricerca della pietra filosofale e dell'elixir vitae (trasmutazione della materia) diventa una formula mitologica del « dibattimento » ideologico (trasmuta-zione della società e della natura umana).

the external conditions it is evident they truly exist these
    [conditions
they existed before us and they'll exist after us here is the
    [debate
liberations frequency and force and agitation empowered and
    [other
aliquot lineae desiderantur
       where you sleep heart cut out
and glued and illustrated with visceral documentation where
    [above all
you see hygenically in the anti-fermentative water but fixed now
those extratemporal dwarfs you know the dwarfs o Ellie
in the polluted air
       in a stable elliptical anatomical crater

---

into the nether world, to the chaos of the historical soul ("Ellie soft body of sinful excrescences/ that we can twirl/ and turn and smell and adore in time"). The sexual hierophany (and demonology) combines with ideology: Foscolo's phrase about poets ("noi che receviamo la qualità dai tempi," "we who receive our quality from the times") and the quotation from Stalin ("the external conditions it is evident they truly exist") are worthy of being inscribed over the gates of Hell. With the reference to the "phlogiston" the alchemical theme is broached: the image of the body, a combustion vessel, evokes the idea of the telluric matrix and the transmutation of nature through fire.

The Faustian adventure is restated in the context of the relation between psychology and alchemy Jung explored. Like depth psychology, alchemy is a *regressus ad uterum*: the effort of uniting the un-unitable is but the integrating work of consciousness with the unconscious. Jung treats alchemical symbols as a collective type of psychic material; so derived by the author these symbols are placed in another circle: the search for the philosophers' stone and for the elixir vitae (transmutation of material) becomes a mythological formula of ideological "debate" (transmutation of society and human nature).

perché ulteriormente diremo che non possono crescere
tu sempre la mia natura e rasserenata tu canzone metodologica
periferica introspezione dell'introversione forza centrifuga
    [delimitata
Ellie tenue corpo di peccaminose escrescenze
        che possiamo roteare
e rivolgere e odorare e adorare nel tempo
        desiderantur (essi)
analizzatori e analizzatrici desiderantur (essi) personaggi anche
ed erotici e sofisticati
        desiderantur desiderantur

Gli homunculi alchemici (« i nani extratemporali ») sono i moti
dell'inconscio, creature del nanismo mentale che non possono crescere
nel cratere lunare (nel paese disfatto), sono anche mostruosamente i
figli spirituali e fisiologici che si dibattono con le condizioni esterne.

Poiché l'*Opus* è soprattutto una psicanalisi patita dal protagonista e
condotta da personaggi (« analizzatori e analizzatrici ») alquanto
lacunosi, la glossa filologica « desiderantur » indica la difficoltà
metodologica del processo d'individuazione. Il transfert filologia =
psicanalisi è indicato fin dal titolo *Laborintus*, tratto dall'omonima arte
poetica di Everardus Alemannus (sec. XIII), e dalla susseguente epigrafe:
« quasi laborem habens intus », che è di un anonimo glossatore di
Everardus.

Il verso usato dall'A. in tutte le sue poesie è un recitativo drammatico
il cui svolgimento poggia su un fondo di armonicità naturale, mentre
il ritmo è assorbito dalla sintassi e dagli chocs semantici. La struttura
metrica è quindi rigorosamente *atonale* e, si potrebbe dire, *gestuale*
(« action poetry », come ha detto Cesare Vivaldi). Presupposto: il rifiuto
della forma ritmica, oggettivamente degradata e ormai condizionante,
secondo l'A., il libero rispecchiamento soggettivo.

as furthermore we'll say that they cannot grow
you ever my nature and you brightened methodological
　　　[song
peripheral introspection of introversion delimited centrifugal
　　　[force
Ellie soft body of sinful excrescences
　　　　　that we can twirl
and turn and smell and adore in time
　　　　　desiderantur (they)
analyzer and analyzeresses desiderantur (they) characters too
and erotic and sophisticated
　　　　　desiderantur desiderantur

Alchemical homunculi ("extratemporal dwarfs") are the motions of
the unconscious, creations of mental dwarfism that can grow only in
the lunar crater (in the decayed landscape); they are also, monstrously,
the spiritual and physiological *children* who grapple with external con-
ditions.

Since the *Opus* is chiefly a psychoanalysis undergone by the protago-
nist and conducted by somewhat sketchy characters ("male and fe-
male analyzers"), the philological gloss "desiderantur" indicates the
methodological difficulty of the individuation process. The transfer-
ence philology = psychoanalysis is hinted at by the very title *Laborintus*,
taken from the so-titled ars poetica of Everardus Alemannus (13th cen-
tury) and from the following epigraph: "quasi laborem habens intus,"
by an anonymous commentator on Everardus' text.

In each of the poems the author's verse form is a dramatic recitative
whose development rests on a foundation of natural harmoniousness,
while the rhythm is absorbed by the syntax and by semantic shocks.
The metrical structure is thus strictly *atonal* and, one might say, *ges-
tural* ("action poetry," as Cesare Vivaldi has called it). A premise here:
the refusal of rhythmic form, objectively debased and now, the author
maintains, conditioning free subjective reflection.

187

2

e una volta Mare Humorum guardami bene (la rottura di una
        [personalità)
e dilatami (tutto suscettibile di assentimento) e combinami
        [in un'epoca
indirizzando i sensi (il tempo dell'occhio che risuona nel
        [quieto addome) e
toccami
                perché io sono al più giusto confine organico sepolcro
complicato per godere e riuscirò dopo la fluida intromissione
una moltitudine riuscirò nella grammatica speculativa e
        [simbolizzato in cifre
terribilmente armoniose di fronte all'eruzione di carbonizzanti
        [passioni
infatti e alle distorsioni relative di fronte a lunghi funghi
        [fumosi

Il romanzetto erotico-demonologico va inteso come una tras-
posizione: la polluzione notturna (naturalmente « absque cogitatione
immunda ») ha valore di « rivolta » misurata sopra una « ideale
esigenza ». L'uomo è « organico sepolcro / complicato per godere »
« in un'epoca » determinata. Così Ellie in figura di polluzione provoca
la « rottura » della personalità e la sua « dilatazione » in « moltitudine ».
Gli epiteti di Ellie—Mare Humorum, Lacus Somniorum—continuano
la geografia lunare. La proposizione scolastica « sed non omnis emissio
—humoris carnalis—est proprie pollutio », ricavata da un 'index rerum'
della *Summa theologica,* è spezzata ad arte.

2

and just once, Mare Humorum, look at me (the fracture of a
     [personality)
and expand me (entirely susceptible to assent) and match me
     [with an epoch
directing my senses (the eye's time that echoes in the quiet
     [abdomen) and
touch me
               because I stand at the most fitting organic
     [boundary sepulchre
complicated for enjoying and I will excel after the fluid
     [intrusion
a multitude I will excel in speculative grammar and
     [symbolized in ciphers
terribly harmonious before the eruption of carbonizing
     [passions
in fact and relative distortions before long, smoky mushrooms

---

The little erotico-demonological romance is meant as a transposition:
nocturnal pollution (naturally "absque cogitatione immunda") func-
tions as a cautious "revolt" over an "ideal need." Man is "organic sep-
ulchre / complicated for enjoying" "with an epoch." Thus Ellie, as
pollution, prompts the "fracture" of the personality and its "multitu-
dinous" "expansion." The epithets for Ellie—Mare Humorum, Lacus
Somniorum—extend the lunar geography. The scholastic tenet "sed
non omnis emissio—humoris carnalis—est proprie pollutio," taken
from an "index rerum" in the *Summa Theologica*, has been deliberately
broken up.

che si gonfiano e indico l'ustione linguistica frammenti che
[costellano
il notturno giardino dei succubi sopra l'atollo delle labbra
[coralline
si impone e oscilla lo spettro maschile con voce telefonica
(sed non omnis emissio dice) dalla casa di giuoco
il compasso scottante io che colloco in calde comunicazioni
[prenotabili
gli opprimenti (humoris carnalis) ed enfiati fantocci
[continuatamente
Lacus Somniorum emuntori (al punto dell'inevitabile invocazione
[è carnalis)
dell'orinazione dell'encefalo in tutta la sua massa precipitabile
è finita è finita la perspicacia passiva primitiva è finita eppure
in uno stadio enunciatamente ricostruttivo di responsabile
[ricomposizione
è finita infine è atomizzata e io sono io sono una moltitudine
attraverso ritentate esperienze Mare Lacus accoglimi (est proprie
[pollutio)

La polluzione notturna è frutto dell'incubo; tutta la proiezione del sogno è confusa, maschile e femminile si scambiano le parti. La «inevitabile invocazione» è il grido dell'estasi erotica, con il suo sfondo rituale, sacrale. (Nella sez. 3: «l'accelerata evocazione delle anime procede mediante l'apparato / escretorio per eccellenza che suggella ritualmente il sacrificio / dello sperma con l'implorazione»). I morti, gli incubi e i demoni sono *evocati* nel delirio della nékyia.
Lo «stadio enunciatamente ricostruttivo» è quello della nuova strutturazione dell'io, della rinascita alchemico-magica. Dopo il coito sognato («fluida intromissione», «compasso scottante») avviene la

that swell and I point to a linguistic burn fragments that stud
the nocturnal garden of victims on the atoll of coral lips
the masculine specter dominates and oscillates with
        [telephone voice
(sed non omnis emissio he says) from the gambling house
the searing compass I who arrange in heated reservable
        [messages
the oppressive (humoris carnalis) and swollen puppets
        [continually
Lacus Somniorum emunctories (at the moment of its
        [inevitable invocation is carnalis)
of the encephalon's urination in all his precipitant mass
it's over it's over this primitive passive perspicacity it's over
        [and yet
in an enunciatively reconstructive phase of responsible
        [recomposition
it's over at last it is atomized and I am I am a multitude
through retired experiences Mare Lacus welcome me (est
        [proprie pollutio)

The nocturnal pollution is born of a nightmare; the entire projection
of the dream is confused, with masculine and feminine parts switched.
The "inevitable invocation" is the cry of erotic ecstasy, with its ritual,
sacred background. (In section 3: "the accelerated evocation of the souls
proceeds by the excretory / apparatus par excellence, ritually sealing
the sacrifice / of the sperm with an imploration"). The dead, the night-
mares and demons are *evoked* in the delirium of the *nékyia*.
The "stadio enunciatamente ricostruttivo" is that of the new structur-
ing of the ego, of alchemico-magical rebirth. After the dream-coitus
("fluid intrusion," the "searing compass") comes the geometricization

il tenero mattino conduce la mastite a visitare il triste cervelletto
sensibile al vento per incantamento est duplex intellectus
e tu ascoltamì bene amore Mare Lacus
      non c'è più divertimento
ridurremo forse la testa umana a secco luogo geometrico ma
comparata con l'ideale esigenza questa rivolta
non avrà fine

---

geometrizzazione della realtà (cfr. « simbolizzato in cifre »). La « casa
di giuoco » nel « giardino dei succubi » indica il lusus erotico (e il lusus
poetico, onde il titolo di *Erotopaegnia* della seconda parte dell'*Opus*);
nella figura onirica che parla « con voce telefonica » c'è un rinvio
demonologico: così nei « funghi fumosi », gli « enfiati fantocci » che
simboleggiano il sesso maschile. La « mastite » è, ovviamente, metafora
dell'emicrania del mattino dopo. Il « duplex intellectus » è dei demoni
(« duplices daemones ») che operano dal sonno sulla coscienza
capovolgendo le situazioni.

the tender morning leads the mastitis to visit the sad
        [cerebellum
sensitive to the wind by incantation est duplex intellectus
and you listen to me love Mare Lacus
                there is no more pleasure
maybe we will reduce the human head to a dry geometric
        [locus but
compared with the ideal demand this revolt
will have no end

---

of reality (cf. "symbolized in ciphers"). The "gambling house" in the
"nocturnal garden of victims" suggests erotic *lusus* (and poetical *lusus*,
whence the title *Erotopaegnia* in the second part of *Opus*); the dream
figure that speaks "with telephone voice" marks a return of victims;
thus in the "smoky mushrooms," as with the "swollen puppets," sym-
bolizing the male sex. The "mastitis" is obviously a metaphor of the
morning-after migraine. The "duplex intellectus" is that of demons
("duplices daemones") who work on consciousness from sleep, revers-
ing situations.

4

e mentre ancora combattono il re e lo scheletro del re con
[storica ironia
di costumi correlati mentre mi appresto alla prefazione
[improbativa
nell'anno della grande monomania e Laszo oscilla all'Eldorado
[Club
con la gola d'oro solitaria vaso della ricostituzione
a scadenza itinerarium rapidamente ballabile
                    tu Ruben
che sei il garantito visionario Filius Hermaphroditus in
[putrefazione
ma in questa νέχυια senza risorse
                    acqua senza coscienza dico
(vivo quando dormo) lasciati vivere
lascia che la vita scorra su te (vivo quando dormo)
con l'epidermide intiera tocchiamo terra
che sarò nella pioggia e nel vento che la luna non entra
nell'acquario ma asciutta
occidit et vivere facit
                    noi les objets à réaction poétique

Il re è una figura archetipica dell'allegoria alchemica, simbolo
dell'inconscio che si fa strada verso la coscienza (cfr. Edipo, Lear,
Dhritaràshtra). Il suo regno è sterile e cela uno stato di potenzialità
finché egli non genera dal proprio cervello un figlio e una figlia destinati
alla *coniunctio oppositorum.*
« Filius Hermaphroditus » simbolizza la totalità, l'androginia primitiva
della divinità lunare (nasce alchemicamente dal matrimonio del sole e
della luna): è l'*οὐροβόρο,* il figlio che diviene il proprio padre (o il re

4

and while the king and the king's skeleton still battle with
    [the historic irony
of correlated customs while I prepare for the improbative
    [preface
in the year of the great monomania and Laszo swings at the
    [Eldorado Club
with his solitary golden throat vessel of short-term
reconstitution rapidly danceable itinerarium
        you Ruben
who are the guaranteed visionary Filius Hermaphroditus in
    [putrefaction
but in this νέχυια without resources
        water without conscience I say
(I live when I sleep) let yourself live
let life run over you (I live when I sleep)
with the epidermis whole we touch ground
for I will be in the rain and in the wind for the moon does not
    [sink
into the aquarium but dry
occidit et vivere facit
        we les objets à réaction poétique

The king is an archetypal figure of alchemical allegory, a symbol of the
unconscious making its way into consciousness (cf. Oedipus, Lear,
Dhritaràshtra). His reign is a sterile one that conceals a state of poten-
tiality, until he begets a son and daughter out of his brain who are
destined for a *coniunctio oppositorum*.
"Filius Hermaphroditus" symbolizes the totality, the primitive an-
drogyny of the lunar god (born alchemically from the wedding of sun
and moon): he is the οὐροβόρο, the son who becomes his own father

riportiamo un linguaggio a un senso morale
che sarò nella lettura discreta del barometro nel dubbio
della metalessi tenace ma in questa morte impropria
dove l'amore non est aurum vulgi

Laszo implicazione dell'indifferente equilibrio della tua anima
erano appunto le propaggini propedeutiche della mia vita
(aspettando la mia vita) che intendevo illustrare
(passerò oltrepasserò la mia vita)
       terra dell'intelletto pratico
fatalmente abortivo
ottimamente
       daremo al mondo il giusto aspetto
quando saranno in ingegnosa congiunzione il figlio insolubile
del re e lo scheletro enigmatico
sempre del re

---

che genera il proprio figlio), cioè l'archetipo della ripetizione-della
nascita. L'intera sezione è intessuta di simboli alchemici (la gola d'oro,
il vaso della ricostituzione, ecc.); Laszo, il protagonista, è una pallida
incarnazione del sole (balla all'Eldorado Club); la « morte impropria »
è la sua discesa agli inferi per trovare l'amore lunare, l'argento vivo
« quod occidit et vivere facit », la pietra filosofale.
« Le but de la véritable alchimie est d'éveiller ce qui dort, de faire
ruisseler l'eau prisonnière dans la terre. En d'autres termes, le sens de
l'alchimie est de réveiller la princesse endormie qui se trouve au plus
secret de l'âme » (M.M. Davy: *Essai sur la symbolique roman*).

return a language to a moral sense
that I will be in the discrete reading of the barometer in the
        [doubt
of the tenacious metalepsis but in this inappropriate death
where love non est aurum vulgi

Laszo implication of the indifferent equilibrium of your soul
were precisely the introductory offshoots of my life
(awaiting my life) that I meant to illustrate
(I will pass I will pass beyond my life)
            land of the practical intellect
fatally abortive
optimally
            we will give the world its best face
when there will be in ingenious conjunction the insoluble son
of the king and the enigmatic skeleton
also the king's

(or the king who begets his own son), i.e., the archetype of the repetition of birth. The whole section is laced with alchemical symbols (the golden throat, the reconstitutive vessel, etc.); Laszo, the protagonist, is a pale incarnation of the sun (he dances at the Eldorado Club); the "inappropriate death" is his descent into the underworld to find his lunar love, the quicksilver "quod occidit et vivere facit," the philosophers' stone.

"Le but de la véritable alchimie est d'éveiller ce qui dort, de faire ruisseler l'eau prisonnière dans la terre. En d'autres termes, le sens de l'alchimie est de réveiller la princesse endormie qui se trouve au plus secret de l'âme" (M.M. Davy: *Essai sur la symbolique roman*).

Ellie mia Ellie mia tesi sei la fine di uno svolgimento civile
la soffocazione di tante leggi esplorate
   la preghiera della meditazione
della mano dell'intolleranza e in prima sede
sei questo linguaggio che partorisce
   portami dunque l'unghia
e la sua filigrana
   le lacune di un bacio o di mille anni
un mysterium tremendum il tiro alla fune
le metamorfosi degli insetti il volume della sfera
   voglio dire
perdita di affettività e stato crepuscolare e incidenza di giudizio
e confessione vistosa glutinosa glutinante
il flessibile amalgama di due punti di coscienza
   voglio l'unità mistica
che insinua pali nella sabbia della volontà impiccatrice
e il dente del gigante
   portami la povertà

Qui Ellie rappresenta la fine di un ciclo storico (una vichiana *età della ragione*); da lei sprigiona il linguaggio « che partorisce », che rispecchia la realtà: Ellie è tale linguaggio, tale realtà.

L'unghia, che è legata alla « mano dell'intolleranza », dà l'avvio a tutte le grazie che Ellie può concedere, a tutte le realtà che essa può generare. Il suo influsso è soprattutto psicologico (anzi psicopatico) e si manifesta nella « perdita di affettività », nello « stato crepuscolare », nell'angoscia dell'impossibile « unità mistica » tra i « due punti di coscienza ».

Ellie my Ellie my thesis you are the conclusion of a civil
    [development
the suffocation of so many explored laws
      the prayer of meditation
of the hand of intolerance and in the first place
you are this language that gives birth
      so bring me then the fingernail
and its filigree
      the lacunae of a kiss or of a thousand years
a mysterium tremendum the tug of war
the metamorphoses of the insects the volume of the sphere
      I mean
loss of affection and dusky mood and incisive wisdom
and ostentatious glutinous glutinating confession
the flexible amalgam of two points of conscience
      I want the mystic unity
that slips stakes into the sand of the annihilating will
and the giant's tooth
      bring me poverty

Here Ellie represents the end of a historical cycle (a Vicoan *age of reason*); she emits language "that gives birth," that mirrors reality: Ellie is that language, that reality.

The fingernail, linked with the "hand of intolerance," launches all the graces Ellie can allow, all the realities she can generate. The influence is chiefly psychological (or rather, psychopathic) and is evidenced in the "loss of affection," in the "dusky mood," in the anguish over the impossible "mystic unity" between the "two points of conscience."

e la figura etimologica che si porta per mano
portami per mano Ruben
        tu stesso Ruben portami per mano
alle miniere degli animali al palco
del trattamento psicoterapico all'esperienza
terrificante dei conflitti
        ah per te ho inventato il rame e la polvere
ho liberato la lettera erre e la lettera ci da un penitenziario
    [di tabacco
ho trascinato lepri e chiodi in Paradise Valley
di te ho anche detto perfectiones intelligibiles
        ho detto
novimus enim tenebras aquas ventos ignem fumum
vediamo insieme il passato il futuro
        ho detto
quoi qu'elle fasse elle est désir improportionabiliter excedens

---

Ruben è un personaggio intermediario della « confessione vistosa »,
probabilmente un amico che partecipa intellettualmente alla relazione
Ellie—Laszo; figura dell'alchemico Hermaphroditus invocata a
sostituire l'influsso di Ellie.
Le lettere « erre » e « ci » sono le iniziali del nome anagrafico di Ellie:
« Paradise Valley », in u.s.a L'idea del nuoto si riferisce alla Palus.
Tenebre, acque, venti, fuoco e fumo sono gli elementi su cui hanno
dominio i demoni.

and the etymological figure that is carried by hand
bring me by the hand Ruben
            you yourself Ruben bring me by the hand
to the animal's mines to the platform
of psychotherapeutic treatment to the terrifying
experience of conflicts
            ah for you I invented copper and dust
I freed the letter r and the letter c from a tobacco penitentiary
I dragged hares and nails into Paradise Valley
I said of you perfectiones intelligibiles
            I said
novimus enim tenebras aquas ventos ignem fumum
we see together past and future
            I said
quoi qu'elle fasse elle est désir improportionabiliter excedens

---

Ruben is an intermediary character of the "ostentatious confession,"
probably a friend involved intellectually in the relationship between
Ellie and Laszo; he is a figure of the alchemical Hermaphroditus in-
voked to supplant Ellie's influence.
The letters "r" and "c" are the initials of Ellie's real name: "Paradise
Valley" is in the United States. The idea of swimming relates to the
Palus. Darkness, bodies of water, winds, fire, and smoke are the ele-
ments the demons preside over.

la nostra sapienza tollera tutte le guerre
tollera la peste mansueta delle discipline
la tua statura mescola pietre sirene pollici bruchi
        oh fermo carcere
dei disegni e dell'utero tempo indicativo fontana che rode e
    [silenzio
e propriamente et os clausit digito
        distratto Laszo pietosamente
per amori per mezzo delle ossa amati
        per mezzo della calce viva
per mezzo dei concerti per violino e orchestra
        per mezzo delle tue lenzuola
per mezzo della Kritik der reinen Vernunft
        amori da ogni cornice
e da ogni tradimento protestati
        amori del tutto principali
amori ecco essenziali promossi da ogni fiore
        ergo vacuas fac sedes
tuarum aurium devi assumere le pietre disperate oh tridente

Il primo verso, dice l'A., è molto autocritico. Si predica ancora di Ellie
(« fermo carcere », « tempo indicativo », « fontana che rode », « silenzio »),
materia prima che « mescola » in sé ogni realtà. Così gli amori sono
amati « per mezzo di » ogni cosa: anche per mezzo dell'austero Kant,
come si addice a un « amore intellettuale ».

« Protestati » come le cambiali. Sul simbolismo litico (« pietre
disperate ») si può vedere in Eliade, *Trattato di storia delle religioni*, Torino
1954. In questa predicazione onirica di Ellie il linguaggio si disgrega e
abortisce.

our wisdom tolerates all wars
tolerates the mild plague of disciplines
your stature mixes stones sirens thumbs worms
                    oh steady prison
of drawings and of the womb indicative tense fountain that
        [gnaws and silence
and truly et os clausit digito
                    distracted Laszo piteously
for loves loved by means of bones
                    by means of quicklime
by means of concertos for violin and orchestra
                    by means of your sheets
by means of the Kritik der reinen Vernunft
                    loves protested by each
frame and each betrayal
                    loves absolutely foremost
then essential loves promoted by each flower
                    ergo vacuas fac sedes
tuarum aurium you have to assume the wretched stones oh
        [trident

The first line, according to the author, is highly self-critical. It is still Ellie that is being referred to ("steady prison," "indicative tense," "fountain that gnaws," "silence") raw material that "mixes" all realities in itself. Thus the loves are loved "by means of" all things: even by means of the austere Kant, as befits an "intellectual love."

"Protested" as bills of exchange are. Concerning the lithic symbolism ("wretched stones") one might consult M. Eliade's *Treatise on the History of Religion*. In this dream predication of Ellie, language disintegrates and miscarries.

delle mie fatiche chimiche ancora e sempre Ellie
mio folto estuario coltivatrice di cicatrici inchiodate
chiedere la notizia delle tue monete infiammabili dei tuoi vuoti
      [porticati
per uno regolamento
         stabilirete il suo gusto
esigere il fallimento dietro la tua età
i fiammiferi con secchezza sotto i tuoi conigli sottrarre

L'ultimo verso è un *nonsense*, che celebra l'*Anima* (nel senso di Jung)
oltre ogni effabilità; cfr. la sez. 23: « et j'y mis du raisonnement e non
basta et du pathétique e non basta / ancora καὶ τὰ τῶν ποιητῶν and
CAPITAL LETTERS... ».

of my chemical labors now and forever Ellie
my lush estuary cultivator of nailed scars
ask about the news of your inflammable coins of your empty
    [arcades
for a rule
        you will establish its taste
demand failure behind your age
dryly extract the matches from under your rabbits

The last line is nonsensical, celebrating the *Anima* (in the Jungian sense)
beyond all utterance; cf. section 23: "et j'y mis du raisonnement e non
basta et du pathétique e non basta / ancora καὶ τὰ τῶν ποιητῶν and
CAPITAL LETTERS...."

ma complicazione come alienazione come aspra alienazione
    [corollario
alienazione epigrammatico epilogo Laszo drammatico addendo
    [compendiario
entro la proporzione erotica limitativo (carcer voluntarius)
    [lineare
(optimae mortis itinerarium) intellectualis est figura
intellectualis seminis seu spermatis punctum
ut duo unum fiant character amoris
          est autem in mari piscis rotundus
risolvere Laszo qui in puncto requiescit nel suo procedimento
    [quasi
la periodica proiezione in figuris et habet in se humidum radicale
dove si scioglie la spiaggia alveolare in indivisibili puncto
in permutazione la permanente alienazione e l'elevazione la
    [cattura
della potente estensione cuius centrum est ubique
et habet in se pinguedinem

Sviluppa il tema della sez. 6 citata nell'introduzione. Qui la complica-
zione (« la tessitura delle idee » della sez. 6) è posta come « alienazione »,
nel senso clinico e della *Verfremdung.* Sul concetto di complicazione
vedi una citazione dal Cusano (da *De ludo globi,* in Cassirer: *Individuo e
cosmo nella fil. del Rinasc.):* « Anima rationalis est vis complicativa
omnium notionalium complicationum »; « Ut duo unum fiant » si
riferisce all'impossibile « unio » mistica e alla complicazione-alienazione
culturale; nella sez. 3: « impossibile parlare di due cose (di una c'est
avoir le sens de l'anarchie) ».

but complication like alienation like bitter alienation corollary
epigrammatic alienation dramatic epilogue Lazso summary
    [addendum
limitative within erotic proportion (carcer voluntarius)
    [linear
(optimae mortis itinerarium) intellectualis est figura
intellectualis seminis seu spermatis punctum
ut duo unum fiant character amoris
         est autem in mari piscis rotundus
resolve Laszo qui in puncto requiescit in his course almost
the periodic projection in figuris et habet in se humidum
    [radicale
where the alveolar beach dissolves in indivisibili puncto
in permutation permanent alienation and elevation the
    [capture
of the powerful extension cuius centrum est ubique
et habet in se pinguedinem

This section develops the theme of section 6 quoted in the introduc-
tion. Here the complication ("the fabric of ideas" of section 6) is pos-
ited as "alienation," both in the clinical sense and as *Verfremdung*. On
the concept of complication, see a quotation of Nicholas of Cusa (from
De ludo globi, in Cassirer, *The Individual and the Cosmos in Renaissance
Philosophy*): "Anima rationalis est vis complicativa omnium notionalium
complicationum"; "Ut duo unum fiant" refers to the impossible mysti-
cal "unio" and to cultural complication/alienation; in section 3: "im-
possible to speak of two things (of one c'est avoir le sens de l'anarchie)."

oh mia carne e perimetro di carne
corticibus carentem e forma equazioni e sistemi di equazioni
organi significanti in situazioni
quorum circumferentia vero nusquam inveniri potest

non altrimenti descrive et chante en imitant il numero del
    [tempo
(à la perfection la nature) Laszo in una tragedia teologica
    [metamorfica
in livido segmento sofferente
    il tempo è numero e numero astratto
per una descrizione del numero negativo descrive la serie del
    [tempo
per una notizia del tempo il tempo immaginario
è spazio in condizione il tempo giusto arbitraria
il solo discorso giusto allora le portrait questo novum organon
    [espressione
de l'artiste-horloger in questi termini espressione di alienazione
espressione del tempo il tuo tempo era la misura di ogni tempo
l'horloge a disposizione astronomique
cerca ancora una disposizione vitale
    in condizione nome astratto arbitraria

« Cuius centrum est ubique... circumferentia vero nusquam inveniri potest » è la definizione di Dio del Cusano; qui definisce il « piscis rotundus », archetipo dell'eroe Laszo (con evidente richiamo cristologico). Tutta la parte seconda (da « non altrimenti... »), che descrive l'implicazione del tempo nello spazio e tratta della supremazia del tempo, è ispirata al celebre alchimista Nicolas Flamel. Il discorso si proietta ora in una teologia *cronica* e procede su piani intrecciati; il

oh my flesh and perimeter of flesh
corticibus carentem and form equations and systems of
    [equations
organs significant in situations
quorum circumferentia vero nusquam inveniri potest

does not otherwise describe et chante en imitant the measure
    [of time
(à la perfection la nature) Laszo in a metamorphic theological
    [tragedy
in a livid suffering segment
        time is number and an abstract number
for a description of the negative number it describes the series
    [of time
for news of time imaginary time
is space in arbitrary condition the right time
the only right discourse then le portrait this novum organon
    [expression
de l'artiste-horloger in these terms expression of alienation
expression of time your time was the measure of each time
l'horloge with astronomique disposition
still seeks a vital disposition
      in arbitrary condition abstract name

"Cuius centrum est ubique... circumferentia vero nusquam inveniri potest" is Cusa's definition of God; here it defines the hero Laszo's archetypal "piscis rotundus" (an obvious Christological allusion). The entire second section (from "does not otherwise..."), describing time's implication in space and its supremacy, is inspired by the renowned alchemist Nicolas Flamel. The discussion now advances into a *chronic* theology, operating on interwoven planes; the theme is the transfor-

significa per una descrizione incompleta della posizione
    [incompleto
negativa per la mia presenza sur le sol espressione
est placée nozione di alienazione l'orologio la sphère celeste
era altissimo senza dignità e oscuro logica o fantastica la
    [proposta
di proposizione di periodo aggiungere cercare o volere o
    [tubercolo
nous apercevons o labirinto un mécanisme impossibile cosa
    [transformateur
du temps solaire en temps vrai
            ahi spirale puncto temporis data
ahi Lacus Moriae
            forzosamente toccare la corteccia congestionata
et imagine decipimur
            et fallimur imagine
ahi additando la sua corruttibile natura sciogliere la
    [dettagliata identità
siquidem de intellectuali puncto habet in se dolcemente
anarchia come alienazione
            rotundae mortis undas necessarias

---

tema è la trasformazione « du temps solaire en temps vrai »: si cerca
un meccanismo che trasformi il tempo in realtà assoluta.
Il *Laborintus* è il novum organon de l'artiste-horloger, dell'alchimista
Laszo-Flamel. È una ricerca condotta in delirio, in alienazione, con
« la corteccia congestionata ». Laszo cerca l'astrazione perché
l'immagine inganna; cerca Dio nella geometria, negli orologi, in mezzo
all'anatomia, in un labirinto.

signifies incomplete by an incomplete description of the
     [position
negative by my presence sur le sol expression
est placée notion of alienation the clock la sphère celeste
was lofty without dignity and obscure a proposal logical or
     [fantastic
of a proposition a period adding seeking or wanting or tubercle
nous apercevons or labyrinth un mécanisme impossible thing
     [transformateur
du temps solaire en temps vrai
          alas spiral puncto temporis date
alas Lacus Moriae
          forcedly touch the congested cortex
et imagine decipimur
          et fallimur imagine
alas pointing at its corruptible nature dissolving the detailed
     [identity
siquidem de intellectuali puncto habet in se sweetly
anarchy as alienation
          rotundae mortis undas necessarias

---

mation "du temps solaire en temps vrai": the search is for a mecha-
nism that can transform time into absolute reality.
The *Laborintus* is the novum organon of the clockmaker-artist, the al-
chemist Laszo-Flamel. It is an investigation conducted in a state of
delirium, in alienation with "the congested cortex." Laszo seeks after
abstraction because images are deceptive; he searches for God in ge-
ometry, in clocks, within anatomy, in a labyrinth.

e ormai per forza di serietà ricuperare ma per produzione
    [potremo
ma contro il mio palato sopra questo orizzonte ma distesa
e un sogno respinto e ormai distesa e sopra questo orizzonte
respinto e per forza di vita e con le mani respinto e produttive
percorsa masticata e sopra questa negazione di orizzonte
    [toccata
e adesso espulsa e sopra questo nulla sive coitus et filiam et
    [mundum
gestavi et sensibilem sopra questo orizzonte e produttivo et
in cerebro meo e ormai sopra questo nulla di nulla e ormai
coniunctio e distesa (coniunctio sive coitus) e permeabile
permeata e sopra questo nulla di orizzonte in incastro
come i giorni permeata e trascinata ormai in me e trascinata
sopra questa negazione di negazione e orizzonte cerebrale e
    [toccare
inghiottire e trascinata fuori e per riprendere (fuori e fuori)
i paesaggi dell'amore e sopra questo composti sopra questo
orizzonte di nulla e sopra questo paesaggio sensibile di nulla

16

and by now by force of seriousness and by production we
　　[will be able to recover
but against my palate over this horizon but extended
and a rejected dream and by now extended and over this
　　[horizon
rejected and by force of life and with the productive hands
　　[rejected
travelled chewed and above this denial of the horizon touched
and now expelled and above this nothing sive coitus et filiam
　　[et mundum
gestavi et sensibilem above this horizon and productive et
　in cerebro meo and by now above this nothing of nothing and
　　　[by now
coniunctio and extended (coniunctio sive coitus) and permeable
permeated and above this nothing of the interlocking horizon
permeated like the days and dragged out by now in me and
　　[dragged
over this denial of denial and cerebral horizon and touch
gulp and dragged out and to resume (outside and outside)
the landscapes of love and above this arranged above this
horizon on nothing and above this landscape sensitive to
　　[nothing

(di negazione e di orizzonte) e sopra e fuori e adesso e ormai
            ma
dentro un sensibile cerchio Ellie dentro un cerchio di nulla
in cerebro meo composta e maturata dentro un cerchio di
            [incastro
tanto cerebrale tanto sensibile e ormai trascinata fuori
tanto fuori e distesa e dentro un cerchio di contatto e di
            [giorni e di
maturazione ma espulsa ma per forza di nulla ma toccata in
            [sensibile
contatto ma ormai per produzione ma ormai sopra un palato
            [permeabile
un serio sogno ma sogno per forza di vita

e ormai un sogno respinto ma in masticazione ma il sogno
ma il sogno stesso era una vita
e masticazione e vita e produzione e sogno in cerebro meo

Il canto celebra la morte mistica (o alchimistica) di Ellie, ritrovata « in
cerebro » e respinta, «trascinata fuori» dal sogno. La mente sostituisce
lo spazio sensibile e si afferma come il « cerchio » dove il sogno è soltanto
sogno e le cose soltanto *res cogitatae* (ma, intanto, idee: ARCHETYPAL
IDEAS). Il cerchio è un'immagine archetipica, è la sfera del reale, il
nulla che divora se stesso. Il « ma ormai » che regge strutturalmente la
poesia indica la ricerca del nuovo tempo, la pressione del tempo contro
il cerchio dello spazio.

(of denial and horizon) and above and outside and now and by
      [now

            yet
within a sizeable circle Ellie within a circle of nothing
in cerebro meo composed and ripened within an interlocking
      [circle
so cerebral so sensitive and by now dragged out
so far out and extended and within a circle of contact and of
      [days and
ripeness but expelled but impelled by nothing but touched in
      [sensitive
contact yet by now through production yet by now above a
      [permeable palate
a serious dream but a dream by force of life

and by now a dream rejected but in mastication but the dream
but the dream itself was a life
and mastication and life and production and dream in cerebro
      [meo

The canto celebrates Ellie's mystical (or alchemistical) death, discov-
ered "in cerebro" and rejected, "dragged out" of a dream. The mind
substitutes perceptible space and asserts itself as the "circle" in which
the dream is merely a dream and things are merely *res cogitatae* (but,
meanwhile, ideas: ARCHETYPAL IDEAS). The circle is an archetypal
image, it is the sphere of the real, nothingness devouring itself. The
"yet by now" that structures the poem points to a search for the new
time, the pressure of time against the circle of space.

soltanto in cerebro meo dove l'orizzonte è seriamente
        [orizzonte
il paesaggio è paesaggio il mundus sensibilis è mundus
        [sensibilis
la coniunctio è coniunctio il coitus coitus
                ma ormai
in un orizzonte orizzontale per forza di serietà ricuperare
ma ormai ricuperare in me per forza di sogno
                ma ormai
i paesaggi del mare e il re marino tutti i paesaggi sensibili
del mare tutti i paesaggi ricuperare in me e lo scheletro maturo
del re marino e lo scheletro cerebrale della figlia del re marino
et in cerebro meo ricuperare in me e respingere nei giorni
e in comprensione e comprensione e comprensione
                ma ormai

Nel finale assistiamo alla traduzione in termini femminili del mito
rappresentato nella sez. 4: il figlio del re è ora la «figlia del re marino»,
lo scheletro enigmatico è «lo scheletro cerebrale» metafisico, maturato
nella trasformazione. Il tema ermafroditico (omo-eterosessuale) riporta
labirinticamente al simbolo di Tiresia (in cui si fondono il polo maschile
e il femminile) in *The Waste Land* di Eliot. Lo scambio delle parti sessuali,
sofferto nelle scene oniriche, è «ricuperato» nella coscienza e *respinto*
nel tempo.

only in cerebro meo where the horizon is seriously horizon
the landscape is landscape the mundus sensibilis is mundus
        [sensibilis
coniunctio is coniunctio coitus coitus
                yet by now
in an horizontal horizon by force of seriousness recover
yet by now recover in me by force of dream
                yet by now
the seascapes and the sea king all the sensitive seascapes
all the landscapes recover in me and the ripe skeleton
of the sea king and the cerebral skeleton of the sea king's
        [daughter
et in cerebro meo recover in me and push back to the days
and in comprehension and comprehension and comprehension
                yet by now

In the ending we witness a translation into feminine terms of the myth
presented in section 4: the king's son has become the "sea-king's daugh-
ter," the enigmatic skeleton the metaphysical "cerebral skeleton,"
reaching maturity in transformation. The theme of the hermaphro-
dite (homo-heterosexual) leads back in labyrinthine fashion to the sym-
bol of Tiresias (in whom the masculine and feminine polarities are
merged) in Eliot's *The Waste Land*. The reversal of sexual parts that
took place in the dream scenes is "recovered" in consciousness and
thrown back in time.

devi conoscerlo e allora mangiano e vieni dunque (oh
    [melodrama!) coraggio!
più facilmente chi mi conduce e allora rinunciano a vedere al
    [loro incongruo
atteggiamento in iterazione i cortili e più ragionevoli
    [digeriscono diventano
in correzione gli amori incatramati malati? e vieni dunque e
    [con buoni
effetti ma anni occorrono ma rimase poi tranquilla per
    [comprenderlo
e fra i tappeti veramente e così entrambi sedemmo e
    [finalmente
al cader del sole ritrovammo il nostro uomo
        e ah perché non mi hai cercato
ieri sera? gridava ah ero in compagnia ah come vedi e del resto
non ci scriviamo quasi più e potrei aggiungere e Moneybags e
    [vieni!
ricordi? lo storpio! e LEGGITOR cortese, hai qui una bella
    [occasione (1781)

Il personaggio centrale di questa sez. è Ruben, l'ebreo; nello sfondo,
sua proiezione e suo *negativo,* è Moneybags (= mucchio di monete), il
capitalista-tipo satireggiato da Marx.
Gli « amori », soggetto-oggetto della prima parte, si prestano a una
lettura polivalente: indefiniti personaggi mangiano e digeriscono gli
amori, oppure (anche) sono amori che mangiano, amori che
digeriscono.
Del 1781, spiega l'A., è il testo nella cui tavola di errata-corrige si nomina
il « LEGGITOR cortese ». Il senso è che al lettore (all'amico) si offre

you have to know him and then they are eating and so you
    [come (oh melodrama!) take heart!
more easily he who leads me and then they decline to the
    [courtyards
in their incongruous attitude in iteration and more reasonably
    [they digest they become
in correction the tarred sick loves? and you come then and
    [with good
effects but years are necessary but then she remained tranquil
    [to comprehend it
and truly among the carpets and thus we both sat and finally
at sunset we rediscovered our man
           and ah why didn't you look at me
last night? he was shouting ah I was with someone ah as you
    [see and as for that matter
we hardly write to each other anymore and I could add and
    [Moneybags and come!
do you remember? the cripple! and courteous READER, you
    [have here a fine occasion (1781)

The main character in this section is the Jew Ruben; in the background, his projection and his *negative* Moneybags, the arch-capitalist satirized by Marx.

The "loves," subject-object of the first part, lend themselves to a poly-valent reading: indefinite characters devour and digest the loves, or (also) are loves that devour and loves that digest.

As for 1781, the author explains that this is the date of the text whose table of errata is addressed to the "courteous READER." The meaning being that the reader (friend) is offered the opportunity to bring his

di esercitar la tua sofferenza e vieni dunque! e ascolta
       ah
era il tentativo di imporre una determinata educazione morale!
e molto rapidamente... ah Moneybags! ora ricordo e ah tu sei
il mio repertorio ontologico ho gridato tu sei oh mio vapeur
       [colonial
(altra espressione equivalente) il mio Ruben! in trascrizione
ora soltanto ti riconosco vapeur de rivière! la mia eresia
       [verissima
la mia necessità e tutta la serietà della vita! e voglio incontrarti!
adesso!
           tout est dans le commencement come sempre
e vieni dunque! questa esperienza sarà di giovamento a un'altra
       [paziente

---

l'occasione di esercitare sul testo la propria sofferenza e pazienza; il
lettore è Ruben, lo storpio è Moneybags.
L'attacco « ah tu sei » riprende per Ruben il tema della predicazione
universale di Ellie. Come ogni altra realtà, Ruben è « vapeur de rivière »,
ma è figura determinata trascritta in una forma riconoscibile (è la
predicazione che permette di riconoscerlo).
L'incontro con Ruben « al cader del sole » è nello stile tragico-epico
dell'esperienza morale. Ruben è il « repertorio ontologico » di Laszo,
e « questa esperienza sarà di giovamento a un'altra paziente », cioè ad
Ellie (o a chi per lei, nel tempo).

to exercise your suffering and so come! and listen
         ah
it was the attempt to impose a specific moral education!
and very rapidly... ah Moneybags! now I remember and ah you
are my ontological repertory I shouted you are oh my vapeur
         [colonial
(another equivalent expression) my Ruben! in transcription
only now I recognize you vapeur de rivière! my truest heresy
my necessity and all the seriousness of life! and I want to
         [meet you
now!
             tout est dans le commencement as always
and so you come! this experience will benefit another patient

---

own distress and patience to bear on the text; the reader is Ruben, the
cripple is Moneybags.

The opening "ah you are" again recapitulates for Rubin the theme of
Ellie as universal predication. Like all other reality, Ruben is a "vapeur
de rivière," yet is a determinate figure transcribed into recognizable
form (predication allowing him to be recognized).

The encounter with Ruben "at sunset" is in the tragico-epic style of
moral experience. Ruben is Laszo's "ontological repertory" and "this
experience will benefit another patient," i.e., Ellie (or whoever at the
time is in her place).

s.d. ma 1951 (unruhig) καί κρίνουσιν e socchiudo gli occhi
οἰ πολλοί e mi domanda (L): fai il giuoco delle luci?
καί τὰ τῆς μουσικῆς ἔργα ah quale continuità! andante κ. 467
qui è bella la regione (lago di Sompunt) e tu sei l'inverno Laszo
    [veramente
et j'y mis du raisonnement e non basta e du pathétique e non
    [basta
ancora καί τὰ τῶν ποιητῶν and CAPITAL LETTERS
et ce mélange de comique ah sono avvilito adesso et de
    [pathétique
una tristezza ah in me contengo qui devoit plaire
sono dimesso et devoit même sono dimesso, non umile
surprendre! ma distratto da futilità ma immerso in qualche cosa
and CREATURES gli amori OF THE MIND di spiacevole
    [realmente
très-intéressant mi è accaduto dans le pathétique un incidente

---

Ars poetica. Appare qui il nuovo personaggio cifrato che sostituisce Ellie:
L (o lambda), che ancora impersona l'archetipo femminile.
I frammenti in lingua greca sono tratti dalla Retorica e dalla Poetica di
Aristotele, quelli in inglese dai neoplatonici di Cambridge (ved. Cassirer:
La rinascenza platonica in Inghilterra e la scuola di Cambridge). La fonte
francese indicata dall'A. è: *Nouveaux entretiens sur les sciences secretes ou
le Comte de Gabalis* (Cologne, 1691).
La trama dei frammenti consente (qui come altrove) una doppia lettura:
riallacciando i piani linguistici e conservandoli frantumati.
« Unruhig » = inquieto (con rifer. alla prima parte del *Faust* di Goethe).

23

n.d. but 1951 (unruhig) καί κρίνουσιν and I squint my eyes
οἱ πολλοί and she (L) asks me: are you playing the game of
    [lights?
καί τὰ τῆς μουσικῆς ἔργα ah what continuity! andante κ. 467
this region here is beautiful (Lake Sompunt) and you are really
    [the winter Laszo
et j'y mis du raisonnement and it's not enough et du
    [pathétique and it's not enough
again καί τὰ τῶν ποιητῶν and CAPITAL LETTERS
et ce mélange de comique ah I'm disheartened now et de
    [pathétique
a sadness ah I hold in me qui devoit plaire
I'm raggedly et devoit même I'm raggedly, not humble
surprendre! yet distracted by futility yet immersed in some
    [thing
and CREATURES the loves OF THE MIND actually unpleasant
très-intéressant and an accident happened to me dans le
    [pathétique

Ars poetica. Here the new encoded character who substitutes for Ellie
enters: L (or lambda), yet another personification of the feminine ar-
chetype.
The fragments in Greek are taken from Aristotle's Poetics and Rhetoric,
those in English from the Cambridge Neoplatonists (cf. Cassirer, The
Platonic Renaissance in England). The author cites his French-language
source as: Nouveaux entretiens sur les sciences secretes ou le Comte de Gabalis
(Cologne, 1691).
The interweaving of these fragments allows (here as elsewhere) for a
two-fold reading: renewing and reconnecting linguistic levels, while
also preserving them as shards.
"Unruhig" = "restless" (from the first part of Goethe's Faust).

che dans le comique mi autorizza très-agréable
a soffrire!

      e qui convien ricordarsi che Aristotile
sì c'è la tristezza mi dice c'è anche questo ma non questo
soltanto io ho capito and REPRESENTATIONS non si vale mai
OF THE THINGS delle parole passioni o patetico per significar
le perturbazioni and SEMINAL PRINCIPALS dell'animo;

                                   et πάθη
tragicam scaenam fecit πάθημα e L ma leggi lambda: in quel
    [momento παθητικόν
ho capito καί κρίνουσιν ἄμεινον egli intende
sempre di significar le fisiche and ALPHABETICAL NOTIONS
    [affezioni
del corpo: come sono i colpi
i tormenti è come se io mi spogliassi le ferite le morti
di fronte a te

      et de ea commentarium reliquit
(de γ.) ecc. de morte ho capito
che non avevo (coloro che non sono trascurati!) mai
RADICAL IRRADIATIONS ecco: avuto niente
e ho trovato (in quel momento); che cosa può trovare
chi non ha mai avuto niente?

      TUTTO; and ARCHETYPAL IDEAS!
this immensely varied subject-matter is expressed!
et j'avois satisfait le goût baroque de mes compatriotes!

Il lago di Sompunt è per la cronaca (e la geografia) in Val Badia.
Il penultimo verso è una citazione da un saggio di H. Read su Klee.

that dans le comique authorizes me très-agréable
to suffer!

      and here we ought to remember that Aristotle
yes there is sadness he tells me there's this too but not this
only I understood and REPRESENTATIONS never takes
    [advantage
OF THE THINGS of passion words or pathetic to signify
the perturbations and SEMINAL PRINCIPALS of the soul;
                         et πάθη
tragicam scaenam fecit παθημα and L read lambda: in that
    [moment παθητικόν
I understood καί κρίνουσιν ἀμεινον he intends
always to mean the physical and ALPHABETICAL NOTIONS
    [affections
of the body: as they are blows
torments it's as if I shed my wounds and deaths
before you

      et de ea commentarium reliquit
(de γ.) etc. de morte I understood
that I never (those who aren't neglected!) had
RADICAL IRRADIATIONS so there: had anything
and I discovered (at that moment); what can he find
he who has never had anything?

      TUTTO; and ARCHETYPAL IDEAS!
this immensely varied subject matter is expressed!
et j'avois satisfait le goût baroque de mes compatriotes!

Lake Sompunt is, for the record (and for geography's sake), located in
Val Badia.
The penultimate line is a quotation from an essay on Klee by Herbert
Read.

ah il mio sonno; e ah? e involuzione? e ah e oh? devoluzione?
    [(e uh?)
e volizione! e nel tuo aspetto e infinito e generantur!
ex putrefactione; complesse terre; ex superfluitate;
         livida Palus
livida nascitur bene strutturata Palus; lividissima (lividissima
    [terra)
(lividissima): cuius aqua est livida; (aqua) nascitur! (aqua)
    [lividissima!
et omnia corpora oh strutture! corpora o strutture mortuorum
corpora mortua o strutture putrescunt; generantur! amori!
; resolvuntur;
        (λ) lividissima   λ! lividissima! (palus)
particolarissima minima; minima pietra; definizione; sonno;
    [universo;
Laszo? una definizione! (ah λ) complesse terre; nascitur!

La fonte latina è il *Comentum* dantesco di Benvenuto da Imola. Questa sez. commenta, infatti, il tema del primo verso della sez. 1 (« composte terre in strutturali complessioni sono Palus Putredinis »). Nella Palus si generano tutte le cose e tutti gli « amori », e insieme « putrescunt ». Le interiezioni rappresentano il più basso stadio del linguaggio, sono forme pre-espressive che indicano una carica passionale non ancora determinata. Il personaggio femminile (Ellie-lambda) è « liquore » (acqua) e « definizione di Laszo », sua essenza e origine, sua madre (« lividissima mater »). Dunque: discesa alle madri; la congiunzione Laszo-lambda è « sonno » e « universo », pietra e liquore originario, essenza-generazione.

ah my slumber; and ah? and involution? and ah and oh?
    [devolution? (and uh?)
and volition! and in your appearance and infinite and
    [generantur!
ex putrefactione; complex soils; ex superfluitate;
        livida Palus
livida nascitur well arranged Palus; very livid (very livid soil)
(very livid): cuius aqua est livida; (aqua) nascitur! (aqua)
    [lividissima!
et omnia corpora oh structures! corpora or structures
    [mortuorum
corpora mortua or structures putrescunt; generantur! loves!
; resolvuntur;
    (λ) very livid λ! very livid! (palus)
minimally particular; minimal stone; defintion; sleep; universe;
Laszo? a definition! (ah λ) complex soils; nascitur!

The Latin source is Benvenuto da Imola's Dante *Comentum*. This section is actually a commentary on the theme of the first line of section 1 ("compound soils in structural complexes are Palus Putredinis"). All things and all "loves" are engendered and, at the same time, "putrescunt" in the Palus. The interjections represent the lowest stage of language, pre-expressive forms suggesting an as yet indeterminate passional charge. The female character (Ellie-lambda) is "liquid" (water) and "Laszo's definition," his essence and origin, his mother ("lividissima mater"). Thus: the descent to the Mothers; the conjunction of Laszo and lambda is "slumber" and "universe," stone and primordial liquid, essence-generation.

ah inconfondibile precisabile! ah inconfondibile! minima!
oh iterazione! oh pietra! oh identica identica sempre;
identica oh! alla tua essenza amore identica!
alla tua vita e generazione! e volizione! (corruzione) perché
      [essenze
le origini; essenze;
           e ah e oh? (terre?)
complesse composte terre (pietre); universali; Palus;
(pietre?) al tuo lividore; amore; al tuo dolore; uguale tu!
una definizione tu! liquore! definizione! di Laszo definizione!
generazione tu! liquore liquore tu! lividissima mater:

ah unmistakable specifiable! ah unmistakable! minimal!
oh iteration! oh stone! of identical identical always;
identical oh! identical to your essence love!
to your life and generation! and volition! (corruption) because
        [essences
the origins; essences;
            and ah and oh? (soils?)
complex compound soils (stones); universal; Palus;
(stones?) to your lividity; love; to our sorrow; you equal!
you a definition! liquid! definition! Laszo's definition
you generation! you liquid liquid! lividissima mater:

Da EROTOPAEGNIA

2

quale raptus (cadde!) pustoloso apparve forse amore (τέχνον)
    [involuta
(cerebrum); (fortitudo) lascìammo la città; (magro corpo!):
    [« res quaedam »;
in telo pustolosa, ut dicunt MEDICI; quel giorno! di ottobre!
    [(caloris!);
(e il quarantesimo giorno...): evacuatum; in acqua fredda
    [(frigida) evacuatum;
che con le pinze prese! (frigida regio); (MCCLVIII) livida! una
    [grossa
formica; un verme; la cosa: avevamo noi (in farmacia) ottenuto;
    [non comprende
(la cosa): sine phantasmate; ma quando vorrà, (con la mano...);
    [quale rictus!,
eccessiva!, ex testiculo (MEDICUS loquitur); umidità (accennò)
    [eccessiva,
destra, in principio: cottiledones debiles (provocatio) avevate
    [ottenuto (spermatis)

L'aborto è raccontato un po' dall'A. e un po' da Alberto Magno
(Quaestiones super de animalibus, MCCLVIII, liber IX, Q. 22). Nell'incontro
col medico (in farmacia) si ottengono spiegazioni circa gli elementi
che influiscono sulle possibilità generative e sull'andamento della
gravidanza. Il medico tranquillizza: la « cosa » è cosa (res quaedam), è
verme da prendersi con le pinze, non può capire, non ha coscienza
(sine phantasmate).

from EROTOPAEGNIA

2

such raptus (he fell!) perhaps love appeared simply (τέχνον)
    [we left
(cerebrum); (fortitudo) the involuted city behind; (lean body!):
    ["res quaedam";
pimple in cloth, ut dicunt MEDICI; that day! in October!
    [(caloris!);
(and the fortieth day...): evacuatum; in cold (frigida) water
    [evacuatum;
that with pincers he seized! (frigida regio); (MCCLVIII) livid!
    [a big
ant; a worm; the thing: we had (in the pharmacy) obtained; it
    [does not include
(the thing): sine phantasmate; but when he pleases, (with the
    [hand...); such rictus!,
excessive!, ex testiculo (MEDICUS loquitur); excessive (he
    [indicated) right
humidity, in the beginning: cottiledones debiles (provocatio)
    [you all had obtained (spermatis)

The abortion is narrated a little by the author and a little by Albertus
Magnus (*Quaestiones super de animalibus*, MCCLVIII, liber IX, Q. 22). The
meeting with the doctor (in the pharmacy) provides explanations about
the elements influencing the possibilities of generation and the pro-
cess of pregnancy. The doctor calms her down: the "thing" is some-
thing (res quaedam), a worm to be handled with utmost care, lacking
comprehension and consciousness (sine phantasmate).

liber IX, Q. 22 : avevate ottenuto, e cadde; quale rictus!
    [quale! de facili
provocationes (avevate ottenuto): de facili, τέχνη! ma il
    [calore! ma (loquitur)
la regione! il vento! et abortiunt, amore; involuto: (e accennò
    [con la mano):
e un verme quindi (con le pinze) prese; apparve in telo,
    [pustoloso τέχνον,
« res quaedam », s'intende, quondam (ex testiculo dextro); (un
    [verme avevamo
ottenuto...); et abortiunt, debiles; et evacuatum, cerebrum;
    [inutilmente, quidem;
(nei giorni che seguirono si dimostrò inquieta, mesta): la cosa
    [non ebbe nome.

liber IX, Q. 22: you all had obtained, and he fell; such rictus!
    [such! de facili
provocationes (you all had obtained): de facili, τέχνη! but the
    [heat! but (loquitur)
the region! the wing! et abortiunt, love; involuted: (and
    [signaled with his hand):
and a worm therefore seized (with pincers); there appeared in
    [cloth, pimply τέχνον,
"res quaedam," of course, quondam (ex testiculo dextro); (we
    [had obtained a
worm...); et abortiunt, debiles; et evacuatum, cerebrum;
    [uselessly, quidem;
(in the days that followed it revealed itself to be uneasy, sad):
    [the thing did not have a name.

4

in te dormiva come un fibroma asciutto, come una magra
        [tenia, un sogno;
ora pesta la ghiaia, ora scuote la propria ombra; ora stride,
deglutisce, orina, avendo atteso da sempre il gusto
della camomilla, la temperatura della lepre, il rumore della
        [grandine,
la forma del tetto, il colore della paglia:
            senza rimedio il tempo
si è rivolto verso i suoi giorni; la terra offre immagini confuse;
saprà riconoscere la capra, il contadino, il cannone?
non queste forbici veramente sperava, non questa pera,
quando tremava in quel tuo sacco di membrane opache.

Nel nato ritorna l'immagine del verme: la «magra tenia», che nel ventre
materno viveva nell'attesa del mondo e delle cose, patisce ora la
delusione di chi trova dinanzi a sé la limitata realtà dell'esperienza.
Potrà riconoscere in questa realtà le immagini (le ARCHETYPAL IDEAS
del *Laborintus*) che nutrivano quell'attesa? Altre cose sperava, un altro
mondo.

4

he slept inside you like a dry fibroma, like a thin tapeworm,
　　[a dream;
now he stamps on the gravel, now he shakes his own shadow;
　　[now he shrieks,
swallows, urinates, having awaited from the start the taste
of camomile, the hare's temperature, the sound of hail,
the shape of the roof, the color of straw:
　　　　　without remedy time
has turned to his days; earth offers confused images;
will he know the goat, the peasant, the cannon?
he did not hope for these shears, for this pear,
when he was trembling in that opaque, membranous sack of
　　[yours.

In the newborn the image of the worm recurs: the "thin tapeworm,"
who lived in the mother's belly waiting for a world and for things, now
suffers the disappointment of someone who faces the limited reality of
experience. Will he then recognize in this reality the images (the AR-
CHETYPAL IDEAS of *Laborintus*) that nourished that wait? He had
hoped for other things, another world.

la cosa come la passa; (la porta appunto); (la coscia);
    [(la finestretta): il pugnale!
(la passa!); e tremando! (proporzioni terribili!); ingigantito!
    [premendo (...);
e la bottiglia appunto:
            nelle latrine; e così appunto; in quell'aria
infetta; lei paziente bianchissima: e come la passa questo
    [pugnale! tremando!

La frase d'apertura (« la cosa come la passa ») è di Giordano Bruno
(forse: *Cena delle Ceneri*) e ha qui un duplice significato: quello originario
(la realtà, gli eventi come effettualmente si svolgono) e quello, del resto
evidente, metaforico-erotico.
Tutto l'episodio, che comincia in questa sez. e si conclude con la sez.
II, è d'ispirazione onirica.

7

the thing see how it moves; (the door to be precise); (the
    [thigh); (the little window): the dagger!
(it moves!); and trembling! (terrible proportions!); huge!
    [pressing (...);
and the bottle to be precise:

        in the latrines; and just so; in that infected
air; she patient, utterly white: and how it moves this dagger!
    [trembling!

The opening phrase ("the thing see how it moves") is Giordano Bruno's
(perhaps from *Ash Wednesday's Supper*) and has a two-fold meaning:
the original one (reality, events as they actually occur) and, quite obvi-
ously now, the metaphorical-erotic one.
The whole episode, which begins in this section and ends in section II,
is dream-inspired.

8

vengono gli studenti; (e in quella buca, oh noi, conclusi!
        [oh noi, viluppo!); stridono:
il tuo nome! (e grido); il tuo nome! (e non risponde: orina):
        le loro teste
emergono, rigonfie; i loro occhi, rigonfi, emergono; si
        [innalzano,
purpurei; oscillanti (prodigiosi) folgorano; (oh lampi!
        [oh cenere!);
nuotano (le loro teste) in quell'aria (oh cenere!) ardendo
        [vibrando!,
sterili;
        parlano gli studenti; il vostro nome! (e gridano);
        [il vostro nome!
(non rispondiamo: orinando):
        le nostre teste soffrono; e adesso parlano :
(le nostre lingue); (e ardendo): oh testes! (gridano); oh testes!
        [e alfine
si stacca (da quel coro) una lingua di cenere: semper curato!
(così appunto grida); semper! e lampeggiando ancora, con
        [robusto singulto,
in quell'aria sterile (lo studente); ne sis! (grida); intestabilis!

L'amplesso avviene in latrine da *Universitas Studiorum*. Gli studenti si
affacciano al sommo della porta e gridano chiedendo il nome ai
protagonisti. « Testes » ha il doppio senso di testimoni e di testicoli;
analoga duplicità assume, in relazione alla bivalenza della parola
« intestabilis », la proposizione (plautina): « sempre curato ne sis
intestabilis » (=procura di non trovarti senza testicoli [o testimoni]; =
procura di non essere maledetto).

8

the students are coming; (and in that hole, it's us, completed!
    [it's us, a tangle!); they shriek:
your name! (and I shout); your name! (and he doesn't answer:
    [he urinates):

              their heads
emerge, swollen; their eyes, swollen, emerge; they arise
purple; oscillating (prodigious) they flash; (oh lightning!
    [oh ash!);
they swim (their heads) in that air (oh ash!) burning vibrating!,
sterile;

     the students speak; your name! (and they shout); your
    [name!
(we don't answer: urinating):

           our heads suffer; and now they speak:
(our languages); (and burning): oh testes! (they shout);
    [oh testes! and at the end
an ashen tongue uncleaves (from that chorus): semper curato!
(just so he shouted); semper! and flashing still, with a strong
    [sob
in that sterile air (the student); ne sis! (shouts); intestabilis!

The intercourse takes place in the toilet stalls of the *Universitas Studiorum*. The students peer over the door and vociferously demand the names of the protagonists. "Testes" has the double meaning of witnesses and testicles; in connection with the ambivalence of the word "intestabilis," the following statement (from Plautus) also takes on a dual meaning: "semper curato ne sis intestabilis" (= Be careful not to find yourself without testicles [or witnesses]; = Be careful not to be cursed).

e oltre la porta a vetri, l'improvvisa piscina; e lei, e nella nebbia,
una volta ancora, e perduta!
            osservavo infatti (e da una di quelle finestrette)
la piazza deserta, i palazzi deformi, crollanti : ancora
         [ascoltavo, ancora
quel silenzio; e quell'aria odoravo, e immobile; e io stesso
         [infatti,
e perduto, ancora; ma oltre i vetri vedi grigiastra l'acqua; vedi
i viluppi di vibrati, di arsi nudi, e ancora:
           ancora il pulito
fiato di lei desiderando; e io stesso, allora, e in quell'acqua,
         [miseramente,
e perduto; e la gola di lei, e ancora, e la pulita, di lei,
         [allora, gola!
dall'acqua, e in un singultio, quegli iracondi, immensi,
         [oscillando, nudi!
tiepido, oh tiepido coro, oh molle, toccando, coro, ciò che
         [nominavano;

La scena d'inferno si è ora spostata in una irreale piscina accademica.
La nebbia grava sulla città, vista attraverso i vetri di una finestra, e
penetra nell'edificio. La piscina è colma di esseri nudi: gli studenti, che
si toccano e ostentano i testicoli. Tutto appare deforme e corrotto; nel
grosso « ventre » della piscina gli studenti conducono i loro giochi
omosessuali. Verso la fine la visione della donna « innescata » e « pressa »
nella bolgia erotica.

9

and beyond the glass door, the sudden swimming pool; and
    [she, and in the fog,
once again, and lost!
        in fact I was watching (and from one of those little
    [windows)
the deserted piazza, the deformed palaces, collapsing: still
    [I was listening, still
that silence; and I smelled that air, motionless; and I myself
    [in fact,
and lost, still; but beyond the panes you see the water grayish;
    [you see
tangles that quivered, burnt nudes, and still:
        still her clean
breath desiring; and I myself, then, and in that water, miserably,
and lost; and her throat, and still, and the throat, hers, then,
    [clean!
from the water, and in a sob, those wrathful, immense,
    [swaying nudes!
tepid, oh tepid chorus, oh soft, to the touch, chorus, what
    [they were naming;

The hell scene has now been shifted to an unreal academic swimming pool. Fog covers the city, seen through windowpanes; it enters into the building. The pool is full of naked beings: the students, who grope each other and show off their testicles. Everything seems warped, corrupted; in the pool's great "belly" the students carry on their homosexual games. Toward the end, the vision of the woman "primed" and "pressed" into the erotic chaos.

coro, ancora: testibus (esplosivi gridando)! testibus (deformi
[toccando)!
testibus (deformi testes!)! et praesentibus, oh!
            e penetrava la caligine;
e lucidissima; e vibrante, allora, ardente, l'acqua; e in calde
[coppe,
copulati; in stridenti vasche, voltolati; urlando, bollenti:
in questo ventre (così allora urlando!) premendo! pressi, allora,
[gemendo;
colando, impressi: oh, frangibili (dissi);
            e vidi lei, innescata, grondando, oh!
(praesentibus testibus vidi); lei vibrata vidi; vibrante; lei
[appunto; pressa.

chorus, still: testibus (shouting explosives)! testibus (deformed
    [to the touch)!
testibus (deformed testes!)! et praesentibus, oh!
        and the soot filtered through;
and most shiny; and vibrant, then, burning, the water; and in
    [hot cups,
copulated; in shrieking basins, rolled about; screaming, boiling:
in this belly (so shouting then!) pressing! pressed, then, moaning;
dripping, impressed: oh, breakable (I said);
        and I saw her, primed, dripping wet, oh!
(praesentibus testibus vidi); I saw her vibrated; vibrating;
    [precisely her; pressed.

e più tardi, in quella nebbia, e in piedi, convulsi; e non
     [convulsi, più tardi,
ancora, e distesi;
        e quelle luci, in quella nebbia! e rovesciate, quelle
     [luci,
sopra l'erba; sopra la pista, soffocate, oscillando; quelle luci!
     [molli!
miseramente vidi lei, ancora, in quella nebbia, e convolta;
e riposando, e in quelle luci, corrompersi! e i cavalli,
     [respirando, ruotando,
decolorarsi (lo steccato di legno, palpitando, riscuotersi!);
     [e quelle molli
luci! disperdersi! in quella nebbia!: oh lago (dissi)! oh perduto!
e sopra quella pista toccavo io! il cavallo! et:
        oh equus (dissi)!
oh corpus (sopra quell'erba, in quella nebbia, dissi!)! oh corpus!
(dissi) oh!; (dissi): ne tangito!; (oh mi lacerava quello zoccolo!);

La piscina è sostituita qui da una pista; vi corrono, come cavalli, gli
studenti. Dopo il coito iniziale, avviene lo scambio onirico della donna
con il cavallo. L'animale adombra un personaggio maschile, lo studente
che troveremo nella sez. 17 (un amico del protagonista che, dice l'A.,
ha una dentatura da cavallo e frequenta le corse ippiche) e che già era
presente nel *Laborintus* (nella sez. 24, per es., come « mendax Equus »).
Il trapasso dall'eterosessualità all'omosessualità significa l'equivalenza

and later, in that mist, and on foot, convulsed; and not
    [convulsed, later,
still, and extended;
            and those lights, in that mist! and overturned, those
        [lights,
on the grass; on the tracks, suffocated, swaying; and those
        [lights! soft!
miserably I saw her, still, in that mist, and convoluted;
and resting, and in those lights, decomposing! and the horses,
        [breathing, wheeling,
decolorating (the wooden stake, quivering, rousing!); and those
        [soft
lights! fading! in that mist!: oh lake (I said)! oh lost!
and on those tracks I was touching! the horse! et:
            oh equus (I said)!
oh corpus (on that grass, in that mist, I said!)! oh corpus!
(I said) oh!; (I said): ne tangito!; (oh that hoof was
        [cutting me!);

The swimming pool is replaced by a track where students are trotting like horses. After the opening coitus, the oneiric reversal between horse and woman takes place. The animal suggests a masculine character, the student we shall find in section 17 (a friend of the protagonist who, the author says, has horse-like teeth and regularly goes to the race-track) and who made an appearance in *Laborintus* (section 24, e.g., as "mendax Equus"). The passage from hetero- to homosexuality signifies

(oh mi torceva!); (oh!); (oh quella lingua!); e respirando,
     [ruotando,
su quella pista; nuotando! et:
               nudus essem (ammisi);
nudus (avvinghiandomi); (e avvinghiato ancora): corpus! ni!
(respiravo, ruotavo; nuotando); me! (nuotando; avvinghiando);
texisses! (respiravo, infine); riposavo; et:
               cerchiamo nel frigorifero
(dissi); oh equus (dissi nuotando)! corpus meum! equus meus!
cerchiamo dunque nel frigorifero! (e ritrovammo la fresca,
     [la dolce erba);
(e vedevo in quell'aria, in quell'acqua, le chiare, le molli
     [luci);
oh mi allontanai, infine, ruotando, nuotando; oh mi
     [allontanavo! oh respiravo!
zoccolo mio (volli esclamare)! corpo mio! (urlai)! oh mia
     [lingua!

---

infernale dei valori sessuali. La proposizione « nudus essem ni me
texisses » deriva dal *Sogno di Polifilo.*
L'immagine del nuoto crea l'equivalente piscina = pista. Scena finale:
si cercano cibi « nel frigorifero » e da buoni cavalli vi si trova l'erba;
quindi il protagonista e il cavallo si fondono insieme: « mio » nell'ultimo
verso esprime l'annullamento dell'io, partecipazione patetica e
confusione.

(oh it was twisting me!); (oh!); (oh that tongue!); and
    [breathing, wheeling,
on those tracks; swimming! et:
            nudus essem (I admitted);
nudus (clutching myself); (and still clutched): corpus! ni!
(I was breathing, I was wheeling; swimming); me! (swimming;
    [clutching);
texisses! (I was breathing, at last); I was resting; et:
            let's look in the refrigerator
(I said): oh equus (I said swimming)! corpus meum! equus
    [meus!
then let's look in the refrigerator! (and we found the fresh,
    [the sweet grass);
(and I saw in that air, in that water, the bright, soft lights);
oh I went away, in the end, wheeling, swimming; oh I was
    [going! oh I was breathing!
my hoof (I exclaimed)! my body! (I shouted)! oh my tongue!

---

the infernal equivalence of sexual values. The statement "nudus essem
ni me texisses" comes from the *Dream of Poliphilus*.
The image of swimming sets up the equation pool = track. Closing
scene: they raid "the refrigerator" for food and, good horses that they
are, they find grass; hence the protagonist and the horse merge: "my"
in the last line expresses the annihilation of the ego, pathetic participa-
tion and confusion.

consistente coda! frigida frusta! oh muscolo! oh pugno!
    [penetrante:
hai bevuto abbastanza (tale l'avvertimento); hai giocato, hai
    [sudato (tale
giuoco giocasti, bestia!); (tale, belva!); mordi il tuo fieno!
    [la tua paglia
calpesta! e scoprimi, adesso, animale!
       (e lo riportavo nella stalla silenziosa);
ma mentre procedevamo mesti attraverso la fosca aula magna,
    [come nitristi,
mia vanga; come, mia piramide, lacrimasti! felice mostro
(dissi); ma quali vipere ci vengono incontro? e gamberi?
    [e mosche?
il coccodrillo vedi! lo scorpione vedi! arrestiamoci! oh questo
    [vivo giardino!
e oh questi funghi, come odorano! cogliamo questi funghi!
    [belli! e gli ovoli vedi!
quanto dilatati! fecondi! qui bene crepitano le nostre secche
    [croste;
felci fioriscono nelle atroci narici; striscia il muschio magro

---

Continua a intervenire, nel gioco erotico, la simbologia maschile (coda, frusta, muscolo, pugno); « scoprimi » vuol dire anche *non coprirmi più*. Il carattere onirico dell'intero episodio si afferma ora nel repertorio « inferiore » degli animali (vipere, gamberi, mosche, coccodrillo, scorpione). Gli animali sono sempre gli studenti, il giardino è la pista-piscina.

II

consistent tail! frigid whip! oh muscle! oh fist! penetrating:
you've drunk enough (such was the warning); you gambled,
        [you sweated (such
a game you played, animal!); (such a game, beast!); chew
        [your hay! trample your
straw! and find me, now, animal!
                (and I was taking him back to the silent stable);
but as we proceeded glumly towards the gloomy great hall,
        [how you whinnied,
my spade; how, my pyramid, you wept! happy monster
(I said); but what vipers are coming towards us? and shrimp?
        [and flies?
you see the crocodile! you see the scorpion! let's halt! oh
        [this living garden!
oh these mushrooms, how they smell! let's pick these
        [mushrooms! gorgeous! and you see the ovules!
how dilated! fecund! here our dry scabs crackle nicely;
ferns bloom in our dreadful nostrils; the scanty moss creeps

Masculine symbology continues to enter into the erotic game (tail, whip, muscle, fist): "discover me" also means *don't cover me anymore*. The oneiric quality of the whole episode is now affirmed by the "lower" inventory of animals (viper, shrimp, flies, crocodile, scorpion). The animals are once again the students, the garden the track/pool.

sopra il palato luteo, lustro; sei già la scolopendra chiara;
　　　　[la sua ghiandola
grinzuta sei; oh squisito grumo, perditi! oh perditi, grumo!
liquida lista! asmatico atomo! oh macchia! oh punto!
　　　　[pungente.

Anche « equus » diventa un repertorio ontologico (thesaurus). Tutto si
metamorfosa. Anche i funghi sono emblemi erotici: funghi maschili e
ovoli femminili. I due personaggi (il protagonista e « equus ») si
trasformano in vegetali e animali dalla forma corrotta. L'ultimo verso
esprime la dissoluzione del sogno.

over the luteous palate, lustrous; you are already the bright
    [centipede; you are its
wrinkled gland; oh exquisite lump, be gone! oh be gone lump!
liquid stripe! asthmatic atom! oh spot! oh point! prickly.

"Equus" also becomes an ontological repertory (thesaurus). Every-
thing metamorphosizes. Mushrooms also are erotic emblems: mascu-
line mushrooms and feminine ovules. The two characters (the pro-
tagonist and "equus") are transformed into the corrupted form of veg-
etables and animals. The last line depicts the dream dissolving.

e nella luce obliqua, infine, dell'obliquo tramonto,
    [nell'accademico,
copulativo colombario; et me, et lo studente (scholasticellulum
    [illum),
(il morbido cavallo, il tenero, l'infantile cavallo); e lei!
infine; lei ahi! columbatim, ovviamente, lei ahi! copulans;
lo studente vidi (dall'urna sua):
        boobus! (ovviamente orinando); (dal loculo suo);
(dal locutorio vidi): boobus! (esclamare); e: ahi! quale, nella
    [luce obliqua,
apparizione!; e in tale occiduo cielo, infine, lo studente:
from « booby » (disse); from « lucus »... (ammiccando disse); e:
    [« boobytrap »
(lei dubitosa aggiunse); aggiunse: from what I see:
        with Caporal and Thor!
with Nike and Matador!; e: boobus! (disse lo studente); from
    [« booboisie »...,

Ritorna la scena della sez. 8 (« nell'accademico copulativo colom-
bario »); la latrina sede di amplessi è anche « urna » locutoria dove
ritroviamo il personaggio femminile e « equus » (lo scholasticellulus,
lo studente) impegnati in una discussione filologica e nell'uso orinatorio
dell'urna. Il « boobus americanus » è il borghese made in USA secondo
un gioco di parole di Mencken: da « booby », stupido, così « booboisie
» sul modello di bourgeoisie. La donna che partecipa alla discussione
si è metamorfosata in studentessa americana. « Boobytrap » è uno
scherzo da ragazzi che consiste nel far cadere qualcosa sulla testa di

and in the oblique light, at last, in the oblique sunset, in the
    [academic,
copulative columbarium; et me, et the student
    [(scholasticellulum illum),
(the soft horse, the tender, infantile horse); and she!
at last; she alas! columbatim, obviously, she alas! copulans;
I saw the student (from his urn):
        boobus! (obviously urinating); (from his burial
    [niche);
(I saw from the parlor): boobus! (exclaiming); and: alas! what
    [in the oblique light,
apparition!; and in such lowering sky, at last, the student:
from "booby" (he said); from "lucus"... (he said winking); and:
    ["boobytrap"
(she added dubious); she added: from what I see:
        with Caporal and Thor!
with Nike and Matador!; and: boobus! (the student said); from
    ["booboisie"...,

The scene of section 8 returns ("in the academic copulative columbarium"); the toilet that was the site of embraces is also a talking "urn" where we find the feminine character and "equus" (the *scholasticellulus*, the student) involved in a philological discussion, while using the urn to urinate in. The "boobus americanus" is H.L. Mencken's pun on the "made in USA" bourgeois, from "booby," a stupid person; hence "booboisie." The woman involved in the discussion is transformed into an American student. A "booby trap" refers to a child's prank in which something is made to fall on the head of someone

from « bourgeoisie », americanus!

americanus boobus with Honest John!

(from « John the Fearful », disse lo studente); (from « dis-honest »,
['Honest);

e: antifrasi (lo studente); (ex. anuresi, disse); e al boobus:
[abbaia!

(disse), abbaia! (from « John the Smuthound », disse lo studente);
[e il boobus:

oh! oh! (ovviamente disse); ovviamente abbaiando, nell'obliquo
[tramonto:

oh! oh!; oh! oh!

---

chi sta entrando da una porta. C'è un gioco di antifrasi parallelo su
« Honest John » (nome di arma atomica americana, come Caporal,
Thor, Nike, Matador) e su « John the Fearful » (il contrario di
Senzapaura). Il « boobus » è trattato infine come cane; « Smuthound »
deriva ancora da Mencken che così designava il moralista borghese:
cane che va a caccia di oscenità, cane da spazzatura. La poesia, che
come si vede è essenzialmente politica e di protesta, si chiude con gli
abbaiamenti del « boobus ».

from "bourgeoisie," americanus!
   americanus boobus with Honest John!
(from "John the Fearful," said the student); (from "dis-honest,"
   ['*Honest*);
and: antiphrasis (the student); (ex. anuria, he said); and to
  [the boobus: bark!
(he said), bark! (from "John the Smuthound," said the student;
  [and the boobus:
oh! oh! (he obviously said); obviously barking, in the oblique
  [sunset:
   oh! oh! oh! oh!

---

going through a doorway. There is a play of parallel antiphrasis in
"Honest John" as the name of an American atomic weapon, like
Caporal, Thor, Nike, Matador, or "John the Fearful" (the opposite of
Fearless). The "boobus," finally, is treated like a dog; "Smuthound" is
also a Mencken term for the bourgeois moralist: a dog that chases
after obscenity, a scavenger dog. The poem, clearly a basically political
protest poem, ends with the barking of the "boobus."

ALPHABETUM

ti attende il filo spinato, la vespa, la vipera, il nichel
bianco e lucente che non si ossida all'aria
                                    ti attende Pitagora
che disse che delle cose è sostanza il numero
                                e tu prendi del polipo
gli otto tentacoli guerniti di ventose e *An die Hoffnung* (op.94)
perché questo, questo lo prendono (essi)
                        lo prendono perché lo trovano

osserva Iside e i costumi abruzzesi, le medaglie per la
        [campagna di Cina
del 1901, la maschera di Peppe Nappa
                            la città di Cannstadt
che fu incorporata nella città di Stuttgart nel 1905
e conoscerai la confindustria e la svastica, il 15 maggio e il
        [24 gennaio
lo spillo di sicurezza che non sa pungere, il lecco lecco e lo
        [Spirito
Santo
        e tu prendi il gliconio e la glicerina, e Hans Pfeiffer

---

Composta nel gennaio 1960, apparve in un volume di litografie di Toti
Scialoja. Il « GRAN PAESE » è il paese di Cuccagna e, per ironia, « dove
si vive »: come l'autore spiega al primogenito Federico, descrivendo la
regione, con il soccorso di illustrazioni d'ogni specie, compreso il
celebre *Lied* di Beethoven. Il 15 maggio e il 24 gennaio appartengono,

the barbed wire awaits you, the wasp, the viper, the white and
lucid nickel that doesn't oxidize in the air
                                        Pythagoras awaits you
who said that the substance of things is number
                            and you take the eight
tentacles of the octopus adorned with suckers and *An die*
      [*Hoffnung* (op. 94)
because this, this they take (they)
                            they take it because they find it

observe Isis and Abruzzi customs, the medals for the China
      [campaign
of 1901, Peppe Nappa's mask
            the city of Cannstadt
which was incorporated into the city of Stuttgart in 1905
and you will know the industrial conglomerate and the
      [swastika, May 15 and January 24
the safety pin that cannot prick, the lollypop and the Holy
Spirit
        and you take the gliconium and the glycerine, and Hans
      [Pfeiffer

Composed in January 1960, it appeared in a volume of lithographs by
Toti Scialoja. The "GREAT LAND" is the Land of Cockaigne and, ironi-
cally, "where one lives": as the author explains to his elder, Federico,
describing this region, with the aid of all sorts of illustrations, includ-
ing Beethoven's famous *Lied*. As we know, May 15 and January 24 are

che nacque a Kassel nel 1907, perché questo, questo lo
    [prendono
(essi), lo prendono perché lo trovano
                    perché lo trovano a lavorare

perché questa è, Federico, la DESCRITTIONE DEL GRAN
    [PAESE: è la targa
automobilistica della provincia di Foggia (FG)
                    è la nave di linea a vapore
1870, è il babbuino, è il bisonte
                e tu prendi gli urodeli e il ministro
Pella, la méthode des tractions rythmées de la langue (due à
Laborde), il Petrus amat multum dominam Bertam
                            perché questo,
questo lo prendono (essi), lo prendono perché lo trovano,
    [perché
lo trovano a lavorare (...)
                    et anderà in pregione.

---

come è noto, alla storia dell'Algeria. Il metodo di Laborde giova
(sembra) a chi ha corso il rischio di annegare. Il « Petrus amat multum
dominam Bertam » è esempio di 'ordo naturalis' nella 'constructio':
« gradus insipidus, qui est rudium », spiega il *De vulgari eloquentia* (II,
VI, 4). Che i lavoratori finiscano in prigione è la maliziosa prova suprema
che si vive proprio nel paese di Cuccagna.

who was born in Kassel in 1907, because this man, this man
  [they take
(they), they take him because they find him
          because they find at work

because this is, Federico, the DESCRIPTION OF THE GREAT
   COUNTRY: it is the automobile
license plate from the province of Foggia (FG)
         it is the steamship
1870, it is the baboon, it is the bison
         and you take the urodeles and the minister
Pella, la méthode des tractions rythmées de la langue (due à
Laborde), Petrus amat multum dominam Bertam
         because this,
this man they take (they), they take him because they find him,
  [because
they find him at work (...)
      et he will go to prison.

---

part of Algerian history. Laborde's method apparently helps who has
risked drowning. The "Petrus amat multum dominam Bertam" is an
example of the "ordo naturalis" in "constructio": "gradus insipidus,
qui est rudium," explains the *De vulgari eloquentia* (II, VI, 4). That the
workers should end up in jail is the supremely wicked proof that we
are indeed living in the Land of Cockaigne.

NANNI BALESTRINI

Translated by Stephen Sartarelli

APOLOGO DELL'EVASO

La massima della mia azione difforme,
infausto al popolo il fiume
che al cinema videro spopolare

il delta, i fertilissimi campi
e i più nocivi insetti (chiara
minaccia ai vizi dei governanti!).

Fra i pampini ovunque liberi
galleggiavano, gonfi—e si fa vano
l'ufficio dello storico. Ma saremo

a lungo preservati dal morso
del tafano azzurro, da iniezioni
di calciobromo, dall'unghie della zarina?

Lucenti strani corpi
violano il cielo; sbanda
il filo di formiche diagonale

Nelle poesie di B. contesti diversi, di epoche diverse, sono *ritagliati*,
frantumati e mescolati fino a perdere il significato originario.
L'ispirazione muove, di volta in volta, da parole e frasi così trattate e
segue la loro tendenza ad aggregarsi secondo linee molteplici di
significazione. È chiaro che l'impulso a quest'opera di « montaggio » è
il vero contenuto della poesia; esso non sussiste come dato personale,

APOLOGUE OF THE FUGITIVE

The maxim for my contrary action,
ill-fated for the people, the river
the movie showed devastating

the delta, the most fertile fields
and insects of the worst sort (a clear
threat to the vices of our leaders!).

Amid the vine leaves everywhere
they floated free, bloated—and the historian's
task becomes pointless. But will we be

protected for long from the bite
of the blue horsefly, from injections
of calcium bromide and the czarina's nails?

Strange, shining bodies
violate the sky; the diagonal
column of ants breaks up

In B's poems different contexts, from different periods, are *cut out*, broken up and mixed to the point of losing their original meaning. The inspiration moves, each time, from words and phrases so treated, and follows their tendency to cluster through multiple lines of signification. Clearly the impulse behind this "montage" work is the true content of the poem; it does not exist as a personal datum, but is rather a projec-

nel cortile riemerso; ancora
il sole sorge dietro
la Punta Campanella incustodita

dai finanzieri corrotti e un argine
ultimo crolla. Lode
a un'estate di foco. S'io fossi

la piccola borghesia colata
nelle piazze fiorite e nei dì
di festa che salvi c'ignora

dalla droga e dalla noia per un po'
d'uva lavata in mare
presso la marcia catapulta; rifugiati

al primo tuono nelle gelaterie—chi fuggirei?
Passato il temporalaccio d'agosto
i graspi giungono a riva

fra i remi ai contrabbandieri salpati
nel novilunio e anzitutto conviene
(usciti dal vico cieco chiamammo

è piuttosto una proiezione di oggetti amorosi, considerazioni di poetica,
preoccupazioni esistenziali e storiche, che tende a risolversi interamente
nella *valenza* dei pezzi montati e nel loro dinamismo interno. Non c'è
dunque lettura obbligata e il lettore non ha da proporsi alcuno sforzo
esegetico (o enigmistico). Si tratta di entrare nell'*ordine aperto* dei
contesti (i cui possibili significati si muovono come le lamine di un

in the reimmerging courtyard; also
the sun rises up behind
Punta Campanella left unguarded

by corrupt coastguards, and one last
embankment collapses. Praise
for a summer of fire. If I were

the petty bourgeoisie pouring
into flowered streets and holidays
ignoring that we are safe

from drugs and boredom for a bit
of sea-washed grape beside
the rotten catapult taking cover

from first thunder in ice-cream shops—who would I
run from? The nasty August storm now past,
grape-stalks float ashore

between the oars of smugglers put to sea
under the new moon, and now's the time
(emerging from the cul-de-sac we called out

---

tion of amorous objects, considerations of poetics, existential and his-
torical concerns, tending toward a full resolution in the *valence* of the
assembled parts and their internal dynamic. Therefore there is no com-
pulsory interpretation and the reader needn't exert any effort at ex-
egesis (or puzzle-solving). It is a matter of entering into the *open order*
of the contexts (whose possible meanings move like the steel plates in

e orme erano ovunque
dell'abominevole uomo delle nevi)
fare l'amore intanto

che sui ponti la Via Lattea dilata.
Il Po nasce dal Monviso;
nuvole... ma di ciò, altra volta.

---

mobile di Calder) e di far funzionare la macchina. Il lettore si affidi all'accogliente autonomia delle diverse cariche espressive, alle sorprese semantiche e sintattiche, all'incerto uso dei pezzi montati con amorevole confusione. Naturalmente, quello che abbiamo chiamato l'impulso-contenuto impone i propri temi. Qui dalla visione iniziale, che cinematograficamente evoca un'alluvione, si prosegue attraverso successive immagini d'acqua e di minaccia fino alla conclusione-rinvio finale.

I versi delle tredici terzine sono tutti di tre piedi o accenti principali. È inutile mettere in rilievo l'evidente atonalismo della struttura metrica di questa poesia, come di tutte le seguenti.

and there were footprints everywhere
left by the abominable snowman)
to make love while

the Milky Way expands over the bridges.
The Po is born on Mount Viso;
clouds... but that's another story.

.

---

a Calder mobile) and making the machine work. The reader should
give himself to the welcoming autonomy of various expressive charges,
semantic and syntactic surprises, the uncertain use of the pieces as-
sembled in fond confusion. Of course what we have referred to as the
content-impulse sets its own themes. Here from the initial vision, which
cinematically suggests a flood, we proceed through successive images
of water and danger to the final ending/postponement.

All thirteen tercets are in lines of three feet or principal stresses. It is
pointless to emphasize the obvious atonality of the metrical structure
of this poem, as well as all that follow.

DE CULTU VIRGINIS

Prima di posare sul sagrato si libra ad ali tese
negli specchi di luce bagnata, rotti da un piede verde;
al *Malcontento Bar* ferisce mortalmente uno sconosciuto
scambiandolo per il suo seduttore.

Altri esempi: torri nel pozzo di San Giminiano, l'amo
al luccio, la rossa in buca. Perciò se al diavolo di Cartesio
(riviviamo il brusco atterraggio che ci lasciò sabato tutti
confusi nelle nostre tenebre

con una gamba ingessata, la penna che macchiò in volo la
          [giacca)
all'ultimo gioco si strappò la membrana—sul Palazzo della
          [Ragione
rivola, proprio quando impugnando l'unica stecca buona
rivinsi al Duca di Sessa

l'abiura. Spesso preghiamo che Dio ci dia una mano
(un cilindro di carta d'amaretto, dateci fuoco in cima,

Numerosi riferimenti di carattere culturale: dal titolo tertullianesco a
Giordano Bruno (« Al Mal Contento », titolo del sonetto di apertura
alla *Cena delle Ceneri),* dal Foscolo (« li lasciò tutti confusi nelle loro
tenebre », detto di Napoleone, alla sua morte) a Stendhal (il verso finale
richiama un passo di *De l'amour);* accenni a familiari giochi « scientifici »
(quello con gli involucri degli amaretti, il diavolo di Cartesio); o richiami
a massime popolari (« ha un piede verde » lo dicono gli egiziani di chi

DE CULTU VIRGINIS

Before stopping in the churchyard she hovers on outstretched
        [wings
in mirrors of wet light, broken by a green foot:
at the *Malcontent Bar* she mortally wounds a stranger,
mistaking him for her seducer.

Other examples: towers in the well at San Gimignano, the hook
in the pike, the red ball in the pocket. Therefore if the
        [Cartesian devil
(we relive the abrupt landing that on Saturday left us all
confused in our darkness

with a leg in a cast, the pen that stained the jacket in flight)
had its membrane torn away in the final game—he flies back
over the courthouse, just when grasping the only good cue
I won the abjuration back

from the Duke of Sessa. We often pray that God will lend us a
        [hand
(if you roll up an Amaretto cookie-wrapper and light it at one
        [end,

There are numerous cultural references: from the title, derived from
Tertullian, to Giordano Bruno ("To the Malcontent," title of the open-
ing sonnet of the *Cena delle Ceneri*), from Foscolo ("He left them all
confused in their darkness," said of Napoleon, on his death) to Stendhal
(the last line recalls a passage from *On Love*); references to familiar
"scientific" demonstrations (the game with Amaretto wrappers,
Descartes' devil); or reminiscences of popular maxims (the Egyptians

attenti! la cenere sale, su quasi fino al soffitto!)
e i bambini imparano che

sbocciano immobili giorni in cui non ricevono doni,
a non calpestare i fiori, strappare ali a gialle farfalle
o fidarsi di uomini che in tasca nascondono molte chiavi
e mutano in una fonte. Un uccello

bianco ogni tanto lacera aquiloni nel sole. TEOREMA:
Francesco Petrarca era forse infelice di non avere il caffè?

---

ha fortuna; mentre altrove chi porta con sé troppe chiavi è un subdolo
individuo). Ma questi inserti sono trattati alla stessa stregua dei brani
di conversazione o di giornale (vv. 3 e 4, per esempio); non hanno cioè
nessun valore di rinvio dotto, erudito, o altrimenti preciso. Ogni strofa
è composta di tre esametri e da un verso finale di tre piedi; due esametri
chiudono le cinque strofe.

look! the ash will rise up almost to the ceiling!)
and children learn

that motionless days spring up where they receive no gifts,
not to step on flowers, tear the wings off yellow butterflies
or trust men who hide lots of keys in their pockets
and turn into fountains. Now and then

a white bird will tear up kites in the sun. THEOREM:
Was Petrarch unhappy because he didn't have coffee?

---

say someone "has a green foot" to mean he is lucky; elsewhere some-
one who carries around too many keys is a shifty individual). But these
intercalations are handled like scraps of conversation or newspaper
(lines 3 and 4, for instance); that is, they have no value as learned, eru-
dite, or otherwise precise allusion. Each stanza is composed of three
hexameters and a final three-foot line; two hexameters end the five
stanzas.

Da IL SASSO APPESO

I

Ma dove stiamo andando col mal di testa la guerra e senza
[soldi?
oltre il tergicristallo ronzante? denotando una reale
e comune volontà di riscatto? che sciocchezze! (né la folla
di sghimbescio parve notare, tutti compresi nei loro
piedi).

Ora comunque allunga le gambe o accavallale bianche,
sbadiglia, guarda nel vetro la paglia che brucia, il fiume
se scorre verdescuro, pensa a qualcosa,
conta i paracarri, fa quel che ti pare:

non c'è pericolo che non arriviamo, pazienti godiamoci il
[viaggio,
godiamoci, non c'è pericolo se ci perdiamo, tanto non si viaggia
(il profilo di un paziente su un carrello attraversando la
[carestia),
tanto non si arriva, arriveremo: all'ameba, alla mecca, alla
[mela,
dietro gli uccelli in fuga bassi dalla città minata, dal
[maltempo.

Il titolo del poemetto evoca una minaccia assurda sospesa a un debole
filo: il « sasso » ha una forza fisionomica arcaica immediatamente
emblematica; nella sua spazialità assurda, verticale, è condensata la
natura minacciosa del tempo, della « stagione piagata ».
A questo tema s'intreccia quello della fuga, che si svolge in molteplici
configurazioni: fuga dai muri, dalla città, dalla terraferma, dal pianeta.

from THE DANGLING ROCK

I

Where on earth are we going with this headache, the war and no
    [money?
beyond the humming windshield-wiper? revealing a real
and common desire for deliverance? what nonsense! (nor did the
    [crowd,
askance, seem to notice, all wrapped up in their feet as they
    [were).

  Now, however, stretch your legs or cross them white,
yawn, watch the burning straw in the glass, if the river
flows dark green, think of something,
count the curbstones, do what you like:

We'll get there, don't worry, relax, let's enjoy the ride,
let's make the most of it, don't worry if we get lost, we're not
    [really travelling
(profile of a patient on a rollaway crossing the famine),
anyway we're not getting there, we'll get there: to amoeba, to
    [Mecca, to apple,
behind the birds fleeing low from the mined city, from bad
    [weather.

The poem's title evokes some absurd threat dangling by a slender
thread: the "rock" has an archaic, directly emblematic physiognomic
power; in its absurd, vertical spatiality, the threatening nature of time,
of the "wounded season," has been condensed.
This theme meshes with that of escape, which occurs in a number of
configurations: as escape from walls, from the city, from the main-
land, the planet.

273

LIETO FINE: cresce (sul concetto di morte non è
necessario alcun chiarimento), cresce nelle tue mani;
elefanti frustano l'aria,
                          l'orizzonte di gomma arancio,
la terra sommersa nei campi. Non c'è bisogno di crederla
un'associazione fortuita. (Le tue ossa nere, la fontana,
le pinne rilassate, me lo figuravo tutto diverso.)

Quei soldati bipedi come corrono guarda appesi alla bufera—
ma cosa ce ne facciamo del pianeta! scompaiono, al diavolo,
        [al bivio.
Gonfio di miele il fazzoletto sul sedile posteriore vuoto
e dopo un'ora ne avevamo abbastanza e continua (non ne
        [usciremo)

fumando e raccontando *quand'ero tossicomane* può
        [continuare
con queste mani sempre pulite seppellivo disseppellivo i vivi...
E continua fino alla fine del continente (e un poco oltre,
aperti gli occhi dentro l'acqua, attenti all'elica e al crampo,
se non ce la fai non importa tanto meglio non ti bagni non
        [sanguini).

Il moto è sempre immerso in un'atmosfera statica: non c'è ritorno ma
neppure uscita; tutto avviene in uno stato di irresponsabilità scelto
deliberatamente (si noti il riferimento alla droga nella sez. i), e non è
che un tentativo di provocare la « corda tesa » e portare al limite lo
stato d'animo di rispecchiamento dell'epoca. Infatti, soltanto con la
fine, « se useremo la lama » recidendo la corda, la fuga si attuerà davvero,
liberandoci dal farnetico di movimenti reclusi in una situazione storica.
Dunque non resta che rifiutare ogni risoluzione, ogni meta della fuga,
e accogliere quest'ultima nel suo incessante mutamento, come
possibilità di conservazione e di sopravvivenza, « senza perderci e senza
arrivare ».

HAPPY ENDING: it grows (the concept of death
needs no clarification), it grows in your hands;
elephants swat the air,

                                  the orange-rubber horizon,
the earth underwater in the fields. No need to believe
this is a chance association. (Your black bones, the fountain,
the relaxed fins: I had imagined him quite differently.)

Those two-footed soldiers, look how they run, hanging on the
        [storm—
but what are we supposed to do with the planet! they disap-
        [pear, to the devil, at the crossroads.
Bloated with honey the handkerchief on the empty back seat
and after an hour we'd had enough and he goes on (we'll never
        [make it through this)

smoking and telling of *when I was an addict* he can go on
with these always clean hands I buried and unburied the living...
And he goes on to the end of the continent (and a bit beyond,
eyes open in the water, mindful of cramps and the propeller,
if you can't manage it, never mind, so much the better, you won't
        [get wet you won't bleed).

Motion is consistently immersed in a static atmosphere: there is no
return, not even an exit; everything happens in a deliberately chosen
state of irresponsibility (note the reference to drugs in section I), and it
is only an attempt to test the "taut rope" and push the mental state of
reflecting the era to its limit. Indeed, only at the end, "if we use the
blade," and cut the rope, will the escape really be able to occur, freeing
us from the ravings of movements shut up in a historical situation.
The only answer then is to reject every resolution, every goal of es-
cape, and embrace this flight in its ceaseless change, as a possibility of
preservation and survival, "without getting lost and without reaching
the rotten snow."

3

Non sanguina più. Non sanguina più nemmeno
c'inghiottisse la frana, ci—
                    ma come fai tu a ricordarti
(gridò dalla vasca) tutti quei nomi? Nella vasca,
lunga otto teste, uscitane, alta diciotto labbri,
l'occhio nello specchio, disegnati, appannato, senza palpebre—
e fuggire l'Europa; oltre il mare

                    c'è il mare;
                              se la corda terrà
dunque riusciremo a uscire se useremo la lama,
asciugati bene all'aria calda, e il naso finto,
respirabile ancora a pena fra i muri gonfi, cerca
la scarpa, la cosa (ma avrà una forma di rosa?),
di fare più in fretta e dove appoggiare le mani,

ma il più in fretta possibile, inutile cercare le chiavi,
e fidiamoci ancora, nonostante, e i colchici (la corda
tesa consumata, la bestia svenata, i crani rapati
nelle valige stipati, macchie nella fotosfera),
                              e l'acceleratore
al massimo dopo lo curva, la folla masticata,

Questa rinuncia alla realizzazione delle possibilità si concreta nel
continuo « ricominciare », nel riconoscere che « non c'è più terra da
scoprire », nell'accettare, di là da ogni finalità, la « tragica finzione » di
fronte alla minaccia sospesa, e nell'esprimerla « con convinzione ».
Il motivo erotico, mentre individualizza i temi di fondo, suggerisce il
fatto oggettivo che minaccia, fuga e sopravvivenza riguardano l'essenza
umana, non la biografia del singolo.

3

He's stopped bleeding. He's stopped bleeding, as if a landslide
were to swallow us, us—

but how on earth can you remember
(she shouted from the tub) all those names? In the tub,
eight heads long, she came out, eighteen lips long,
designed lips, eye in the mirror, misted over, lidless—
and fleeing Europe; beyond the sea

there's the sea;

if the rope holds out
we'll manage to get out if we use the blade,
dry yourself off well in the hot air, while the fake nose,
still barely breathable between the swollen walls, looks
for the shoe, the thing (but will it have the shape of a rose?),
looks to hurry up and where to put one's hands,

to hurry up as much as possible, no point in looking for the keys,
let's keep trusting, all the same, and the autumn crocuses
(the taut rope frayed, the beast bled dry, the shaved heads
stuffed in the suitcases, spots in the photosphere),

and the pedal

to the floor after the curve, the chewed-up crowd,

This forswearing of achieving possibilities takes shapes in a continual
"starting over again," the realization that "there is no land left to dis-
cover," in accepting, beyond all finality, the "tragic put-on" confront-
ing the threat hanging in front of us, and expressing it "with convic-
tion."

The erotic motif, while individualizing the basic themes, suggests the
objective fact that threat, escape, and survival concern the essence of
humanity, not an individual biography.

la benzina che basti fino al molo, agli incroci senza esitare
di questo tempo tutto perduto e pochi anni di vita
in queste viscere viola il cielo si sfiora coi capelli
(ogni passo una candela, le ascelle brucate, dalle mie ossa;
l'immenso lupo: lui ci ha seguiti? lui ci manda? dopo
i calcoli invernali? gli esatti incassi? le verifiche?);

                                le foglie
pendono un poco e cadono sull'erba alta e non volano
via; sulla neve nere croste; ricordati
data, meta, uomo;
               il verso del montone
(insopportabilmente acuto); scorda di non
                             dare il tuo nome;
mordendo il labbro inferiore; non franerà più nemmeno.

5

Senza ritorno colando nel collo della bottiglia, nella stagione
     [piagata
(il testo è redatto in un linguaggio corrente, con ortografia
     [corretta)
e continuiamo in ogni caso e senza perderci senza arrivare sulla
     [neve imputridita
ricominciando, « ma mentre stiamo andando col mal di testa »
     [(l'originale lezione)

L'intero poemetto consta di cinque sezioni di 5/6 strofe ciascuna. Ogni
strofa è composta prevalentemente di 5/6 versi (quasi tutti di 5/6 accenti
principali).

the gasoline that lasts as far as the pier, at the intersections
        [without faltering
with this time all wasted and few years to live
in these violet entrails the sky is grazed by the hair
(every step a candle, the armpits nibbled, by my bones;
the immense wolf: was it he that followed us? sent us? after
the winter estimates? the exact grosses? the audits?);

                                        the leaves
sag a little and fall on the tall grass and don't fly
away; on the snow, black crusts; remember
date, destination, man;
                        the ram's call
(unbearably shrill); forget about not
                                giving your name;
biting your lower lip; it won't even crumble any more.

5

Dripping through the bottle's neck with no return, in the
        [wounded season
(the text is written in a flowing style, with correct spelling)
and we keep going at any rate, without getting lost and with-
        [out reaching the rotten snow
starting over again, "and as we are going along with a
        [headache" (the original lesson)

The entire poem consists of five sections of 5-6 stanzas each. Every
stanza is composed for the most part of 5-6 lines (almost all with 5–6
principal stresses).

la storia (gli occhiali) la natura (per sempre) il fare (calpestati)

e camminiamo silenziosi su suole di feltro. Arturo è scalzo.
Poi si diresse (quel venerdì) verso il corpo salato, le tue così
      [calde,
le mani ovvie... prendilo per le caviglie, prendilo per il collo
      [sottile,
le gambe sul soffitto, l'inguine arancio nel silenzio docilmente
dove pende la vita spaccata,

                        e lasciare l'Europa cariata,
sulla pioggia fuggendo lo scafo l'urlo del pianeta sulla fascia
      [di nubi i verdi mari.
Non c'è più terra da scoprire. Dunque guardati attorno. La
      [luce spenta. Affila
le unghie di riso, afferra la scarpa, la sciarpa che sfugge
la gravità (non c'è più posto per tutti), le tue meningi, i tuoi
      [remi, le tue rotule,
(*Non ridere* disse nel palco mentre) la tua gialla, la tua nave

laggiù galleggiante; un'altra sigaretta; la tua navigazione;
sai cosa ti aspetta; dunque guardati attorno; la luna;
                   [l'argomento.
Eccoci infine discutiamo, non per i soldi questa volta
      [sufficienti
per la birra e la benzina; o la frana che importa—la piena che
avanza... non ricordo più bene di cosa si trattava... a passo
d'occhio... (ma lasciatemi parlare)... a perdita d'uomo...
      [un'altra strofa:

history (the glasses) nature (forever) the making (trampled)

and we walk silent on soles of felt. Arturo is barefoot.
Then he headed (that Friday) toward the salty body, your hands
    [so hot
and obvious... grab him by the ankles, grab him by his slender
    [neck,
legs on the ceiling, the orange groin tamely in the silence
where shattered life hangs,

                  and leaving decayed Europe,
over the rain fleeing the boat the planet's howl over the layer
    [of clouds the green seas.
There is no land left to discover. So look around you. The light
    [gone out. Sharpen
the fingernails of laughter, grab the shoe, the scarf that defies
gravity (there's not enough room left for everybody), your brains,
    [your oars, your kneecaps,
(*Don't laugh* he said in the box while) your yellow, your ship

afloat over there; another cigarette; your navigation;
you know what awaits you; so look around yourself; the moon;
    [the subject-matter.
Here we are, arguing again, not about money, which we've got
    [enough of this time,
but about beer and gasoline; who cares about the landslide—
    [the advancing
spate... I forgot what it was all about... at an eye's
pace... (please let me speak)... as far as the walking can see...
    [another stanza:

Abbondanti cespugli di ginestre fanno tutto giallo e non ne
        [vale
la pena, né quel sasso maledetto col suo spago che dondola
        [teso,
e noi senza partire dunque l'intero pomeriggio fissando
        [i corvi alti,
ogni parola con convinzione, e una nuvola, una tragica
        [finzione, la cosa
appesa (lasciatemi finire), o un'altra cosa, fino a averne
        [abbastanza.

Lush broom bushes glow all yellow and it's not worth
the trouble, nor is that damned dangling rock with its string
        [hanging taut
while we without ever leaving therefore staring the whole
        [afternoon at ravens high above,
each word with conviction, and a cloud, a tragic put-on, the
        [hanging
thing (let me finish), or something else, until we've had enough.

Da FRAMMENTI DEL SASSO APPESO

A 2

          e con queste parole (in primo piano
taceva il mondo intorno   a lui taceva il mondo
          per renderlo amorfo
                    manipolando il
   [mosaico e
          la stesura)
rossa e spessa (viste dal basso)   gli spettatori non
   [videro altro
      nel ventre riempito dalla neve
tutte si accesero le luci

B 4

Il suo viso esprime una grande sofferenza,
uno dopo l'altro si tirano fuori in fretta;
          biologicamente lo stesso
(lo stordimento dei paesaggi, la malinconia dei bastimenti)
punto di vista   uno sforzo continuo, pensino quello
             che vogliono. Nel solco della tradizione
   comédie à tiroir,
   tutto diverso:

L'indeterminatezza di questi frammenti nasce dalla tensione tra le parole (che sono nette e precise ma sintatticamente *sospese*) e gli spazi bianchi. Questi ultimi, evidentemente, non hanno alcuna funzione

from FRAGMENTS OF THE DANGLING ROCK

A 2

         and with these words (in the foreground
the surrounding world was silent   for him the
   [world was silent
        to render it formless
              manipulating the
  [mosaic
       the draft)
red and thick (seen from below)   the spectators saw
   [nothing else
     in the snow-filled belly
all the lights came on

B 4

His face expresses great suffering,
they are drawn out one after another in a hurry;
        biologically the same
(the bewilderment of the landscapes, the melancholy of the ships)
point of view   a constant effort, let them think
          what they want. In the wake of tradition
  comédie à tiroir,
  entirely different:

The indeterminacy of these fragments comes out of the tension between words (which are neat and precise and yet syntactically *suspended*) and the blank spaces. The latter, clearly, have no symbolic function,

là seduto schivando
Il filo a piombo nell'età schizofrenica
(in fretta fino al collo l'impermeabile proseguendo impotente
la folla crepitava adagio una
dopo l'altra sui moli massacra e paziente onde lentamente)
qui in basso

[leggendo
Il suo trucco era un garbo del cuore

C 5

attraversata di corsa la crosta sottile, l'ombra ondulata,
tutto dire tutto previsto
di corsa le fanerogame e i poliziotti bisogna
la morte che è un esilio, la vita che è un momento attraversata
(evitare i giochi di luce e preferire il massimo d'illuminazione)
conservati i soli lineamenti

Lugubre l'eco riflessa
del muro crollato del muro anzi dissanguato.

---

simbolica, di suggestione o rarefazione, non servono cioè a creare un
prolungamento, uno *sfumato* intorno alle parole scritte: indicano
soltanto lacune, parole irrimediabilmente mancanti; o sono sospen-
sioni, salti, fratture nel tessuto poetico. In margine, è da notare che i

C 1

seated there dodging
The plumbline in the age of schizophrenia
(in a hurry up to his neck the raincoat proceeding powerless
the crowd softly crackled one
after another slaughters on the piers and patient slowly waves)
reading here below
Her make-up was a kindness of the heart.

C 5

the thin crust crossed in a rush, the rolling shadow
saying all, foreseeing all,
in a rush spermatophytes and policemen we must
death which is an exile, life which is crossed for a moment
(avoid plays of light and prefer maximum lighting)
only features preserved
Gloomy the reflected echo
of the crumbled wall, rather, the bloodless wall.

---

either evocative or rarefying, that is, they do not serve to create a delay, a protraction, a *sfumato* around the written words: they merely indicate gaps, irreparably missing words; or they are suspensions, leaps, skips, fractures in the poem's structure. It should be noted in passing

I soldati facevano la guerra oppure
                    per fare più in fretta
        involontario e continuo facevano a grande altezza
                        vista da fuori facevano in costume
    tuttavia   sale fumo
            sopravvivendo è stato convenuto
        un altro di troppo a meno che   si sedette per terra
                    (visto sempre dal sasso)

E 3

senza far nomi, si nutrono soprattutto, non nominando i fatti
(mentre   i problemi si risolvono
era sceso per asciugare   l'occhio rarefatto
la macchina)   non già fornendo nuovi dati
            razzi, frange   sul muro strisce albe
e notti variano per pochi segni crepuscolare!
                        o il telefono tace,

---

frammenti consentono una lettura in più direzioni, anche verticalmente
e diagonalmente; anzi includono e suggeriscono al lettore il concetto
dell'alea o meglio della scelta interpretativa tra immagini e «fatti verbali
» fissati dai sintagmi.

The soldiers made war or rather
                    to hurry it up
unintentionally and continually they made at great height
                        seen from outside they made

    [in costume
nevertheless   smoke rises
        in surviving it was agreed
    another too many unless   he sat on the ground
                    (still seen from the rock)

E 3

without giving names, they feed themselves above all, not
    [mentioning facts
(while   problems are resolved
he had gone down to dry   the rarefied eye
the car)   providing no new facts
        rockets, frills   white streaks on the wall
and vary by few signs crepuscular!

                    or the telephone falls silent,

---

that the fragments allow for interpretation in several directions, verti-
cal as well as diagonal; indeed they include and suggest to the reader
the concept of chance or better, of interpretive selection between im-
ages and "verbal facts" set up by the syntagms.

Da CORPI IN MOTO E CORPI IN EQUILIBRIO

Avremmo potuto farne a meno,
gli alberi fanno troppo rumore,
ma cosa ci stanno a fare

i cavalli, ciascuno per suo conto
avremmo finito per perderci,
fare ritorno, fare

tutto quello che vuoi, certe
volte gli alberi riescono
a crescere in direzione del cielo

aspirando l'esplosione nell'istante
inatteso, aspettando che finisca
di piovere, ispirati dall'istinto

correndo da una parte all'altra
ispidi, istigati dall'isteria,
il cuore pieno di bottoni,

le dita immerse, anguiformi,
com'erano belle dalla barca,
soffiamoci sopra, fine.

È curioso notare l'intrusione dei cavalli, che ritornano soli o in
compagnia di altri animali in più d'una poesia di questa serie.
L'apparizione incongrua delle bestie nella coscienza è un sintomo di
depressione e di ansietà. Il cavallo, come creatura infernale o

BODIES IN MOTION AND BODIES IN EQUILIBRIUM

We could have done without it,
the trees make too much noise,
but what are the horses

doing there, each going his own way
we would have ended up getting lost,
going back, doing

whatever you like, some-
times trees manage
to grow skywards

inhaling the explosion in the unexpected
instant, waiting for the rain
to stop, inspired by instinct

running this way and that
bristly, spurred by hysteria,
heart filled with buttons,

fingers immersed, serpentine,
they were so lovely from the boat,
let's blow on them, the end.

It is curious to note the intrusion of horses, who come back alone or
accompanied by other animals in more than one poem in this series.
The incongruous appearance of animals in our consciousness is a symp-
tom of depression and anxiety. The horse, as an infernal creature, or

Quante volte me lo
al cavallo che si era avvicinato
al rumore del muro crollato

e afferrò la maniglia scricchiolante
col pacco sotto il braccio—e posarlo
dove l'aveva preso e nessuno

(ci sono tante sedie) lì c'era
a ricevere, controllare, a dire.
Che cosa. (Me lo disse: rimani?)

Dunque un po' di silenzio, dunque la
colazione: e prenderne per conservare
la razza, il sesso, la statura

a manciate per fare più
in fretta galoppi anche se
appiccica alla pelle, poiché ha fine.

La seconda ragione (fu
sul punto di andarsene, ma vivacemente):
. . . .

antifrasticamente come creatura solare, è una « grande immagine »
presente in una infinità di miti e leggende. Messaggero di morte o
demone della tempesta, ha sempre carattere di cauche-mar e
simboleggia il tempo; ed è forse particolarmente significativo ritrovarlo

How many times did
at the horse that had come near
at the sound of the crumbled wall

and he grabbed the creaking handle
with the package under his arm—and to put it
back where he had got it and nobody

(there are so many chairs) he was there
to welcome, supervise, to say.
What. (But he said it: Will you stay?)

Thus a bit of silence, thus
breakfast: and take some to preserve
race, sex, stature

by handfuls to hurry up
the gallop a bit even though
it sticks to the skin, since it ends.

The second reason (was
about to leave, though spiritedly):

. . . .

---

by antiphrasis a solar creature, is a "great image" present in countless
myths and legends. A herald of death or storm-demon, the horse al-
ways has the character of the cauche-mar and symbolizes time; and it
may be particularly significant to find the creature here in a context

Le ore bianche, contraffatte,
l'attesa nei guanti, gli elastici,
primaverile, gli artigli, facile

come raggiungerti, come
sganciare la bomba, la
durata la ripetizione,

l'altra ragione è fuggiamo finalmente,
non c'è che un modo per farti felice
e un altrove, un colore c'è sempre

di mare, un po' di tempo passato,
bevuto, qualsiasi cosa si è
rotta, tutto questo tutto

per cosa? L'incidente. Ogni cosa
rinviene al suo posto. Inconsueta.
E pretesto. Bottiglia. Sarebbe stato meglio

(spesso ne faccio a meno)
se lì si fosse arrestato il vortice,
questa voglia di vetro, di

---

qui in un contesto che, a rigore, rifiuterebbe il simbolo, giacché le pa-
role-immagini hanno perso per l'A. la primordiale carica semantica
per conservare il loro puro residuo semiologico, di segni o engrammi
astratti e arbitrari. In realtà, la presenza insensata di oggetti, animali,

The hours of white, counterfeited,
the gloved wait, rubber-bands,
springlike, talons, easy

how to reach you, how
to drop the bomb, the
length of time the repetition

the other reason is we flee at last,
there's only one way to make you happy
and an elsewhere, there's always a color

of sea, a bit of time past,
drunk, something has
broken, all this all

for what? The accident. Every thing
falls back into place. Unusual.
And pretext. Bottle. It would have been better

(often I do without it)
if the vortex had stopped there,
that craving for glass, for

---

which should, strictly speaking, reject the symbol, since image-words
[*parole-immagini*] have lost their primordial semantic charge for the
author, retaining their pure semiological residue as abstract and arbi-
trary signs or engrams. In reality, the senseless presence of objects,

Invece di un vero cieco
la pioggia è ancora caduta
su tutta la strada e l'animale

osservato seppe cosa fare,
noi tutti qui intenti con tutti
questi fili sul prato sulla riva

della buca azzurra dell'anima,
che cosa vi mancava, qualora
ciò che importa non è l'incidente,

purché non si rimetta a piovere
ora che scoperto il gioco
occorre continuare? a

legare? legalmente portiamo
l'opinione in su e in giù per le scale,
pianerottolo, ringhiera e libero

accesso, a meno che nella torre,
ma veramente si tratta, mai paura,
d'impacchettare, annodare e non guardare.

---

eventi che invadono il tessuto immaginativo e lo bucano a mo' di tarli
si rivela il nucleo essenziale di questi corpi o costellazioni di « particelle
strane »: simboli di un mondo scomparso (« ma chi li ha visti mai? »).
[p. 300]

Instead of a real blindman
the rain still fell
on the whole street and the animal

observed knew what to do,
all of us here engrossed in all
these lines on the lawn on the bank

of the blue hole of the soul,
what were you missing, in case
what matters is not the accident,

as long as it doesn't start raining again
now that the cards are on the table
must we go on? tying

up? we lawfully hold
the opinion up and down the staircase,
the landing, bannister and free

access, unless in the tower,
but it never really boils down, never fear,
to packaging, knotting and not looking.

---

animals, events invading the imaginative fabric of the poem and eating away at it like moths, reveals the essence of these bodies or constellations of "foreign particles": symbols of a vanished world ("but really who has ever seen [the horses?]"). [p. 301]

I delegati sono cinquemila,
uomini e donne, alcuni
per il freddo, il ladro, la balbuzie,

tutti gli altri hanno avuto ragione
e se ne sono andati tuttavia
e noi siamo rimasti qui tutti

seduti oppure in piedi oppure
a un più attento esame rivelano
la mancanza di affettività, chissà

quando li rivedremo
e il mondo riavrà pace
e nessuno voleva restare

e così nessuno è restato, tuttavia
essi sono ritornati e senza
ritrovarci, noi ingrati, noi calvi,

pudibondi, le dita immerse, raramente
si lamentano, non esprimono desideri,
non hanno alcuna esigenza.

L'intrusione di altre parole-chiave si spiega con ragioni del tutto soggettive: « bottone », per esempio, è una parola che ha un bel suono secco e sicuro, specie dopo l'approccio un po' grave, una parola che indica un oggetto dallo stile sincero, elegante, pratico e domestico senza essere crepuscolare, e l'A. mostra di amarla molto mettendola dove può andar bene.

298

There are five thousand delegates,
men and women, some because
of the cold, the thief, the stutters,

all the others were right
and they went away all the same
and we all stayed behind

sitting or else standing or
upon closer examination they show
a lack of affect, who knows

when we will see them again
and the world will have peace again
and nobody wanted to stay

and so nobody stayed, however
they came back and did not
find us there, we ingrates, bald,

bashful, fingers immersed, rarely
do they complain, they express no desires,
they make no demands.

The intrusion of other keywords attests rather to the author's feelings
for certain linguistic creatures: the recurrence of *"bottone,"* "button,"
for example, can be explained by the characters of the word itself, which
has a stark, solid sound, especially after the somewhat heavy start, and
which denotes an object that is pure, elegant, practical, domestic.

Una volta o l'altra il tendine
è spezzato, la falange recisa
rincorre il vento nella gabbia

e ostinato sempre lo stesso
uccello, l'aria da respirare
nella bocca piena di sangue

e sopra il corpo a coda di rondine
minuto per minuto spiegazzando
un'estate e i licheni filamentosa

incrostati, incastrati, le contrazioni
tutte le volte che tossisci
ora gialli ora verdi ora mai

perduti dal gancio penzolanti
i pescecani che affiorano, sfiorano
carne a forza di dirlo,

ma in fondo chi li ha visti mai
i cavalli? l'estate fu calda,
la folla camminava adagio.

Un procedimento stilistico frequente, qui come nella serie successiva, è la registrazione (drammatico-umoristica) di imprevisti grammaticali e sintattici: l'A. si sforza di cogliere le parole al momento della pronuncia, di caricarle della tonalità imprecisa che hanno allorché vengono scelte per « comunicare »; tali registrazioni fanno ondeggiare la struttura linguistica e metrica con effetti simili a quelli che ottiene il clown con il suo uso incongruo e sciolto degli oggetti. Il verso di questi *Corpi* ha tre accenti.

Sooner or later the tendon
is broken, the severed phalanx
chases the wind in the cage

and stubborn always the same
bird, the air to breathe
in a mouth full of blood

and over the dovetailed body
minute by minute wrinkling
a summer stringy and the lichens

inlaid, waylaid, the contractions
every time you cough
now yellow now green now and forever

lost hanging from the hook
the sharks that surface, caress
meat by saying and saying it,

but really who has ever seen
the horses? the summer was hot,
the crowd walked along slowly.

One frequent stylistic procedure, here as in the following series, is the recording (dramati-comical) of sudden grammatical and syntactical contingencies: the author attempts to seize the words in the moment of their utterance, to charge them with the imprecise tonality they have when they are being chosen in "communication"; such records create a 'ripple' in linguistic and metrical structure with effects like those a clown achieves in his agile and incongruous use of objects. The verse lines of these *Bodies* have three stresses.

Da L'ISTINTO DI CONSERVAZIONE

I

Questi sono i nodi, queste le cicatrici,
gli abiti che hai indossato, la stagione inattesa
sull'asfalto dove ancora vivremo, quella nuvola
che abbastanza somiglia alla teiera già

fredda, con la faccia di uno che sta male,
azzurro come il ristorante, la distanza,
sebbene siano le nove, i preparativi
pressoché ultimati, papaveri distillati,

credendo ai miei occhi, sporgendo dal tetto
sulle cime di pini recisi, ma
inganni il titolo, garanzia ai passanti,
che quasi tutti se ne sono andati, si annidano

necessari e la barca che tu non trovi
più ma necessaria perché attraversiamo
quantunque noi non guardiamo e dove
vediamo se pure non c'è rimedio e passano

Nelle poesie di questo gruppo i versi hanno quattro accenti e sono
raccolti in strofe perfettamente omogenee. Fin dalla sez. I si può notare
come gli aggregati sintattici siano disposti secondo un ritmo interno
che s'insinua nella rigida struttura metrica portando a un risultato di
uniformità percorsa da rapide e sottili vibrazioni che lasciano avvertire
la « direzione » tematica senza fissarla. L'ultimo verso è un tipico

from THE INSTINCT OF SELF-PRESERVATION

I

These are the knots, these the scars,
the clothes you put on, the unexpected season
on the asphalt where again we will live, the cloud
that rather resembles the teapot already

cold, looking like someone who feels ill,
blue as the restaurant, the distance,
although it's nine o'clock, the preparations
almost done, distilled poppies,

believing my eyes, jutting from the roof
at the tops of felled pine trees, but
let the title deceive, a guarantee to passersby
who have almost all left, they lie hidden,

necessary and the boat you can no longer
find though necessary because we are crossing
but not watching and wherever
we look although there's no solution and still

The verses in the poems of this group are in four stresses and orga-
nized into perfectly homogeneous stanzas. From the very first one can
observe how the syntactic clusters are arranged according to an inter-
nal rhythm that works its way into the rigid metrical structure, creat-
ing a uniformity traversed by fleeting, subtle vibrations underscoring
the thematic "direction" without narrowly confining it. The last line is

ancora, incerti i luoghi dove
confini nettamente segnati ci rivelano...
Poi il cielo dovrà pur mutare. Come io potrei
cambiare di colpo, e pochi se ne

accorgerebbero, il tonfo che fruga ancora
sordo le ore del pomeriggio, e profondo
e i sassi che hai sotto la schiena o la fuga
di sostantivi corrosi dalle stravolte strutture—

comunque niente di nuovo, la pomice
sui gomiti, se non c'è posto che per uno di noi
e appena uscito di casa s'imbatte,
tu t'imbatti, se hai capito quanto ti aspetto.

4

Qui conta come (può un pesce vivere
a lungo sulla sabbia secca? dormire
senza cuscino?) la vita dell'uomo è
tutta un tentativo (non ne ho la minima
idea, non sono mai stato così triste);

---

esempio di finale a sorpresa, che risolve con una brusca e immotivata
interruzione l'andamento aperto della composizione.
  « Qui conta come... » (sez. 4) è un avvio frequente nelle rubriche del
Novellino. C'è in tutta la poesia un senso di oppressione, una « pena »

they pass, uncertain the places where
clearly marked boundaries give us away...
Later the sky will still have to change. As I might
suddenly change, and few would

notice, the thud still dull and deep
that rummages the hours of the afternoon,
and the stones under your back or the corroded
nouns fleeing contorted structures—

nothing new in any case, pumice
on the elbows, if there's only room for one of us
and one step out of the house he runs into,
you run into, if you know how much I've been waiting for you.

4

Herein is told how (can a fish live
for long on dry sand? sleep
without a pillow?) human life is
all an attempt (I have no idea,
I've never been that unhappy);

---

a typical example of surprise ending, resolving the open movement of
the composition with an abrupt, unmotivated interruption.
"Herein is told how..." is a common beginning for the rubrics of the
Novellino. The whole poem is pervaded by a sense of oppression, a

tuttavia una volta si era travestito
da lattaio, d'altra parte (cercai una posizione
più comoda sulla sedia) non può vivere a lungo
(passammo il resto della notte seduti,
straziati dalla fame, aspettando l'alba).

Salì dunque fino all'ultimo piano,
come gli alberi più alti nella neve
(descriveteci i luoghi che vi circondano se possibile),
e la lancetta sembrava girare troppo adagio;
nessuno lo vide, dormono tutti.

(La stessa sensazione, dunque state seduti,
dubitatene; sbottoniamo altre settimane,
e ancora la ferita, il raffreddore, mani
aperte che sporcano le acque, sempre che
non ci abbiano seguiti. Rossa come un cavallo).

La febbre alta come la neve, un solo bottone
pensò. Un enorme risparmio di tempo.
Un cavillo—prego? galoppa (e
parliamone pure, il personaggio merita
di essere ricordato). Salì fino all'ultimo.

---

metrica; ogni slancio è sùbito soffocato da un inciso o da un crudo mu-
tamento sintattico o da una presenza assurda (come il lattaio). Di qui il
valore tematico della frase: « la vita dell'uomo è tutta un tentativo ».
Le immagini finali liberano fantasiosamente l'intricato contesto.

nevertheless, he once dressed up
as a milkman, on the other hand (I tried to find
a more comfortable position on the chair) he cannot live long
(we spent most of the night sitting down,
racked with hunger, waiting for daybreak).

So he went up to the top floor,
like the tallest trees in snow
(describe the places around you if you can),
and the clock's hands seemed to turn too slowly;
nobody saw him; all are asleep.

(The same feeling, so remain seated,
cast doubt on it; let's unbutton other weeks,
and still the wound, the common cold, open
hands that dirty the waters, provided
we haven't been followed. Red as a horse).

Fever high as the snow, only one button
he thought. A great deal of time saved.
A quibble—beg pardon? gallops off (well
let's talk about it, the character deserves
to be remembered). He went up to the top.

---

metrical "pang of affliction"; every impulse is checked, immediately
choked by parentheses or by a crude syntactic shift, or by some absurd
presence (like the milkman). Whence the thematic value of the phrase:
"human life is all an attempt." The last images fantasically free up the
poem's intricate contextuality.

Perforata la sottile lamiera (potrei
avere qualcosa da bere?) nei ritagli
di tempo (non risponde) strappa i rami
ai boschi (una lisca nel palato) su una slitta
carica di neve (è scomparso) sbucato

da chissà dove (e ossicini sul pavimento
dappertutto) e la grandine sul prato spuntata
nel paesaggio pitturato; in forma di gocciola,
altissimo torreggiante campanaro, giacendo
in fondo alla torre, bevendo a grandi sorsi.

    5

Sul pelo dell'acqua avanzare la pinna,
non si dovrebbe incoraggiare la gente a farlo,
dopo lui giunse (osserviamoli) tutta vestita di
(mentre) con un mazzo di rose bianco,
sull'arenile c'erano ancora le aste; non si tratta

di un bisogno puramente sensuale (per gli antichi
Garamanti, il problema della comunicabilità); lasciamo
che la natura segua il suo corso, seguiamo
senza candele la direzione del naso, la cera
cavata dalle orecchie, le otto differenti

Nella sez. 5 brani di giornale, frammenti di conversazione, còlti nel
loro essere puramente lessicale e asintattico, sono spinti istericamente
(talvolta con grande delicatezza) in un mare di ambiguità. Ad esempio,
l'accenno alle « otto posizioni » è un punto di passaggio dal precedente
tema sessuale al morto che giace « con gli occhi supini »; ma è anche in
relazione al « cono d'ombra » (posizioni astronomiche). Del resto,

Having punctured the thin plate (could I
have something to drink?) in the remnants
of time (he doesn't answer) he tears branches
from the forests (a fishbone in the palate) on a sled
full of snow (he disappeared) popped out

from who knows where (and little bones all over
the floor) and the hail in the meadow popped up
in a painted landscape; in the form of a drop,
tall towering bell ringer, lying
at the bottom of the tower, drinking in great gulps.

5

On the water's surface the fin advancing,
people should not be encouraged to do it,
later he arrived (let's observe them) all dressed in
(while) with a white bouquet of roses,
the booms were still on the sandy shore; it's not a question

of a purely sensual need (for the ancient
Garamants, the problem of communicability); let
nature take its course, let's follow
without candles the nose's direction, the
wax extracted from ears, the eight different

In this poem passages out of newspapers, scraps of conversation, seized
in their purely lexical and asyntactic being, are pushed hysterically (and
sometimes with great delicacy) into a sea of ambiguity. For example,
the allusion to "eight positions" is a transitional point from the pre-
ceding sexual theme of the dead man lying "with eyes turned upwards";
but it also relates to the "cone of shadow" (astronomical positions).

posizioni; nel cono d'ombra della terra
giace aperto, con gli occhi supini, l'acqua
non era molto alta, in piena bocca (due o più volte)
trafiggendo il cervello; fanno il bagno una volta
il mese, e poi Nadar lo fotografò.

Appressandosi la notte la folla va diramandosi;
ripulito del sangue delle sue vittime
(non sono in grado di dire con altra intonazione),
qualche volta considerato peccaminoso, è un semplice
problema matematico. Tu pensi? io credo

avesse molti tentacoli, un crepitio più intenso
delle fiamme proseguendo il gioco e le parole
echeggiarono per le gallerie lunghe della mente.
La febbre nel sangue (non posso leggere),
l'intossicazione sul fiume, la prima volta verdissimi;

poi prese tutte le misure (per continuare), e sempre
più di quanto non avrebbero sperato i piedi
dissipati, le mani minuziose i vari modi
di innescare l'esca, infatti l'ultimo
inverno si è fermato di colpo nella gabbia.

---

questa osservazione—così come molte altre che si potrebbero fare
(violando in un certo senso l'intimazione contemplativa e la assoluta
agibilità del testo)—non esaurisce evidentemente la capacità di
significato *non lineare* delle immagini e dei loro stravolti lineamenti.
Nella molteplicità di lettura vanno infatti considerati gli scambi
grammaticali di numero e di genere e quelli di tempo e luogo. Perché
la scelta di queste *misure?* « Per continuare », lo dice il testo. Che cosa?
La vita, la poesia, l'amore, il mondo.

positions; in the earth's cone of shadow
lies open, with eyes turned upwards, the water
was not very deep, fully in the mouth (twice or more)
piercing the brain; they bathe once
a month, then Nadar photographed them.

The night drawing near, the crowd is dispersing;
cleansed of the blood of its victims
(I'm incapable of using any other intonation),
sometimes considered sinful, it's a simple
problem of mathematics. You think so? I believe

it had many tentacles, a sharper crackling
of the flames continuing the game and the words
echoed through the long tunnels of the mind.
Fever in the blood (I can't read),
intoxication on the river, very green the first time;

then he measured all of it (to continue), and always
more than would have been the hope of the squandered
feet, the meticulous hands the different ways
of loading the muzzle, indeed the last
winter he stopped suddenly inside the cage.

Moreover, this observation—like many others one could make (vio-
lating in a certain sense the text's contemplative intimation and its
absolute operativeness)—obviously does not exhaust the images' *non-
linear* capacity for meaning, or their distorted features. In the multi-
plicity of possible readings the grammatical switches of number and
gender and those of time and place are in fact taken into account. Why
the choice of these *measures*? "To continue," as the text tells us. What?
Life, poetry, love, the world.

DE MAGNALIBUS URBIS M.

Dionisa Cisqua La Pavana La Chessa
e 120.000 uomini che stanno
sotterrando le acque gli archi distruggendo
(li circonvolge puzzo d'eresia) belando
per un bacio tra i vasi vincerà negli affari
sulla coscia di coccio sterla per natura

la didattica formica dialetticamente la mosca
insieme per caso nella nebbia delle cose
con compassione spietata riconoscenza ricatta
come 120.000 pecore automatiche
coloro che amanti erano della vita
così da rendere insufficiente l'opera di spazzatura

De Magnalibus urbis Mediolani è l'opera di Bonvesin da la Riva, al quale
si accenna nel penultimo verso (nel contesto numerose citazioni e
riferimenti: all'ordine degli Umiliati, cui Bonvesin appartenne, nel verso
4; la vittoria della «didattica formica» sulla mosca, nel verso 7; i fantasmi
che fanno trasalire i viandanti notturni, nel verso 15; il taglio della
carne—una delle *Cinquanta cortesie da osservare a mensa*—nel verso 22;
la manipolazione latina nel terzultimo verso).

DE MAGNALIBUS URBIS M.

Dionisa Cisqua La Pavana La Chessa
and 120,000 men who are
burying the waters the arches destroying
(a smell of heresy surrounds them) whining
for a kiss among the vases will triumph in business
on the earthenware thigh by nature a skylark

the didactic ant dialectically the fly
together by chance in the fog of things
with ruthless compassion recognition blackmails
how 120,000 automatic sheep
those that were lovers of life
so as to render the work of sanitation insufficient

De Magnalibus urbis Mediolani is the work of Bonvesin de la Riva, to whom homage is paid in the next-to-last line (in this context, numerous quotations and allusions: to the Order of the Humiliated, the Umiliati, to which Bonvesin belonged, in line 4; the "didactic ant's]" victory over the fly, in line 7; the phantoms who frighten the nocturnal wayfarers in line 15; the meat-carving—one of the "Fifty Courtesies to Observe at Table"—in line 22; the Latin in the third to last line).

nell'aria nebbiosa di un mattino sgozzate
dopo 6 ore di agonia non ti guardano in faccia
o forse sarà un legno o frasca o altra ombria
dietro i tergicristalli in agguato: non sanno nemmeno
chi sei (ecco quella del duca Melzi guarda
sigilli del) le pupille a un ideale lontano

semaforo e comprandoci ingurgitandoli tutti:
però taglia alla femna la carne vergozevre
che scese fitta e insistente per tutta
la giornata dietro pallida i vetri succhiando
che per essi non sorge sui grattacieli
lividissima tellus: l'architettura è morta

le ondulazioni di frequenza si propagano da un capo
all'altro e solo dopo le 23 la colonna
eretta accennò a diminuire: la bianca
nel 1630 visitatrice e
col bottone sostituì un buongoverno al vecchio
sulle spalle che abbandoniamo voltate all'arco

I nomi di femmine in apertura: famose prostitute e usuraie milanesi
dell'800; « sgozzati dopo 6 ore di agonia » si riferisce alla colonna infame
« eretta nel 1630 »; diversi brani son tratti dalla descrizione di una
nevicata nel « Corriere della Sera » del 14 gennaio 1895; altri frammenti
riguardano il Foscolo a Milano.

in the foggy air of a morning their throats slit
after 6 hours of death-agony they don't look you in the face
or perhaps it's a stick or frond or other shade
behind the windshield wipers lying in wait: they don't even know
who you are (here's Duke Melzi's dame, keeper of the
seal of) the pupils to a remote ideal

traffic-light and buying us swallowing them all:
but it cuts the woman's shamebad flesh
that fell thick and insistent for the whole
back pale day the windows sucking
which for them does not grow on skyscrapers
lividissima tellus: architecture is dead

the frequency waves travel from one end
to the other and only after 11 p.m. did the erected
column show signs of shrinking: the white
in 1630 visitress and
with a button replaced the old with good government
on shoulders that we abandon turned toward the arc

The women named in the first line are famous nineteenth-century
Milanese prostitutes and usurers; "their throats slit/ after 6 hours of
death-agony" refers to the notorious column "erected in 1630"; vari-
ous passages are taken from a description of a snowfall in the "Corriere
della Sera" of January 14, 1895; other fragments concern Foscolo in
Milan.

della pace fuggitivi (un bovarismo del ns.)
e all'arruginito sistema spagnolo e attraverso
il valico di Chiasso una città sfuggiamo
avversa al mondo o verso mezzanotte sebbene
più rada e avversi a lui gli eventi poste
le sue forze al servizio continuava a scendere:

lautamente indebitato disperatamente innamorato
eliminano le notti tristi le tossine
ma io ho perduto la mia libertà: exige
sic faciens mercedem o peggio more
virili (con lui comincia la letteratura milanese)
pochissimi broughams continuarono il servizio:

Si tratta di una poesia melodrammaticamente antimilanese; ma senza
odio-amore, nel senso che l'avversione è ironizzata e a tratti resa
grottesca per evitare l'urto frontale con un rivale massiccio e al tempo
stesso sfuggente. Va osservato che anche qui gli inserti culturali sono
stemperati e assorbiti nel magma formicolante e dilatato del contesto,
e che il loro valore sta tutto nel particolare tono e alone di « frase
usata ».

of peace fugitives (our author's Bovarism)
and from the rusty Spanish system and through
the Chiasso pass we flee a city
averse to the world or around midnight though
sparser and events averse to him and having put
his powers to work he continued to descend:

magnificently indebted desperately in love
toxins eliminate unhappy nights
but I have lost my freedom: exige
sic faciens mercedem or worse more
virili (Milanese literature begins with him)
very few broughams remained in service:

What we have here is a melodramatically anti-Milanese poem—but
one without love-hate: the aversion has been ironized and at times
made grotesque in order to avoid head-on collision with a reality at
once bulking and elusive. Note that even here the cultural interpola-
tions are diluted or melted down, absorbed into the teeming, dilating
magma of the context, and that their value resides entirely in their
peculiar tone, their aura, of being "hackneyed phrases."

ANTONIO PORTA

Translated by Paul Vangelisti

EUROPA CAVALCA UN TORO NERO

1   Attento, abitante del pianeta,
      guardati! Dalle parole dei Grandi
      frana di menzogne, lassù
      balbettano, insegnano il vuoto.
      La privata, unica, voce
      metti in salvo: domani sottratta
      ti sarà, come a molti, oramai,
      e lamento risuona il giuoco dei bicchieri.

2   Brucia cartucce in piazza, furente
      l'auto del partito: sollevata la mano
      dalla tasca videro forata.
      Tra i giardini sterili si alza
      altissimo angelo, in pochi
      l'afferrano e il resto è niente.

3   In su la pancia del potente
      la foresta prospera: chi mai
      l'orizzonte oltre l'intrico scorgerà!
      Fruscia la sottoveste sul pennone,
      buone autorità, viaggiano in pallone,
      strade e case osservano dall'alto,

Emblematica *suite* di episodi di cronaca. La strofa 1 è ispirata alle conferenze al vertice e alle prevaricazioni del potere politico. Nella 2 è isolata una visione ingenuamente manichea, l'angelo che si leva nella piazza dove avviene uno scontro di fazioni. La 3 presenta le autorità in pallone sopra la foresta del traffico che esse guardano compiaciute.

EUROPE MOUNTS A BLACK BULL

1   Careful, people of the planet,
look out! from the words of the Great
a landslide of lies, on high
they mumble, they teach the void.
Put the private, single voice
in a safe place: tomorrow it will be
taken, as from many, by now,
and lament sounds in the tinkle of glasses.

2   Waste bullets in the piazza, the official
car burns out of control; they saw the hand
drilled lifted from the pocket.
From the sterile gardens rose
the most holy angel, a few
nab him and the rest is nothing.

3   Upon the paunch of the powerful
the forest prospers, who can never
spot the horizon beyond their intrigue!
The underwear rustles on the flagpole,
decent officials go on a balloon ride,
streets and houses they see from on high,

Emblematic *suite* of news items. The first stanza is inspired by summit
conferences and prevarications of political power. Stanza 2 offers a na-
ively Manichaean vision, the angel who rises in the piazza where fac-
tions are clashing. Stanza 3 presents the authorities riding in a balloon
over a forest of traffic they observe contentedly.

gli uomini sono utili formiche,
la folla ingarbugliata, buone
autorità, cervello di sapone,
sopra le case giuocando scivolate.

4   Un incidente, dicono, ogni ora,
    una giornata che c'era scuola nell'aria
    un odore di detriti, crescono
    sulla piazza gli aranci del mercante.
    Il pneumatico pesantissimo (tale
    un giorno l'insetto sfarinò)
    orecchie livella occhi voce,
    le scarpe penzolano dal ramo,
    evapora la gomma della frenata.

5   Il treno, il lago, gli annegati,
    i fili arruffati. Il ponte nella notte:
    di là quella donna. Il viola
    nasce dall'unghia e il figlio
    adolescente nell'ora prevista dice:
    « Usa il tuo sesso, è il comando. »
    Dentro la ciminiera, gonfio di sonno
    precipita il manovale, spezzata la catena.

6   Cani azzannano i passanti, uomini
    raccomandabili guidano l'assassino,

La 4 e la 5 evocano incidenti tipici della nostra organizzazione; nella 5
tra l'incidente ferroviario e l'infortunio sul lavoro s'incastra
un'immagine di prostituzione. Nella 6: persecuzione razziale, abuso

people are necessary ants,
the mixed up crowd, decent
officials, soap for brains,
playing merrily above the slipping houses.

4   An accident, they say, every hour,
on a day when there was school in the air
an odor of debris, the vendor's
oranges grow in the piazza.
The tremendous tire (the same
one day pulverized an insect)
levels ears eyes voice,
the shoes dangle from the branch,
the rubber evaporates from the skid.

5   The train, the lake, the drowned,
the ruffled wires. The bridge at night:
the woman in the next room. Purple
springs from the nail and the adolescent
son at the appointed hour says:
"Use your sex, that's an order."
Inside the smokestack, bloated with sleep
the laborer is flung headlong, the chain broken.

6   Dogs snap at passersby, trustworthy
men guide the assassin,

Stanzas 4 and 5 evoke incidents typical of our social structure; in stanza
5, an image of prostitution is set between the train accident and the
industrial accident. In the 6th: racial persecution, police abuses, viola-

fuori, presto, scivoli.
Negri annusano il vento.
Ambigua è la sciagura,
le sentinelle, i poliziotti.
I due voltarono le spalle.
Rete, sacco: volati
in basso come pompieri.
Spari. Vibra l'asfalto,
alla porta di una casa, il tonfo.

7   Con le mani la sorella egli
spinge sotto il letto. Un piede
slogato dondola di fuori.
Dalla trama delle calze sale
l'azzurro dell'asfissiato. Guarda.
Strofina un fiammifero, incendia
i cappelli bagnati d'etere
luminoso. Le tende divampano
crepitando. Li scaglia nel fienile,
il cuscino e la bottiglia di benzina.
Gli occhi crepano come uova.
Afferra la doppietta e spara
nella casa della madre. Gli occhi
sono funghi presi a pedate.
Mani affumicate e testa
grattugiata corre alla polveriera,

---

della polizia, violazione della dignità e assassinio insensato. Il
protagonista della strofa 7 è un pazzo che fa saltare un paese dopo aver
ucciso la sorella. Nella 8 un uomo è investito da un'esplosione nucleare.

outside, soon, you slip.
Negroes sniff the wind.
The calamity is unclear,
the sentries, the policemen.
The two turned their backs.
Net, sack: hit
the ground like firemen.
Shots. The asphalt shivers,
at the door of a house, the thud.

7   With his hands he jams his
sister under the bed. A foot
dislocated dangles out.
From the mesh of stockings rises
the asphyxiated azure. Look,
he strikes a match, lights
the hair wet with bright
ether. Curtains burst into flame
crackling. There in the barn tossed
the pillow and the bottle of gasoline.
The eyes crack like eggs.
He grabs the double-barrel and fires
into his mother's house. The eyes
are mushrooms kicked to pieces.
Smoked hands and grated
head he runs to the magazine,

---

tion of dignity, and senseless assassination. The protagonist of stanza 7
is a madman who blows up a village after killing his sister. In 8 a man
is struck by a nuclear explosion. Stanza 9 recounts a suicide. In the

inciampa, nel cielo lentamente
s'arrampica l'esplosione e i vetri
bruciano infranti d'un fuoco
giallo; abitanti immobili
il capo basso, contando le formiche.

8   Osserva della notte l'orizzonte,
inghiottita la finestra dal gorgo del cortile,
l'esplosione soffiò dal deserto
sui capelli, veloce spinta al terrore:
tutto male in cucina, il gas
si espande, l'acqua scroscia,
la lampada spalanca il vuoto.
Richiuse la porta dietro a sé,
e gli occhi punse il vento dell'incendio
corso sugli asfalti, macchiato d'olio:
saltati i bottoni alla camicia estiva
la ferita si colora, legume
che una lama rapida incide.

9   Vide dal suo posto le case
roventi incenerirsi e in fondo alla città
i denti battono sotto le lenzuola
e guizzano i corvi dall'ombellico.
L'A è finestra e oltre
s'agita la pianura di stracci.
L'O s'apre chiamasi

La 9 racconta di un suicidio. Ultima strofa: una folla raccolta su un prato
attende la fine, la parte virgolettata è un passo dei Salmi, alle immagini
di terrore risponde una voce « Sì » (è la vita che vuole continuare).

stumbles, slowly the explosion
ascends to the sky and the windows
burn shattered with a yellow
blaze; motionless inhabitants
heads down, counting ants.

8   Observe the horizon at night,
      the window swallowed by the whirlpool of the courtyard,
      the explosion blew in from the desert
      to the hair, thrust quick to terror:
      all wrong in the kitchen, the gas
      expands, the water pours out,
      the lamp throws the emptiness open.
      He closed the door behind him,
      and wind from the fire pricked his eyes,
      run over the asphalt, spattered with oil:
      buttons missing from the summer shirt,
      the wound colors, legume
      sliced open by a swift blade.

9   From his place he saw the red-hot
      houses reduced to ash and at the city's end
      teeth clatter beneath the sheets
      and ravens dart from the navel.
      The A is window and beyond
      the plain of rags starts to stir.
      The O splits open and is called

---

final stanza, a crowd gathered on a meadow waits for the end; the
passage in quotations comes from the Psalms, to whose images of ter-
ror a voice answers "Yes" (it is life with its will to go on).

lago ribollente fango.
« Galoppate a cammello nel deserto! »
Fa acqua l'animale sventrato
dal taxi furibondo: si ricordò
d'avere atteso tanto, la gola
trapassa il sapore dei papaveri sventolanti:
cala veloce nelle acque dietro
l'auto impennata, volontario
palombaro, con un glù senza ricambio.

10   Un coro ora sono, ondeggianti
nel prato colmo di sussulti.
« Lo zoccolo del cavallo tradisce,
frana la ragione dei secoli. »
Urla una donna, partorisce,
e un bambino percosso dalle cose.
Con un colpo di uncino mise a nudo
l'escavatrice venose tubature,
e radici cariche di schiuma
nel vento dell'albero antico
spasimano, gigante abbattuto.
Quattromila metri di terriccio
premono le schiene, e un minatore
in salvo ha mormorato:
« Là è tutto pieno di gas. »
Un attimo, prima di scivolare
nella fogna gridò: Sì.

A definire la metrica valgono le ragioni narrative: i tre accenti (che
talvolta si riducono a due) scandiscono con incisiva rapidità la
cinematica dei fatti.

lake of boiling mud.
"Ride a camel into the desert!"
The animal drips water disemboweled
by the furious taxi: he recalled
having waited a long time, the throat
pierces the taste of flapping poppies:
he slides quick into the water inside
the rearing car, volunteer
diver, without a spare gurgle.

10   A chorus they are now, waving
in the field full of trembling.
"The horseshoe betrays,
the reason of centuries caves in."
A woman screams, gives birth,
to a beat-up boy.
With a thrust of the scoop the power shovel
bares veinous water mains,
and roots of the ancient tree
heavy with scum spasm
in the wind, a crashing giant.
Four thousand meters of earth
push on their backs, and a miner
back safe murmured:
"It's all full of gas in there."
The moment, just before slipping
into the sewer he yelled: Yes!

Narrative logic serves to define the metrics: the three stresses (at times reduced to two) scan the kinematics of events with incisive speed.

VEGETALI, ANIMALI

Quel cervo la vigile fronte penetrata nei dintorni
nel vasto prato rotondamente galoppando
s'avviò; a volo le lunghe erbe
da ogni parte afferrava finché l'erba
cicuta lo pietrificò. L'albero l'ossatura allargava
cercando spazio tra gli alberi; con il ciuffo in breve
di un palmo l'altezza superò della foresta:
due guardie forestali quello segnarono col marchio.
Che alla scure segnala il punto dell'attacco.
L'insetto giallo sull'albero strisciava
ad alte foglie ampie come laghi:
a ciondolare. Intervenne a schizzargli la schiena
il becco del Bucorvo rosso e curvo come un ponte
d'avorio. Quel fiore foglie e petali distese
fino a inverosimili ampiezze: sostare vi potevano
colibrì e lo spesso gregge degli insetti.
Sciocco ed arruffone, recidendolo, l'esploratore
ne, con violente ditate, fece scempio.
Quel topo gli occhi aghiformi affilò
una veloce nuvola fissando che gonfiava salendo,
esplodeva sibilando nell'aria violenti pennacchi:
allo scoperto rimasto, topo del deserto, dall'attento
falco fu squarciato. L'uccello il folto
dei cespugli obliò, un lunghissimo verme
succhiò dalle zolle: due amici monelli
appostati gli occhi riuscirono a forargli
sulla gola inchiodandogli la preda dal becco
metà dentro e metà fuori.

VEGETABLES, ANIMALS

That deer watchful forehead penetrated in its surroundings
in the vast meadow circularly galloping
set out; in flight, grabbing long
grasses on every side until the hemlock
grass petrified him. The tree stretched the bones
seeking space among the trees; by a slight tuft
of a palm it surpassed the forest's height:
two rangers left a mark on that one.
Which to the ax marks the point of attack.
The yellow insect crept in the tree's
high leaves lavish as lakes:
dawdling. Red and curved like an ivory
bridge the hornbill's beak came to splatter
its back. That flower leaves and petals opened
to an incredible width: they could hold
hummingbirds and heavy swarms of insects.
Thick-headed and bungling, snapping it off, the explorer
wreaks, with rough fingers, havoc.
That rat needle-like eyes sharpened
fixed on a fast cloud that swelled rising,
exploded hissing rough feathers through the air:
desert rat, caught in the open by a watchful
falcon, was ripped apart. The bird the thickness
of the bush forgot, sucked a very long
worm from the sod: two rascally friends
lying in wait succeeded in piercing
its throat nailing the prey in its beak
halfway in halfway out.

LA PELLICCIA DEL CASTORO

1   La zebra scatta e s'avvicina,
la coscia allunga le strisce
lucide e accorcia, fa esplodere
lo zoccolo cartucce di sabbia,
fa un rombo di gole penetrate
da una mano abile che nuota
agitando le dita per pescare
la lingua disciolta nella saliva
bollente tra i denti alla deriva.

In gola penetra scuotendo
le anche l'animale impellicciato,
dilata la bocca dell'esofago,
lo stomaco si distende, in attesa
d'essere venduto e lavorato
come pelle per guanti.

2   La caccia alla balena ha inizio
sul mare innestato di vele
che l'incavo del vento carica di mare.

Gli animali sono qui (a differenza della poesia *Vegetali, animali,* dove il tema è proprio una tragedia naturale) simboli erotici, trasposizioni che penetrano l'atto amoroso sollecitandolo dall'interno. Si può notare che la violenza erotica, in contrasto con quella civile e allucinata in *Europa,* ha un suo ritmo sinuoso e una torbida coerenza.

La metrica è leggermente variata nelle tre parti. Nella 1: tre accenti che strutturano il racconto emblematico scivolando attraverso gli enjambements con effetto ossessivo e penetrante. Nella 2: da due a

THE BEAVER SKIN

1   The zebra leaps and draws near,
the thigh extends the bright
stripes and constricts, the hoof
explodes bullets of sand,
throats rumble penetrated
by an able hand that swims
wiggling the fingers to fish out
the tongue dissolved in boiling
saliva floating between the teeth.

     The furry animal penetrates
the throat shaking the haunches,
the esophagus' mouth dilates,
the stomach distends, waiting
to be sold and worked
as a skin for gloves.

2   The whale hunt starts off
on a sea fitted with sails
the cavity of wind loads with sea.

The animals here (unlike the poem "Vegetables, Animals," the theme
of which is in fact a natural tragedy) are erotic symbols, transpositions
penetrating the love act. Note that the erotic violence, in contrast to
the civil and hallucinatory violence in "Europe," has its own sinuous
rhythm and a rather murky coherence.
The metrics vary somewhat among the three parts. In part 1: three
stresses structure the emblematic narrative slipping across the
enjambments penetratingly and obsessively. In 2: between two and four

Stiamo vigili al comando, i ghiacci
inviano bagliori circondando la rotta.
Scoppia la bufera e la nave capriola,
la vista indebolisce, la gola
si torce, rigagnoli scendono sulle gambe,
la schiena del cetaceo splende
all'improvviso, incalziamo con gli arpioni
e primi si bucano i seni
gonfi e teneri, seconde
le coscie lucide, e rovescia
il ventre, le braccia
allunga all'indietro: « Issiamola
a bordo, divoriamo! »

3   Veloce s'avvicinò e strinse piano
con le dita i rami carichi di frutti,
la dura scorza dell'albero feriva
la guancia e le piume, in vortice cadendo,
innumerevoli e calde impedivano il respiro:
il succo stillava sugli occhi e nella gola
e fu costretto, infine!, a strangolare il serpente
imbecille accorso ad impedire la raccolta:
ora che l'albero si faceva tenero
e abbracciato cedeva piegando le sue fibre!

---

quattro accenti, con effetti più dinamici adatti all'ambientazione
esterna. Nella 3: quattro accenti che danno stabilità alle immagini e
ampliano le risonanze fantastiche del racconto. Per la 4 valgono le
ragioni della 1.

We are ready for orders, the ice pack
flashes all around our course.
The gale breaks and the ship reels,
sight grows weak, throats
tighten, water streams over our legs,
all at once the whale's hump
glistens, we chase it down with harpoons
and the breasts swollen and tender
are the first to get holes, next
her bright flanks, and she goes
belly up, arms
stretching back: "Hoist her
aboard, time to devour!"

3   Quick he approached squeezed easily
with the fingers the branches heavy with fruit,
the rough treebark scratched
the cheek and the feathers, falling in a whirl,
numberless and hot made breathing hard:
the juice trickled into the eyes and throat
and he was driven, at last! to strangle the stupid
serpent come in to stop the harvest:
now that the tree was growing soft
and hugged it yielded surrendering its fibers!

---

stresses, with more dynamic effects to suit the external setting. In 3:
four stresses which give stability to the images and broaden the tale's
fantastical resonances. For section 4 the same logic holds as for section 1.

4   Nel canneto penetra in corsa
perché le colombacce schiamazzino
in fuga: prima alla zampa
della grù cerca d'afferrarsi,
adagiata, poi, stretta
all'albero cedevole: finché
non scoppino in gola liti
e grida di castori che forzano
l'uscita nel singhiozzo lacrimoso.

Le gambe, intanto, scavano
le talpe e le mele dei seni
gratta la zampa dell'orso:
il fango caldo di palude
dove affonda, sospinto
dal vento che l'increspa,
sopra gli occhi si placa arrovesciati,
filtra nella chiostra dei denti.

4   He penetrates the canebrake on the run
      because the doves squawk
      as they take off: first he tries
      snatching the crane's foot,
      set down, then, fast
      against the yielding tree: until
      burst from the throat arguments
      and invective of beavers that force
      the flow of a tearful sob.

      Moles, meanwhile, dig up
      legs and the bear's paw
      rakes the breast apples:
      the hot mud of the swamp
      where he sinks, wafted
      by the wind that parches it,
      above his overturned eyes he calms,
      filters through the arch of his teeth.

DI FRONTE ALLA LUNA

Qualcosa si farà: quanto
sarà necessario. Che cosa, non ha importanza.
Sali in elicottero e osserva, non
ricordare nulla. Scendi e fai a pugni.
Ricorda: dopo le violenze occorre
una doccia bollente. Libera dal sudore.

Il diavolo è importante, forse.
Riconoscilo, dapprima, con:
le punte dei capelli, i peli.
Se punge osservando di spalle.
Sulla bilancia getta il poco che rimane
e muoverà la spinta

I mezzi sono molti e diversi:
miscelando tre quarti di nitro
e un quarto di metalli. S'introducono

Il titolo è tratto da un scultura di Carlo Ramous: piena di ferite, di
tagli, di fremiti che percorrono l'immagine nello spazio; quasi fosse la
luce della luna a scoprirli. E c'è il senso di una presenza calcarea,
contratta, rattrappita (volendo trasporre l'idea che dà la luce lunare
all'oggetto che essa illumina). Così l'uomo si presenta con tutte le sue
piaghe « di fronte alla luna »; anch'egli è pieno di ferite, esce da una
lotta sostenuta contro la sua epoca, in mezzo a una società sorda
distratta e crudele, che non ha neppure il tempo o la voglia di
disprezzare il poeta e la cultura di verità che egli rappresenta, o vorrebbe

IN FRONT OF THE MOON

We will do something: as much
as necessary. What is not important.
Go up in a heliocopter and watch, don't
remember anything. Come down and throw punches.
Remember: after violence you need
a hot shower. To free you of sweat.

The devil is important, maybe.
First, recognize him, by:
the ends of the hair, hairs.
If it pricks observing backwards.
On the scale he throws the little left
and the push will move

The means are many and different:
mixing three quarters nitro
and a quarter metals. They are placed

The title is taken from a sculpture by Carlo Ramous: full of wounds,
edges and shivers traversing the image in space; as though moonlight
were being shed upon them. And there is the sense of a calcinous,
contracted, shrivelled presence (if one wishes to transpose the idea
the lunar light gives to the object it lights). Thus man is presented
with all his sores "in front of the moon"; he too is full of wounds, born
of a struggle with his own era, in an unresponsive, distracted, and cyni-
cal society, with neither time nor desire to despise the poet and the
culture of truth which he represents. At best this society purports to

nel foro. O si affitti un aereo,
l'esplosivo precipita con violenza.
Ma la violenza serve o forse no.
Passeggiamo ai giardini, indifferenti.

Avvertimento, utile: la società
materasso, gommapiuma, carta
assorbente. Pedate con rabbia e macchie
d'inchiostro: il poeta scatta
di forza, approda tra i nemici,
annega nel coktail, senza saperlo.
Suggerimenti indispensabili provengono
dal *barman*: lo stupro ha efficacia.

L'azione sottile tramava, ispirato;
corrompere e impadronirsi dei comandi,
imprimere una direzione
Le gambe non sorressero inclinando
e roteando; un gran mal di capo, i denti
oscillanti pungevano i capelli,

---

ridurla a divertimento giullaresco. Perciò la poesia è costruita di episodi
« violenti » a cui fanno seguito futilità o frustrazioni, per una sorta di
contrappasso: dopo i pugni il lavacro « civile » della doccia; dopo
l'apparizione del diavolo e il ricorso all'esplosivo, l'indifferente
passeggiata ai giardini; ai grandi progetti l'irrisione di un banale
malessere (il mal di capo, il mal di denti) che li svuota di energia; e poi
la società « carta assorbente » e il gesto irresponsabile dello stupro
suggerito da un barman (in figura di abietto confidente e consigliere
del borghese da *night club*).

in the hole. Or you rent a plane,
the explosive falls violently.
But violence works or maybe not.
Let's stroll in the gardens, indifferent.

Warning, useful: the mattress
society, foam rubber, blotting
paper. Angry kicks and ink
spots: the poet snaps
hard, lands among enemies,
drowns in the cocktail, without knowing.
Indispensable suggestions originate
from the barman: the rape works.

The subtle action thickens, inspired;
to corrupt and get the hang of orders,
to fix a direction
the legs didn't hold tilting
and whirling; a great headache, the teeth
slipping pricked the hair,

---

turn the poet's culture into a comic entertainment. Thus the poem is
composed of "violent" episodes which end in futility or frustration, in a
sort of retaliation; after coming to blows, there is the "civil" cleansing
of the shower; after the apparition of the devil and the recourse to the
explosive, the indifferent walk in the gardens; against grand designs
the mockery of a common ailment (head- or toothache) draining them
of energy; and then society as "blotting paper" and the irresponsible
gesture of the rape suggested by a bartender (in the guise of an abject
confidant and advisor to the bourgeois habitué of the nightclub).

le pupille, la lingua, bianca.
Né sciocco era sperare

Sù di corsa per le scale, sbaglia
La porta! quella di ferro,
una mano sul tavolo, nell'inchiostro versato.
Lo schiaffeggiano calmi due uscieri
canuti rimproverando a bassa voce.

Incontratolo: « L'attendo, venga a trovarmi. »
Quello è il rappresentante, onnipossente.
E invece: « Cosa vuole mai tanghero. »
Nel ricevitore strida di un animale
soffocato da un cumulo di ovatta. « Vedremo. »

La carta gialla del foglio, è la missiva.
Un buco nel muro, il rutto: accidenti!
a che cosa è servita. Forse un telegramma
o frequenti cartoline postali, era il meglio.
È tardi, rinviamo a domani, dopodomani.

Dal contesto degli episodi si districa il personaggio del poeta, che vorrebbe servire alla società e ridiventare una presenza nel mondo umano; eccolo, invece, di fronte alla luce irreale come spezzato. A lui si riferiscono le frasi: « Non è possibile continuare a parlarvi », « va morendo, se vivere era possibile ». Ritrova però una via alla ragione di esistere nel compito ultimo dell'arte: scoprire l'immagine dell'uomo. La poesia è quasi un dialogo, uno scontro diretto con la società; non vuol essere autobiografica se non nel respiro mozzato, nell'angoscia del personaggio che non riesce a parlare e subisce lo stato di violenza-

the pupils, the tongue, white.
Nor was it silly to hope

Up the stairs in a hurry, wrong
Door! the steel one,
a hand on the table, in the spilled ink.
Calm the two white-haired doormen
slap him scolding in a low voice.

Having met: "I mean it, come over sometime."
That's the sales rep, almighty.
Instead: "What the hell do you want hick."
The shriek in the receiver of an animal
suffocated by a heap of padding. "We'll see."

The yellow slip of paper is the missive.
A hole in the wall, the belch: damn!
what is served. Maybe a telegram
or frequent postcards was best.
It's late, leave it for tomorrow, after tomorrow.

Out of the context of episodes the character of the poet is unravelled;
though he would like to serve society and once more become a pres-
ence, we find him shattered in this unreal light. It is to him the sen-
tences refer: "It's not possible to keep talking to you," "he's about to
die, if living were possible," and yet his reason for being is the ultimate
task of art: to discover the image of man.

The poem is almost a dialogue, a direct clash with society; it seeks to
be autobiographical only in its cut-off breath, in the anguish of the
character who cannot summon speech and who endures in a state of

Acquista il biglietto. Il luogo
non è lontano, laggiù. Per
svelare la soluzione. Rintraccerà
chi ha grandi poteri e usando la forza
e l'astuzia farà che gridi:

Il porto cui le vele e i venti!
Giuochiamo ai pirati, al contrario.
Ormai c'è tutto: manca tutto.
Così, allontanato definitivamente:
« Non è possibile continuare a parlarvi. »

La linea congiunge i due punti sulla carta:
alla fine della corsa veloce, insonne,
appoggiato ad un muro divora il suo cibo.
Poi domanda, gli occhi volgendo gravi, ancora sveglio,
innumerevoli indicazioni di una certa importanza.
Disteso sul prato va morendo, se vivere era possibile,
agitato lievemente

---

indifferenza. I punti in cui viene a mancare una conclusione (sottolineati
dal fatto che manca la punteggiatura o non v'è nulla dopo i due punti)
indicano che l'azione è arrestata, il pensiero incapace di continuare, di
trovare una soluzione o un appoggio.
(Ci si potrebbe chiedere se l'A. pensa che col mutare della società tutto,
o l'essenziale, potrebbe risolversi. In effetti, il suo atteggiamento è più
una protesta morale che un chiaro indirizzo ideologico. Da una parte,
il poeta deve « aspirare alla giustizia anche se, raggiunta, possa
esautorarlo »; dall'altra, sembrerebbe restargli pur sempre aperta

Buys a ticket. The place
isn't far, down there. To
uncover a solution. He will trace
who has great power and using force
and cunning he will have him shout:

The port where the sails and the wind!
Let's play pirates, instead.
Now there's everything: everything missing.
Like this, definitely withdrawn:
"It's not possible to keep talking to you."

The line joins the two points on the map:
at the end of the race, swift, sleepless,
leaning against a wall he gulps his food.
Then he asks, eyes turned somber, still awake,
numberless directions of a certain importance.
Lying on the grass he's about to die, if living were
      [possible,
a little excited

---

violence and indifference. The points where it lacks a conclusion (points
underscored by the absence of punctuation or by the fact that nothing
follows the semicolons) indicate that action is halted, thought unable
to advance, find any solution or a support.

(One might well ask if the author thinks that everything, or at least
what is essential, could be resolved with societal change. In effect, his
attitude is more a moral protest than a clear ideological direction: the
poet must "aspire to justice, even if, once it is attained, that justice
may strip him of authority"; on the other hand he is left with "the

Nelle fauci del lupo le travi incarnate,
con l'ugola insegna ad ululare
e può giovare: introdurvi adagio
una mano e svellere le corde vocali, ingoiarle,
proseguire la corsa e l'avventura: capiranno!
I lettori improbabili; e poi cosa cambia?
Ma scoprire, almeno, è il fine dell'arte,
l'immagine di
        uomo
        noi.

---

l'alternativa del racconto fantastico e amoroso ». Ma, in conclusione:
« ciò che conta è lo specchio del momento in cui l'artista penetra e si
consuma. Se anche gli emblemi della violenza nascessero dalla
condizione stessa del mondo, sempre vi si dovrebbe opporre il coraggio
della parola »).
La poesia è impostata su tre accenti, con qualche irregolarità dove il
ritmo è rallentato. I tre accenti regolano il ritmo epico-narrativo e i
rapidi tratti dialogici; le spezzature sono sollecitate dal racconto stesso
nei momenti di sospensione accennati più sopra a proposito della
punteggiatura.

In the wolf's jaws the rafters incarnate,
with the throat he teaches how to howl
and it can be useful: introduce a hand
slow and uproot the vocal chords, swallowing them,
go on with the race and the adventure: they will know!
The improbable readers; and then what changes?
But the end of art is, at least, to discover
the image of
     man
     us.

---

alternative of the fantastic tale or love tale." In conclusion: "what counts is mirroring the moment in which the artist penetrates and is consumed. Even if the emblems of violence were born from the world's very condition, one would still have to counter it with the courage of the word."

The poem is built on three stresses, with certain irregularities where the rhythm slows down. The three stresses regulate the epic-narrative rhythm and the rapid passages of dialogue: the breaks are prompted by the tale itself at the moments of suspension cited above in the remark about punctuation.

MERIDIANI E PARALLELI

I

L'esplosione dell'albero, estate, il castello carico di storia:
la passeggiata del granduca, libri, umanisti; cani
corrono il gran parco,
un alterco più dietro...
Per la strada al passaggio impietrì
della giovane musa, ostinato
l'inseguì, poi, sicuro di non raggiungerla.
Tentò un camion di travolgerlo,
sparì al di là del traffico
e una ferita nel dolente capo
attraversato da un'escavatrice. È vero,
raggiungere voleva il filo dell'Adriatico
e scovar lì notizie,
come chi su di una nuvola scruta la trascrizione di sé.

Sembrò per un momento l'appagasse
il mare di tulipani, il prato del castello tenuto verde al mattino
dove di sé tutto obliò.
Sconosciuto rimase l'autore del delitto: e la sega
partendo di fianco riuscì a lacerare, il tutto sanguinolento
abbandonando nell'ombra.

Contrappone la condizione poetica di un Ariosto a quella di un
Montale: l'artista del Rinascimento fantasioso e aristocratico al poeta
moderno, arido e crepuscolare. Le due condizioni si fondono nel

MERIDIANS AND PARALLELS

I

The tree's explosion, summer, the castle loaded with history:
the grand duke's stroll, books, humanists; dogs
run the great park,
a quarrel further back...
Along the road petrified by the young
muse's passing, obstinately
he followed her, then, sure of not catching up.
A truck tried to run him down,
disappeared beyond the traffic
and a wound in the painful head
gone across by the steam shovel. True,
he needed to reach the thread of the Adriatic
and dig up some news there,
like someone on a cloud watches transcriptions of himself.

For a moment it seemed he would be satisfied
by the sea of tulips, the castle's lawn kept green in the morning
where he forgot all about himself.
The author of the crime remained unknown: and the saw
starting from the side was able to lacerate, leaving it
all bloody in the shade.

The poem contrasts the poetical condition of an Ariosto to that of a
Montale: the fanciful, aristocratic Renaissance artist to the arid and
crepuscular modern poet. The two conditions merge in the character

2

Salito a bordo s'avvia: senz'intoppi il motore lo conduce
nell'aria di un aperto mare trapassato
da alti pali di ronzanti telegrafi.
Fermo ad ascoltare. L'onda, leggera, borbotta.
Ormai in navigazione, coperto di sale, prosegue
e pensa intanto ad una terra
come l'antico folle scopritore:
d'alberi nuovi si vela l'orizzonte,
d'uccelli. Galleggiano gusci scagliati da un vento.
E là doveva giungere e approdare? Eretta
nell'isola rapidamente una tenda,
visse per anni, impazzito.
Sparsi, attorno, cadaveri a migliaia, di pappagalli.

---

personaggio che insegue una follia di scoperte nelle terre equatoriali
dell'immaginazione, e che un camion tenta di travolgere. Il viaggio
d'evasione termina sopra un'isola, tra i morti pappagalli, dove il
navigatore è dignitosamente impazzito. Il finale sembra concludere in
favore di un'attività fantastica, indica la possibilità di una presenza
simbolica.

2

Once on board he sets out: without falter the engine carries
    [him
into the air of an open sea crossed
by high poles of humming telegraphs.
Stopped to listen. The wave, mild, mumbles.
Now underway, covered with salt, he sails on
and meanwhile thinks of a land
like the ancient crazy discoverer:
the horizon veiled in new trees,
in birds. Shells float tossed by a wind.
And there was he to reach and land? Right away
he raised a tent on the island,
lived for years, insane.
Scattered around, thousands of cadavers, of parrots.

---

pursuing a folly of discoveries in the equatorial realms of the imagina-
tion, and whom a truck tries to run down. The journey of evasion
ends on an island, among dead parrots, where the navigator has, with
great dignity, gone insane. The finale seems to opt for fantastic activ-
ity, hinting at the possibility of a symbolic presence.

CONTEMPLAZIONI

1   Si torce la striscia rettilinea
in sinusoide sbavata linea

che inciampa alla prima curva
(non correre, sciocco, in curva)

batte sul petto di un uomo
e un kg. di coke con un suono

sul selciato precipita balzando
di zoccolo una nuvola alzando

come un deposito di lunghe fruste:
e gli zoccoli dei cavalli robuste

sparano mazzate sulla fronte,
battono forte sul ponte,

tra le ciglia folte del pazzo
scava lento il suo strazio

Il tema è lo sforzo di inserire in un linguaggio chiuso una realtà che si
sfalda. L'uso delle rime serve da collegamento o ponte ritmico tra le
immagini che nascono come in un gioco di scatole cinesi. La sequenza
delle immagini è dettata sia dal suono che dall'analogia. Quest'ultima
ha qui semplicemente una funzione discorsiva, a dilatazione del tema;

CONTEMPLATIONS

I   The rectilinear stripe twines
in a sinusoid smeared line

that stumbles at the first curve
(don't speed, stupid, on a curve)

beats on the chest of a man
and a kg. of coal with a bang

rain bouncing on the clod
raising a hoof's cloud

like a deposit of long whips:
and the horses' hooves trip

heavy blows to the head,
beat hard on the spread,

among the madman's thick lashes
pain slowly flushes

The theme is the effort to insert into a closed language a disintegrating reality. The use of rhyme serves as a bond or rhythmical bridge between images that emerge as though in a game of Chinese boxes. The sequence of images is dictated both by sound and analogy. The latter simply has a discursive function here, elaborating the theme; all

l'unghia che scopre il cervello
dal fondo tenero per un secchiello

verdognolo, colmo di sabbia bagnata
da farci sopra una rabbiosa pisciata.

2   L'alto pilone, o torre, piegato sfilaccia
le giunture, polvere e ferro, schiaccia

gli aurei fili, un tram; impedisce
il volo dei piccioni, contorta marcisce

la carcassa, le formiche sono all'opera,
le mosche scavano con la zampa e l'acido opera

in profonda erosione. Il vasellame polverizzato
fa montagna, come in un puzzolente mercato

i rosi dai topi oggetti rivenduti.

---

non hanno niente da vedere con il procedimento ermetico. Il titolo, in confronto al contesto, indica un'ascesi inversa, una pura volontà di guardare il « male ». Dietro il discorso dilatato e distruttivo sta il senso del nostro vivere.

Il metro e la rima hanno qui valore preponderante, quasi di ordine

from the nail that reveals the brain
with a bottom too soft for a stained

bucket, with wet sand from the abyss
over which to take a mean piss.

2   The high pylon, o tower, bent frays
     the joints, dust and steel, splays

     the golden threads, a tram; clots
     the pigeons' flight, contorts rots

     the carcass, the ants are at the opera,
     the flies dig their feet and acid operates

     in deep erosion. The pulverized dinnerware
     makes mountains, as in a foul open-air

     market the gnawing of rats resold objects.

---

these have nothing to do with the hermeticist process. The title, in
relation to context, shows an inverse ascesis, a pure will to look squarely
at "evil." Behind the expanded and destructive discourse lies the mean-
ing of our life.

Meter and rhyme take on the greatest value here, as though part of

3   La carne si conserva in scatola.
     Filacciosa galleggia nella scatola

     e i polipi che sfaldano il coltello
     ruotano con misura in un macello

     ristretto, rigurgito ribollente,
     a pezzi si incagliano nel dente.

     D'olio l'indice si unge
     urta la latta si punge:

     la carne marcisce in scatola,
     vomito spalmato da una spatola

     contro uno stomaco insanguinato.

---

misurato a racchiudere lo sfacelo, a fissare impavidamente la materia
che marcisce. C'è come uno scontro tra questi elementi formali e il
contenuto, col risultato di suscitare un'impressione di visione allucinata,
di follia articolata e circoscritta.

3 Meat is conserved in a tin.
   Stringy meat floats in the tin

   and the knife the octopi trite
   rotate precisely in a tight

   slaughterhouse, boiling backwash,
   stuck on the teeth like goulash.

   With oil the index is greased
   bashed the can is creased:

   the meat rots in the tin,
   vomit with a shovel thinned

   across a bloody stomach.

---

some moderate order able to contain the decay, keep together the rotting material. There is a clash of sorts between these formal elements and the content, suggesting a hallucinatory vision, an articulate, restrained madness.

LA PALPEBRA ROVESCIATA

I

Il naso sfalda per divenire saliva e il labbro
alzandosi sopra i denti liquefa la sua curva masticata
assieme alle radici spugnose mordenti sulla guancia
la ragnatela venosa: nel tendersi incrina la mascella,
lo zigomo s'impunta e preme con la forza dell'occhio
contratto nell'orbita dal nervo fino in gola
percorsa nel groviglio delle voci dal battito incessante.

2

Il succo dalle radici striscia lentamente sù per le vene,
raggiungendo le foglie fa agitare. Con la scorza che ingrossa
cresce la polpa del legno, dilata la fibra succosa
e gli anelli che annerano e irrigiditi incrinano e un taglio
netto guizza sul tronco maturo come colpito da una scure.

Il titolo indica uno sguardo che fissa, stravolto, la realtà. La poesia è
stata suggerita da certe soluzioni materiche di opere informali. La
progressione delle immagini sembra seguire un *itinerario* simbolico
preciso: il cancro che corrode la tela della vita. La prima strofa sul
volto e la gola, l'albero della seconda, i bruchi della terza e le tende in

THE EYELID INSIDEOUT

1

The nose flakes to become saliva and the lip
lifting above the teeth chewed its liquified curve
together with the spongy roots bitten the poisonous
web on the cheek: in stretching the jaw-bone cracks,
the cheek-bone sticks and presses with the strength of the eye
contracted in the socket by a nerve all the way in the throat
overrun in the tangle of voices from the incessant throbbing.

2

The juice from the roots creeps slowly up the veins,
reaches the leaves it stirs. With the bark thickening
the wood pulp grows, the sappy fiber expands
and the rings that blacken and hardened crack and a clean
cut springs through the mature trunk as if struck by an ax.

The title indicates a troubled gaze fixed on reality. The poem was sug-
gested by certain ways action painting handles its medium. The pro-
gression of images seems to follow a precise symbolic *itinerary*: the
cancer eating away the canvas of life. The face and throat of the first
stanza, the tree of the second, the caterpillers of the third and the tents

3

I bruchi attaccano le foglie, i bruchi urtano col muso,
masticano l'orlo vegetale, mordono le vene dure
e lo scheletro resiste. Sbavano il tronco, deviano, nella ricerca,
scricchiola la fibra meno tenera e ingurgitano il verde,
        [l'argento,
inarcano le schiene bianche, l'occhio fisso nell'incavo:
fan piombare gli escrementi giù dal ramo, sazi, si gonfiano,
riposano sullo scheletro sgusciato, distesi sul vuoto masticato.

4

Le fibre della tela distesa lungo i vetri fermi sul viale
rigato da molecole di nafta lentamente calano
e inguainano il ferro e il legno, roteano nel soffio caldo dell'aria,
gonfiano la molle superficie, graffia e lacera la trama,
i fili si torcono e il foro si spalanca. Nello squarcio
condensa viscido molecolare, aderisce la vetrata al cancro
        [della tela.

---

una stanza dell'ultima: sono temi dello sguardo che unifica,
volontariamente o involontariamente, i fenomeni.
Il verso ha cinque accenti che formano una curva di penetrazione
minuziosa. La trama dello sguardo lento e preciso si dilata
progressivamente.

3

The caterpillars attack leaves, caterpillars push with snouts,
chew the vegetal border, chomp on the hard veins
and the skeleton resists. They slobber the trunk, veer, in
        [search,
less tender fibers creak and they gulp down the green, the
        [silver,
they arch their white backs, the fixed eye in the hole:
they let the excrements fall from the branch, full, they swell,
rest on the shelled skeleton, stretched out on the chewed
        [emptiness.

4

The fibers of canvas stretched along the still windows on the
        [street
streaked with molecules of naphtha slowly droop
and they sheathe the wood and steel, rotate in hot puffs of air,
swell the soft surfaces, the plot scratches and cuts,
the wires twist and the hole opens wide. In the rent
molecular slime condenses, glass wall sticks to the canvas'
        [cancer.

---

of the final stanza: these are themes of the gaze that unifies phenom-
ena, voluntarily or involuntarily.
The line has five stresses that chart a carefully penetrating curve. The
plotting of this slow, precise gaze progressively expands.

DIALOGO CON HERZ

« Fui preso dal terrore divenendo lepre,
e accettare, poi, entrò nelle abitudini. »
« Fosse vero potrei uccidermi. » « Qual è
il destino delle lepri? » « La morte semplice. »
« Mi possedeva una paura rivoltante, squittivo,
di notte, e brucavo le foglie, di cavolo
e di tabacco. D'inverno consumai le riserve. »
« Non voglio divenire lepre, ma uccello
e impigliarmi tra le spine. » « La lepre muore
di freddo, di fame, di vecchiaia o fucilata.
Basta agli uccelli, spesso, un forte
vento notturno, tramontana tra le anitre
congelate. » « Herz, disse sulla terrazza,
verremo risucchiati da una grondaia in un giorno
di pioggia, emblema di violenze. »

« Desideravo da tempo essere assorbito
dagli alberi: divenire uccello e in mezzo
al fogliame estivo scoprire un cunicolo,

È un vero dialogo tra due amici; alcuni luoghi (l'albero, la terrazza, il ciclista) si richiamano a una cronaca precisa. La poesia sonda il significato della realtà: il destino umano e quello animale sono congiunti, ma l'uomo tenta di valicare la condizione di natura, il regno dell'arbitrio, e in questa ricerca ha un attimo di speranza e di felicità. Il dialogo è percorso dal senso della fragilità, dell'impotenza e della miseria, cui però supplisce l'amore intellettuale.

DIALOGUE WITH HERZ

"I was terrorstruck becoming a rabbit,
and accepting, then, was a matter of habit."
"If it were true I might kill myself." "What's
the fate of rabbits?" "Simple death."
"A disgusting fear had hold of me, I squealed
in the night, and chewed on leaves, of cabbage
and tobacco. That winter I used up the reserves."
"I don't want to become a rabbit, but a bird
and get caught in the thorns." "The rabbit dies
of cold, hunger, old age or shot down.
Often, for birds, a strong night wind
is enough, a northern blow among the frozen
ducks." "Herz, he said on the terrace,
we're going to be sucked down a drain on a rainy
day, an emblem of fury."

"For a while now I've wanted to meld
with the trees: to become a bird and in
the summer foliage find a tunnel,

This is a true dialogue between friends; some places (the tree, the terrace, the cyclist) refer to an exact chronicle. The poem plumbs the meaning of reality: human destiny and animal destiny are conjoined, but man attempts to overcome the condition of nature, the realm of chance, and in this quest enjoys a moment of hope and happiness. The dialogue is pervaded by a sense of frailty, impotence, and wretchedness that is, however, compensated by intellectual love.

giungere al fondamento. » « Toccare le radici
e assaggiare le sostanze minerali. » « La vecchia
abbaia, hai detto, e lo scemo ha battuto
la ruota contro il muro. Stizzito solleva
la maschera dall'asfalto, ricade nell'incertezza
di un universo in furioso divenire. »
« Mi è impedita la chiarezza. Mi insinuo lateralmente.
Scivolo nuotando tra alghe pericolose.
Penetro in una fogna. Affondo
in fitte vegetazioni, mi riempio
di formiche e di foglie. Mastico piume,
è quasi la conoscenza: la luce
del giorno tra le fessure e la polvere
si solleva in un formicolìo di protezione
e di salvezza. »

Per i capelli ci afferra il vento, è vero,
dietro la nuvola si arresta un cielo specchiante:
nell'ombra maculata fu raggiunto dalla voce di Herz.
La sera, in terrazza, continuarono, felici:
« Avrà mai fine l'arbitrio del giorno e della notte? »

Herz significa *cuore*, naturalmente, richiama le onde omonime. Questo
nome, con le implicazioni suggestive che comporta, contribuisce a
quella amplificazione del reale che è in sostanza il tema della poesia.
L'ultimo verso è una contaminazione da Novalis: « Bisogna sempre
che torni il mattino? / Non ha fine l'arbitrio terrestre? » (trad. Poggioli).

reach the ground." "To touch the roots
and taste the nourishing substances." "The old hag
barks, you said, and the idiot has crashed
the wheel into the wall. Irritated he takes
the mask off the pavement and again tumbles into the
     [uncertainty
of a universe in furious becoming."
"I'm kept from clarity. I slide sideways.
I slip swimming through dangerous seaweed.
I push through a sewer, I sink
in thick vegetation, I fill up
with ants and leaves. I chew feathers,
it's almost like knowing: the light
of day through crevices and dust
rises in a swarm of protection
and salvation."

The wind grabs us by the hair, it's true,
a flashing sky hangs behind the cloud:
in the dappled shadow Herz' voice found him.
Evening, on the terrace, they will go on, happy:
"Will the abuse of night and day ever end?"

Herz means *heart* and also, of course, recalls the waves of the same
name. This name, with the implications it bears, contributes to that
amplification of the real that is the essential theme of the poem. The
last line is a corruption of Novalis: "Must morning always return? Is
there no end to earthly power?" [*translator's note: arbitrio* in Poggioli's
translation, but the lines— actually prose, from part 2 of the *"Hymnen
an die Nacht,"* though there are line breaks here— read "Muß immer
der Morgen wiederkommen? Endet nie des Irdischen Gewalt?"]

IN RE

Lo sguardo allo specchio scruta l'inesistenza.
I peli del sopracciglio moltiplicano in labirinto,
l'occhio nel vetro riflette l'assenza,
nel folto i capelli, temporanea parrucca,
sgomentano le mani: cadono sulle guance.

L'inquietudine prolungata mette in evidenza
il mortale infinito dei pori dilatati,
l'estrema avventura di un oggetto che si trucca,
sceglie una direzione inconsapevole o folle.

Dietro il lavabo il corpo in oscillazione
sfugge l'abbaglio, rivoltante presenza
indicatrice e lampante. Nella camera a vuoto
tra le piume mulina la soffocazione.

IN RE

The look at the mirror searches nonexistence.
The eyebrow's hairs multiply in a labyrinth,
the eye in glass mirrors absence,
in the thick of it the hair, temporary wig,
appalls the hands: they fall on cheeks.

The prolonged uneasiness is evidence
of the mortal infinity of dilated pores,
the extreme adventure of made-up object,
picks a direction ignorant or foolish.

Behind the washbasin the swinging body
flees the dazzle, revolting presence
indicative and clear. In the nothing room
among the feathers the choking twirls.

APRIRE

Dietro la porta nulla, dietro la tenda,
l'impronta impressa sulla parete, sotto,
l'auto, la finestra, si ferma, dietro la tenda,
un vento che la scuote, sul soffitto nero
una macchia più scura, impronta della mano,
alzandosi si è appoggiato, nulla, premendo,
un fazzoletto di seta, il lampadario oscilla,
un nodo, la luce, macchia d'inchiostro,
sul pavimento, sopra la tenda, la paglietta che raschia,
sul pavimento gocce di sudore, alzandosi,
la macchia non scompare, dietro la tenda,
la seta nera del fazzoletto, luccica sul soffitto,
la mano si appoggia, il fuoco della mano,
sulla poltrona un nodo di seta, luccica,
ferita dal chiodo, il sangue sulla parete,
la seta del fazzoletto agita una mano.

Le calze infila, nere, e sfila, con i denti,
la spaccata, il doppio salto, in un istante, la calza maglia,
all'indietro, capriola, poi la spaccata, i seni
premono il pavimento, dietro i capelli, dietro la porta,

È il racconto incalzante di varie « aperture » sulla realtà: un delitto
(ventre lacerato, calze sporche di sangue), una vetrata spezzata, un
muro sbrecciato, una porta che si apre o non si apre.
Il ritmo, scandito da quattro accenti, è al tempo stesso largo e ossessivo:

TO OPEN

Nothing behind the door, behind the curtain,
the fingerprint stuck on the wall, under it,
the car, the window, it stops, behind the curtain,
a wind that shakes it, a more obscure
stain on the black ceiling, a handprint,
he leaned on rising, nothing, pressing,
a silk handkerchief, the lamp swings,
a knot, the light, ink-spot,
on the floor, above the curtain, the scouring pad,
on the floor drops of sweat, rising,
the stain won't rub out, behind the curtain,
the black silk of the handkerchief, shines on the ceiling,
the hand comes to rest, the fire in the hand,
a silk knot on the armchair, it shines,
wounded, now the blood on the wall,
the handkerchief's silk waves a hand.

She slips on the stockings, black, and slips them off, with her
    [teeth,
the splits, the double-somersault, in an instant, the tights,
backwards, caper, then the splits, the breasts
press on the floor, behind the hair, behind the door,

Here we have a pressing narrative of various "openings" onto reality:
a crime (a belly slit open, blood-stained stockings), a broken window,
a wall chipped away at, a door that may or may not open.
The rhythm, with its four stresses, is at once stately and obsessive: the

non c'è, c'è il salto all'indietro, le cuciture,
l'impronta della mano, all'indietro, sul soffitto,
la ruota, delle gambe e delle braccia, di fianco,
dei seni, gli occhi, bianchi, contro il soffitto,
dietro la porta, calze di seta appese, la capriola.

Perché la tenda scuote, si è alzato dalla poltrona,
il vento, nello spiraglio la luce, il buio,
dietro la tenda c'è, la notte, il giorno,
nei canali le barche, in gruppo, i quieti canali,
navigano, cariche di sabbia, sotto i ponti,
è mattina, il ferro dei passi, remi e motori,
i passi sulla sabbia, il vento sulla sabbia,
le tende sollevano i lembi, perché è notte,
giorno di vento, di pioggia sul mare,
dietro la porta il mare, la tenda carica di sabbia,
le calze, di pioggia, appese, sporche di sangue.

La punta, la finestra alta, c'era vento,
si è alzato adagio, stride, in un istante,
ovale, un foro nella parete, con la mano,
in frantumi, l'ovale del vetro, sulle foglie,
è notte, mattina, fitta, densa,
di sabbia, di diamante, corre sulla spiaggia,
alzato e corso, la mano premuta, a lungo,

---

la monotona progressione delle virgole, insinuanti intervalli, carica di tensione la spinta iniziale alla ricerca dell'apertura; i singoli oggetti si presentano e ritornano, nell'iterazione degli attributi e dei genitivi oggettivi, come per un reciproco desiderio di contatto. La stanza, la

it's not there, there's the backward somersault, the seams,
the handprint, backwards, on the ceiling,
the wheel, of legs and arms, sideways,
of breasts, the eyes, white, against the ceiling,
behind the door, silk stockings hanging, the caper.

Because the curtain flutters, it rises,
the wind, the light in the fissure, the dark,
behind the curtain there is, the night, the day,
boats in the canals, in bunches, the smooth canals,
they sail, loaded with sand, under the bridges,
it's morning, the iron steps, oars and motors,
the steps on the sand, the wind on the sand,
the curtains float their edges, because it's night,
day of wind, of rain on the sea,
the sea behind the door, the curtain fills with sand,
with stockings, with rain, hanging, stained with blood.

The point, the high window, there was wind,
he got up slowly, screeches, in an instant,
oval, a hole in the wall, with the hand,
in shatters, the glass oval, on the leaves,
it's night, morning, crowded, dense, clear,
of sand, of diamond, he runs on the beach,
got up and running, the hand pressed, a long time

---

monotonous progression of commas, insinuating intervals, gives tension to the initial thrust to find an opening; the individual objects are presented and return, in the iteration of attributes and objective genitives, as though out of reciprocal desire for contact. The room,

fermo, contro il vetro, la fronte, sul,
il vetro sulla mattina, premette, densa,
la mano affonda; nella terra, nel vetro, nel ventre,
la fronte di vetro, nubi di sabbia,
nella tenda, ventre lacerato, dietro la porta.

Ruota delle gambe, la tela sbatte nel vento,
quell'uomo, le gambe aderiscono alla corsa,
la corda si flette, verso il molo, sulla sabbia,
sopra le reti, asciugano, le scarpe di tela,
il molo di cemento, battono la corsa,
non c'è che mare, sempre più oscuro, il cemento,
nella tenda, sfilava le calze con i denti,
la punta, ha premuto un istante, a lungo,
le calze distese sull'acqua, sul ventre.

Di là, stringe la maniglia, verso,
non c'è, né certezza, né uscita, sulla parete,
l'orecchio, poi aprire, un'incerta, non si apre,
risposta, le chiavi tra le dita, il ventre aperto,
la mano sul ventre, trema sulle foglie,
di corsa, sulla sabbia, punta della lama,
il figlio, sotto la scrivania, dorme nella stanza.

---

tenda su una parete, il soffitto dipinto di nero, il fazzoletto, l'episodio
di una danza e di uno strip-tease, il molo, la spiaggia, la pioggia sul
mare: tutti questi elementi si « aprono » oscuramente in una reciproca
vicenda che sbocca nell'apertura della fine. Il figlio che dorme sotto la
scrivania attende una risposta alla domanda: che cosa riusciremo a
trovare?

motionless, against the window, the forehead, upon,
the glass upon the morning, he pressed, obscure,
the hand sinks deep, in the earth, in the glass, in the belly,
the forehead of glass, clouds of sand,
in the curtain, lacerated belly, behind the door.

Wheel of legs, the canvas slaps in the wind,
tha man, his legs follow the course,
the rope coils, toward the breakwater, on the sand,
on the nets, drying, the cloth shoes,
the cement breakwater, they break into a run
there's nothing but sea, always darker, the cement,
in the curtain, slipped off the stockings with her teeth,
the point, has compressed an instant, a long time,
stockings stretched out on the water, on the belly.

Over there, he squeezes the knob, towards,
there's none, neither certainty, nor exit, on the wall,
the ear, then to open, an uncertainty, doesn't open,
answer, the keys between the fingers, the belly open,
hand on the belly, trembles on the leaves,
rushing, across the sand, the point of the blade,
the son, under the desk, sleeps in the room.

---

the curtain on a wall, the black-painted ceiling, the handkerchief, the
episode of a dance and a striptease, the pier, the beach, the rain on the
ocean: all these elements "open" obscurely into a reciprocity that cul-
minates in the ending's opening. The son sleeping under the desk waits
for an answer to the question: what will we come up with?

Il corpo sullo scoglio, l'occhio cieco, il sole,
il muro, dormiva, il capo sul libro, la notte sul mare,
dietro la finestra gli uccelli, il sole nella tenda,
l'occhio più scuro, il taglio nel ventre, sotto l'impronta,
dietro la tenda, la fine, aprire, nel muro,
un foro, ventre disseccato, la porta chiusa,
la porta si apre, si chiude, ventre premuto,
che apre, muro, notte, porta.

The body on the rock, the blind eye, the sun,
the wall, was sleeping, head on the book, the night on the sea,
behind the window the birds, the sun in the curtain,
the eye even darker, the cut in the belly, under the fingerprint,
behind the curtain, the end, to open, in the wall,
a hole, belly dissected, the door shut,
the door opens, it shuts, belly compressed,
that opens, wall, night, door.

Antonio Porta

For the last two or three seemingly pivotal years, any writer who has set himself unusual goals in his verse-writing has found himself faced with several problems of various kinds, among them: the void opened up when the *fourth generation* sunk altogether as heirs of a Montale they misunderstood, attentive only to the surface of "social" events, unable to plunge into reality; the lack of a penetrating language, in the desert of flaccid forms; a declaration of general bewilderment arising from distress over the mass of new facts and impulses astir more or less everywhere, nurturing the germs of future developments: perhaps the most important being an awareness of the need to participate in the movements and upheavals of society (later we shall see *how*, but, in any case, it remains a healthy opposition to those piéces-de-résistance of the *I* that are forever being reheated and served up as first-rate dishes while in reality one instinctively refuses them): a general distrust in literature, which is isolated and unheard, and distrust in the writer's very tasks, to which the bankruptcy of *neorealism* contributed. These tasks, in fact, must be reexamined so that people may realize, with less insistence on immediate results, how complex and demanding they are, and how extraneous to political practice.

It is essential, then, to add more personal situations to the general picture, such as the lack of critical assistance, of free, disinterested contacts, and convergences necessary to the poetic enterprise; from this point a second sort of problem has taken hold, one which might be defined as a sort of 'solution,' limited to the small group of friends (in fact the only one that counts), who write in the way we approve of.

The negative basis to the problems of such a 'solution,' irrational in part, is the aversion to the *I-poet*, the one who tells us his life story. What happens to such a poet is, insofar as it happens to him, extremely interesting. He belongs to that troop of neo-Crepusculars who have themselves photographed in rather sharp profile against the background of emblematic rivers.

Don't suppose this is the normal aversion to fathers and love of grandfathers: the grandfathers inspire no more sympathy, which at most goes out only to very distant ancestors. Under irrational guises lies the adequate motive, the necessary cause: the lesson has been learned that making poetry requires other starting points, a different substance (without denying the importance of the promptings that come from personal reactions, which can sometimes be a vital question in the moment of getting down to writing, resolved by an indispensable awareness that obviously suggests choosing certain directions rather than others). One is, in short, made aware of the importance of the *external event*, which we feel affects the community and no longer only the figure of the isolated poet: it is there we are measured as human beings. It is useful to specify that one wishes, precisely, to define *images* of man or of mankind in general, of things and facts operating outside and inside existence.

This is how the *poetics of objects*, poetry *in re*, not *ante rem*, has been interpreted. The objects and events selected and composed into one rhythmic *unicum*—these do manage to plunge us into reality.

Naturally, we must note parenthetically, one never starts out with "poetry" as a deliberate aim. One assumes that "poetry" is found *after*, in verse possessing strength and density, authentic violence, torment or resentment towards the world of things.

The *poetics* of objects must again be directly linked with the problem of *the true* or of *truth*, in symbiosis with the quest for images and the need for penetration. Ultimately one wants to

379

find something. The things we plot and maneuver, or that plot and maneuver us, certainly bear a relation to the truth: and precisely to approach the truth we make use of *the true*, which we perceive in objects and in events. It is by this route that one can first sketch out our image and even perhaps intuit the truth. To make proper use of *the true* it is necessary to gather together a whole strand or line of discoveries, fleshing out one's findings in every possible direction, opening oneself to many points of view, rejecting the univocity of the neo-classical poet.

The events, objects, emblems of the true are, then, material to be worked in an almost artisanal fashion: almost, because in entering directly into the problems of expression, into linguistic investigations, one should emphasize the fact that, by unconditionally assuming accentual metrics, one does not confer on these problems the value merely of order or "measure." Accentual metrics are primarily a method of penetration. To vary the number of stresses is like varying the thickness and depth at which a drill works, to vary rhythm is like adjusting a wave-length, perceived as apt from a certain point of view.

This explains the choice of accentual metrics. Furthermore, it leaves a certain margin of freedom necessary to us, and functions as a tool of expression, mobile and penetrating, just as our investigations avoid approximations and phonic license, overly diffuse meaning. It also gives verse the vigor a drilling-tool needs, a vigor the common run of twentienth-century epigones have lost. In choosing three or four or five stresses for a poem, one is able to use various rhythmic means, which function on different levels, and excavating reality, discover the contemporary world.

In summing up this line of inquiry one must emphasize the need for *objective poets*, both in Eliot's sense of the term, and in the sense of a constant commitment to *others*—to a *heteronomous* art. Hence the creation of *characters*, of a protagonist who, moving among words, moves as we ideally do in the sphere of reality, as we see all people moving, if with varying degrees of awareness. How complex and contradictory, ambiguous and elusive these characters turn out depends on their mode of being: as faithful mirrors of a contemporary situation.

Thus they complicate language, and above all syntax, which is as it were the net that captures them, and thereby defines them, in the effort to adhere to truth—not some naive, needlessly feared dive into the sea of objectivity, but an articulation of knowledge, in our own *present moment*.

LANGUAGE AND OPPOSITION

Nanni Balestrini

One is sometimes given to notice with amazement, in the scle-
rotic, automatic abuse of hackneyed phrases and conventional
expressions that form the basis of common spoken language, a
sudden click of unexpected juxtapositions, of unusual rhythms,
of involuntary metaphors; or we are struck and startled by cer-
tain confusions, repetitions, broken or contorted phrases, ex-
cessive or inexact adjectives or images, whenever we hear them
floating on the surface of the anemic, amorphous language of
daily conversation: extraordinary apparitions that illuminate
facts and thoughts from odd angles.

The need to make immediate use of words actually leads to
an approximation, a too little or too much, of the original con-
tent of the communication—it even alters that communication,
forcing it along new directions. The necessity to submit to *time*
profoundly differentiates spoken from written language, which
presents the possibility of a deferred version, with changes, in-
tercalations, deletions. What is said, on the other hand, is said
for ever, and can be corrected only by further additions, that is,
through a continuation in time.

It is here that the idea of a poetry having a different genesis
and life originates. A poetry apparently less refined, less pol-
ished, neither enamel nor cameo. A poetry nearer to the ar-
ticulation of emotion and thought in language, a confused and
still fermenting expression, bearing the signs of its detachment
from the mental state, signs of a not quite achieved fusion with
the verbal state. The structures, still shaky, proliferate unpre-
dictably, in unexpected directions, far from the initial impulse—
a true adventure. And ultimately what gets transmitted by lan-

guage will no longer be thought and emotion, which have been the germ of the poetical operation, but language itself generating a new, unrepeatable meaning.

And the result of this adventure will be a new light on things, an opening amid the dark cobwebs of conformities and dogmas that relentlessly envelop what we are and where we live. It will be a possibility of effectively *opposing* the continual sedimentation that language's inertia abets.

All of which contributes to regarding language as the object of poetry, language understood as *verbal fact*, i.e. not used instrumentally, but assumed in its totality, escaping the accidentality that from time to time makes it reproduce optical images, narrate events, purvey concepts.... These aspects now occupy the same plane as all other properties of language, just as other properties—sonic, metaphoric, metric, etc.—tend to be regarded as pure pretext.

The fundamental attitude thus becomes one of getting poetry to "prod" words, to lay an ambush for them at the very moment they are bound up in sentences, to do violence to the structures of language, pushing all its properties to the breaking point. Such an attitude is meant to stimulate these properties, the intrinsic and extrinsic charges of language, and to provoke the unprecedented, baffling cruxes and encounters that can make poetry a true whip to the reader's brain, a brain that gropes through daily life immersed in commonplaces and repetition.

Poetry therefore as *opposition*. Opposition to the dogma and conformity that waylays us, that hardens the tracks behind us, that entangles our feet, seeking to halt our steps. Today more than ever this is the reason for writing poetry. Today, in fact, the wall we hurl our works against repels the crash it receives, gently, pliantly opens, not resisting blows—all the better to entrap and absorb them; often enough it actually keeps and annexes

383

them. So it is necessary to be much shrewder, suppler, more skillful, in certain cases more ruthless, and to keep in mind that a direct violence is utterly useless in an age that's laid slimy quicksand at our feet.

In an era so unprecedented, unpredictable and contradictory, poetry must more than ever be alert and profound, unobtrusive and mobile. It must not try to imprison, but rather to follow things, it must avoid becoming fossilized in dogmas, and must instead be ambiguous and absurd, open to many meanings and averse to conclusions, in order to reveal, by an extreme adherence, what is intangible and variable in life, and ultimately to provide an antidote to the spiritual atrophy by which we are incessantly besieged, in the attempt to separate us from that which is human.

SYNTAX AND GENRES

Elio Pagliarani

It is pointless to deny the equation lyric = poetry without reinventing the literary genres. And this has already been historically demonstrated: time and reality having been entrusted with breaking down a barrier, poetry broadens its contents, yet cannot do so without correspondingly broadening the poetic vocabulary. But to enrich the vocabulary does not necessarily mean enriching speech, it can even mean creating upheaval and confusion. No word has an unlimited capacity for adaptation (and the more that capacity exists, the more semantically debased the word becomes; every word has its precise syntactical problems, moves in its own *syntactic area*. And lexical expansion postulates a syntax of the sentence, not only of the single phrase. The various syntactic solutions impress speech with different tension, duration, rhythm: this tonal designation and structural specification belong by definition to the literary genres. The reinvention of genres is thus the necessary consequence of the fullest and most varied syntactic modulation of poetic speech following its lexical enrichment.

The equation lyric = poetry (the part for the whole) has, among its most specious corollaries, the identification of the *kind* of lyric with the *genre* of lyric, where the first term, however, qualifies the genre as a psychological category, the bearer of determined contents of the poetic work (dramatic, epic, lyric, didactic, etc.) and the second qualifies the genre as the bearer of stylistic traditions (sonnet, ode, longer poem, etc.)— the distinction implying, among other things, the positive nature of rhetorics. Now, the *genres* of the longer poem, the *kind* of didactic and narrative poetry, are the very instruments certain poets have been using quite deliberately in recent years to transfer into poetic discourse the present contradictions in the language of class. They use a plurilinguistic lexical material (just as the *genre* "chapter," or "art prose," was the instrument, between the two world wars, of the inverse operation, for 'impoverishing' and rarefying prose itself).

Obviously plurilinguistic experimentation has monolinguistic expression as its intrinsic teleology; but with our literary tradition it will take time to "rinse our linen in the Arno"! [trans. note: Manzoni's metaphor for Tuscanizing his own language] time which can be put to good use if we also pursue Eliot's remark about the social force poetry acquires when it is given theatrical form (a force that breaks through the audience's stratifications). But perhaps the only way to speed things up is for there to be an objective necessity for writing tragedies.... I would say we now have the requisite tools for the *genre* of the "verse drama."

"ACTION" POETRY?

Edoardo Sanguineti

I was not the person who schemed up the notion my title doubtfully suggests: on the contrary, it was actually proposed by various parties, and with a different intention, in relation to my *Opus metricum*. Vivaldi, for instance, has described my work as a "philological *collage*," automatic in its application of terms and stylistic tones, creating an *"action poetry,"* if we may speak of poetry using terms borrowed from art criticism, and he goes on to say: "moving beyond the facile, all too convenient schema of 'experimentalism' to describe Sanguineti's work to date, the most apt definition would seem to be precisely that of *action poetry*, that is, poetry motivated and justified by its own "making," by its conveying to the reader the processes and operations the poet has used in writing, thus implicitly criticizing them." Leonetti, on the other hand, in one of his *semantic analyses*, limits his approval to the "useful and vital" character of the segment of my work represented by *Erotopaegnia*. His approval becomes dubious given his earlier charges (against *Laborintus*), a work which he "certifies as being 'abstract expressionism': it is unlikely," Leonetti adds, "that he will give it up." These two positions already, objectively, mark the furthest limits of the question, the horizon upon which move both Vivaldi's concerns about a suspected on-going betrayal on my part of the poetics of *action poetry*, and Leonetti's concerns about my improbable, definitive uprooting from such an aesthetic position (or one very close to it). I apologize to the reader if terms like abstract expressionism and action painting will be used here, not to say interchangeably, but, as it were, "in brackets"; they are and should be "bracketed" in view of the rigorous, technically proper use they are put to in art criticism).

This is not the place for me to discuss the methodological problem which this notion, in and of itself, raises in general. I shall only say that if, in composing *Laborintus*, I made intentional references to certain technico-expressive situations in other arts (music no less than painting), and notably to the situation of abstract expressionism, this was due, if for no other reason, to the mere fact that it was considerably harder to refer to contemporary poetical examples in the years 1951-54. A crisis of language, such as I perceived myself to be defining and enacting in my verses, found comfort and analogy in related pictorial (and musical) experiments much more than in literary experiments: the private reference to other artistic situations was a way of breaking, in solitude, the very solitude of the poetics in which I found myself virtually cast.

And what helps me in that language crisis I've defined and enacted is Zanzotto's quip, when he said my *Laborintus* would be worthy of punishment, were it not for "the earnest transcription of a nervous breakdown." My response to this would be that, yes, *Laborintus* was redeemed in that regard, but with one signficant correction: namely, that the so-called "nervous breakdown" I 'earnestly' tried to transcribe was an objective historical "breakdown." With a good bit of arrogance, I might avail myself, without a single modification this time, of the memorable words of Tristan [trans. note: the Tristan of Leopardi's "Dialogue Between Tristan and a Friend," Cecchetti's translation]:

Now I've changed my mind. But when I wrote that book, I had this foolish idea in my head, as I told you. And I was so convinced that I would have expected anything but to see someone else doubt my observation on the subject, for I thought the conscience of each reader would quickly attest to their veracity. I only imagined that the usefulness or the harmfulness of such observations might be questioned, never their truthfulness. As a matter of fact, I thought that since the ills of life are common to all, my grieving words would echo in the heart of everyone who would listen to them.

Because when there is talk in *Laborintus* of "alienation," in the strict sense, both the obvious clinical meaning (the "breakdown," deliberately aggravated and provocatively emphasized) and the otherwise also technical meaning of "Verfremdung," comprising in turn both the sociologically diagnostic sense of the Marxian concept ("Veräusserung"), and the derivatively aesthetical one ("estrangement"), of Brechtian provenance (and adapted admirably by Adorno, among others). The language crisis, as a critical crisis (as language criticism) was meant to express, as a poetics (and it is obviously not my job to discuss the result), an "objective" state of alienation. Insofar as it was experienced directly, and, indeed, 'earnestly,' this alienation was meanwhile, far from being repressed, "subjectively" metamorphosed into a "breakdown," offering the richest possibilities for reflection. The estrangement was meant, and I think had to be experienced primarily as estrangement not from poetry (even if this was obviously the necessary risk: yet a common one for a good many other much more cautiously founded positions on poetics), but from *one particular*, historically concrete poetry, from a literary poetics, *one particular* idea of lyric poetry. In presenting itself polemically as dissenting from poetry understood in absolute terms, this other poetry documents and reflects the estrangement posited *in re*, *a parte subjecti*, and *a parte objecti*, in the historical dialectic. These superstructural effects which the crisis of *one particular* given language has demonstrated in the other arts, as a sort of crisis of language, were for me to be found in comparing *one particular* poetical language (or better, a plurality of historically available languages), in the hope, as I stated on another occasion, of "turning the avant-garde into museum art": an expression, I must admit, somewhat more evocative than clear. For me this was a matter of superseding the avant-garde's formalism and irrationalism (and finally the avant-garde itself, in its ideological implications), not by a repression, but by formalism and irrationalism itself, heightening their contradictions to a practically unprecedented degree, turning their meanings around, working on their very own anarchist postulates, but carrying them to a degree of subversive historical consciousness. *Laborintus* was thus the description of an estrangement endured with a consciousness of estrangement, indeed with a willfully inoculated consciousness, if such a thing can be, in particularly massive doses, for analytical-experimental purposes: pathetic and pathological were terms that operated in conscious, strict mutual conjunction that, to say the least, was well aware of the etymological link between the pathetic and the pathological. I am speaking, moreover, of an historical etymon, not a mere philological one: speaking in the radical (structural) sense of historical materialism.

It seems clear to me then that, since we can now begin to see that anyone in the 1950s who sought to fling himself with a happy optimism onto a "constructive" terrain, refusing the ways of action poetry, (or, more exactly, lest we forego that marvelous "junctura," of abstract expressionism), was bound to mistake (and this really did happen) the regression toward decadentism as a "progressive" solution, passing *à rebours* over the "free" terrain of the European avant-garde. As if the real issue, in terms of open historical dialectic, were not, as in reality, of crossing beyond the avant-garde, but rather of shrinking back further behind it, plunging into that acritical formalism for which people have meanwhile demonstrated the most virtuosic verbal horror (and this happened all the more painfully as that formalism was suffered unconsciously), to find oneself later, at the end of this splendid journey, only dashed once more against the inevitable rock of irrationalism. To turn the avant-garde into museum art meant (on the level, of course, of intentional poetics, since this is what we are necessarily talking about), recognizing the error of regression; it meant suddenly throwing oneself head first into the labyrinth of formalism and irrationalism, the Palus Putredinis of anarchism and alienation, with the hope I refuse to consider illusory of eventually getting out of it once and for all, if with sullied hands, yet ultimately with even the mire truly left behind. To this end the strict poetics of *action poetry* was destined to be abandoned, beyond *Laborintus*, while the fine mud stains remain—and no doubt will remain—on our sullied hands. This is not a matter just of an insuperable margin of alienation that remains for us to suffer (which one cannot hope idealistically to elude by the noble paths of Reason). It is this, but also something more. It is an awareness of the fact that, for us, today, there is no such thing as the purely pathetic, only the pathologically estranged pathetic: that innocence is not possible: that form never arises except when it issues from the formless, and on this formless horizon, whether we like it or not, there is ours.

Edoardo Sanguineti

I. "The novel, having reached its culmination, is returning to its origins and revealing its original nature": that is, its mythical nature. These, as is well known, are Kerényi's words, in a letter to Thomas Mann of 1934[1]: and we would like to adopt them here as a starting premise. At the moment we are scarcely interested in the simple suggestion of so fixed a conceptual connection. It can be integrated, in any case, with Mann's later caution to Kerényi, in 1941: "Psychology is the means to wrest myth from the Fascist obscurantists and 'transfunction' into humanity"[2]: whereupon we would like immediately to avoid all the ambiguity which may already surround our chosen title—for example, after a book like Barthes' *Mythologies*[3]. Here, however, we do not intend to follow a psychological direction. Nor do we wish really to discuss Kerényi's thesis, or Mann's, or those of Barthes, or the very horizon, vast as it is, inscribed between boundaries so symbolically determined. In the opening statement it would be necessary immediately to correct, or so it seems, the notion of "culmination," which is so precarious in historical usage, if it is understood, as it seems to be in this case, in an objective sense: this may be a matter, by way of hypothesis, of a "culmination," if you will, of consciousness, of a recovery of that awareness of an "original nature" (of poetry proper, we must add immediately, no less than that of novelistic creation), in turn decipherable (much more adequately than in the sense of Jung's archetypes—or, perchance, of Heidegger's

1. *Romanzo e mitologia*, Milano, 1960, p. 32.
2. *Op. cit., p.* 83.
3. Paris, 1957.

"essential essence," precisely of the *Wesen der Dichtung*) in the sense of Vico's fourteenth axiom ("the nature of things is none other than their birth in certain times and under certain aspects...").

But as for the Barthes of *"Le mythe aujourd'hui,"* let us say that his pages serve much better as an attempt (apparently unconscious) at an aesthetic foundation than as a definition of the tasks of a mythologist in contemporary society: again the admirable contact provoked (restored) between *mythe* and *exemple* would suffice, in whose contact we gain, to take Barthes' text at its word, a crucial characterization of the "producteur de mythe." It is known, however, that for Barthes, the *exemple* of the "producteur de mythe" is, then, mythically, the "rédacteur de presse" (operating, in Barthes' myth, anonymously, "chez le coiffeur," through—I take the exemplary example—of "un numéro de *Paris-Match"*) but one is immediately tempted to ask: why this rather than, say, Goethe in the library, through a book on *Dichtung und Wahrheit?* As anyone can see, though, Goethe would hardly tolerate the radical epithet of "cynique."

Still, if one were to concede for a moment the legitimacy of such a substitution of persons: we would like to try ourselves to repeat the gesture in parallel and proportionate fashion, and thus to translate. The one who, as mythologist, assumes the *démystifiante* function ("en démasquant l'intention du mythe") is simply the historian (on the 'exemplary' side of our schema, obviously, in the guise of a literary critic). Whence, rightly, "il déchiffre le mythe." But Barthes, for his part, adds, "il comprend une déformation," since as we know, for Barthes mythology can be understood only as mystification and, by extension, the understanding of it can be concretized only as an intelligence and a pointing out of the deformation that occurs. In the terms of a Della Volpe, more simply perhaps, this would mean participating in an adequate passage by way of paraphrase from the organic contextual level to the omnitextual level (critical paraphrasis of multiple meaning as explication of the act of taste).[4] Or again (and this is Barthes the mythologist's third point) one should note: the one who responds to the myth's constitutive mechanism (who submits to that mechanism), to its dynamic, is "le lecteur du mythe," who reads the myth as a story at once true and unreal.[5]

The greatness of Barthes the demystifier resides, among other things, in his own mystification: assailing art (for in fact it is art that he assails) as a symbolic-exemplary construction, under the species of myth, he actually reestablishes the equation of poetry and mythology in the negative. It is Ermione, in other words, who falls into the category assigned to the photographic image of "Paris-Match": but that category is the same as the one operative, to say the least, in the mythopoesis of Felicita. And the divergence may be seen by critical (historical)[6] paraphrase, not by a categorical route. Obviously Barthes, who is concerned with myth *aujourd'hui*, transforms into negative ones those categories that are the simple operative (formative) symbolic schemas: obviously, confronted with the ridiculous, monstrous repertoire of a certain bourgeois (bourgeois-fascist) mythology with which we are all familiar (and which the French mythologist deciphers admirably), he could only conceive of mythical formativity as a form of de-formation. And the confusion between particular historical phenomenology and the generally operative determination implies, to cite somewhat at random two consequences: the optimistic positive (and once more categorical) interpretation of contemporary poetical language as resistant (albeit with difficulty) to the myth (but also, in

4. *Critica del gusto*, Milano, 1960, pp. 112–122.
5. *Mythologies*, Paris, 1957, pp. 235–236.
6. I must refer to my *Da D'Annunzio a Gozzano*, in "Lettere Italiane," January – March 1959.

Barthes' view, resistant with consistency, insofar as it tends to an essential silence), and the interpretation, truly mythological (and fortunately so) of the socialist revolution as the destruction, not of a qualified bourgeois (-fascist) mythology, but *a priori* and universally, of myth as such. Thus Barthes is forced to align himself (albeit unconsciously), in the way we have just described, among the theorists of the imminent death of art.

II. The mythopoeic character of the work of art (poesis = mythopoesis) explains the dialectical autonomy of the mythological superstructure (i.e., quite simply, the fact that it can be thought of as a historical continuum, at least within the horizon of a given and structurally founded periodization) as the dialectical autonomy of an operative (formative) system of symbolic *exempla*; that is (Barthes again suggests) as the positing of a (determined) *sign* as *signifier* (of some ulterior, undetermined *signified*), as SIGN ("un système sémiologique second"). This mythical mystification (but mythic for us in a neutral sense), precisely that of art, is achieved according to a multiplicity of techniques in whose historical phenomenology one can already detect a particular tendency of the superstructure, that is, an impulse (structurally given and conditioned) that only a metahistorical illusion (this being truly mystifying, in the proper sense of the term) can hope to fix and specify outside of an articulated dialectical system. The mystificatory intentionality (symbolic-exemplary) operates, historically, within determinate instrumental (linguistic) horizons, or better yet, evolves out of such horizons, tending always to be fixed (in relation to stabilizing structural impulses, whereby technical fixation reflects sociological fixation) in a tradition, perpetually susceptible (in keeping with the basic impulsive motion) to becoming crystallized more or less rigidly, or to be enriched in various ways, or metamorphosed and perhaps ultimately dispersed, or finally to die. From this point of view an aesthetic tradition is, like any other cultural tradition, the reflection of a movement (even, hypothetically, a revolutionary one) in the economic structure, and is defined as the *surviving* result (insofar as it actually has been transmitted as identical) of the dialectical components in question, in a circle sociologically definable (since structurally definable) as homogeneous.

It seems equally clear to us that the mystifying intentionality, in its historical superstructural concreteness, should articulate its own instruments and operative techniques in relation to the possibilities of semic and symbolic (i.e. SEMIC) communication, of communication, that is, of mythical (and non-mythic) languages presented socially, synchronically, and more or less separately, by the different classes. All this because the technical horizons are always plural in terms of the plurality of the classes and the circles sociologically definable as homogeneous, with such plurality manifesting or concealing itself (in myth too) in terms of concrete social relationships and the actual dialectical possibilities established among and within the classes, and in terms of the evolution of such relationships and possibilities.

What is said here of mythical techniques in general still holds true in particular for all the specific aspects of the linguistic systems in each manifestation: namely, to grasp quickly an extremely familiar dichotomy, as the history of forms and the history of contents. The technico-instrumental tradition (that is, of forms that immediately present themselves as "poetic," i.e., as mythopoeic: for example, the sonnet or the polyptych) and the symbolic-imaginative tradition (i.e., of contents that immediately present themselves as "poetic," i.e. as mythopoeic: for example, the legend of Oedipus or the Annunciation), continually suggest formal genres and imaginative categories (rules and models), which are presented, to the producer and consumer

396

alike of *exempla*, as intrinsic guarantees of a mythological mystification, and determine a more or less characterized sociological ritual. With this in mind let us try to reread Manzoni's letter *On Romanticism* (1823):

This system of imitation [...] based upon the *a priori* supposition that the classics discovered all genres of invention, and each type within them, exists from the time of the revival of letters; it has never perhaps been elaborated in a perfect theory, yet it has been, and still is, applied in a thousand cases, implied in a thousand decisions, and scattered through all of literature. And without such means, would it otherwise ever have occurred to modern poets, for example, to represent shepherds, in the conditions and guises found in the eclogues, or in compositions of a similar kind, from Sannazaro to Manara, if, before the former, or after the latter, there had not been other bucolic poets, whom I have either not known or forgotten? And since, from blind and crudely literal imitation one easily slips into caricature, it happened, one fine morning, that all the poets of Italy, by which I mean those who had composed either many or few Italian verses, transformed themselves (ideally, that is) into so many shepherds, inhabiting a region of the Peloponnesus, with names neither ancient, nor modern, neither pastoral, nor anything else; in almost all their compositions, of whatsoever genre, and on whatsoever subject matter, they would speak, or stick in, some hint about their flocks and their bagpipes, their pastures and their huts. And such a fashion was able not merely to endure quietly for a generation, but to hold out firmly against the judicious, brilliant mockery of Baretti, and survive even him.

Admirable documentation, this, of a polemically very elegant awareness of the death of a tradition (indeed, the supreme document of its kind known to us), with a view toward constituting a different tradition, another (as the historian knows quite well) "system of imitation," differently articulated, because it is not

397

only founded upon other technico-instrumental and symbolic-imaginative elements, but on other interpretations of the elements themselves, their meaning and their interrelation. But to return now to our argument, we should consider another example. In nature, at the utmost, there may occur in a certain rock formation a presence able to suggest, within a determined technico-expressive horizon, a mythical presence: concretely, a *sculpture*. Necessarily the *sculptor* (i.e. the mythpoeic producer who presents himself, in such a society, as potentially capable of guaranteeing professionally his own mythpoeic ability), should he ever come upon this exemplary rock formation, might offer it today, say, in an exhibition space as a *sculpture* (even if, hypothetically, he were to show it explicitly as a found object), so that the intentionality of the mystification devised for this natural presence also became evident, giving the consumer the chance to perceive it as an *exemplum*, and thus to accept it as such (or, conversely, of course, reject it as such). Every society, in fact, or better, every social class, constructs in its history and tends to codify its own coherent system of mythological mystifications, of varying effectiveness and richness, and it is *from out of* that system (i.e.—dynamically, however—*in* that system) that the mythological operation is made possible (that is, concretely recognizable, and thus potentially transmissible), both in its active articulation, i.e., both as production of symbols (poesis, creation), and also passively, in the immediate form of fruition. And production and fruition, it is hardly necessary to point out, take on constantly different forms and meanings (and interrelation) in relation to their historical position, that is, their particular self-configuration with regards to the social structure and the related general system of ideological superstructures.

Thus when a historical society receives, within its own systems of mythical mystification, the mythic products of earlier or (structurally) different societies, or of different classes or groups, constituting itself, precisely through this, as a historical society conscious of its own aesthetic historicity (by virtue of a structure that can determine, in its dialectic, such an ideological possibility in general), these products, insofar as they are immediately open to use, since they evidently have been alienated by their prior superstructural and ideological context, and diverted by the particular position that they have occupied in that context, immediately deform the mythical import of which they are the bearers. Here we operate on the hypothesis that among possibilities of deformation the most frequent and likely one has not materialized: the pure and simple manifestation of the product as instantly devoid of mythical possibilities, of mythical signification. (But it is not at all exceptional for a linguistic object to acquire a historical charge it originally lacked in a different historical context: a given archaeological find, read as simple *sign* when it was first produced, and even possibly produced without any mystifying intention, enters into an expressive system which can take it to be a homogeneous sign, that is, assume it as mythically contextual in the proper sense.) A corollary to this: that the lack of all mythopoeic intentionality may very well be found in the producer of the linguistic object—which doesn't prevent the consumer's egoism from perceiving, in an identical or different historical context, indifferently, a symbolic significance that remains, in direct experience, insensitive to the etymon (if it comes to be known) of the product in question. By the same token everyday experience confirms how little the full consciousness of the producer's intentionality matters to the reader of myths whenever he fails to read any symbolic signficance (no matter how the responsiblity of the failed mythical communication should then be defined); in other words: however much it matters to that reader, whenever he tries to understand the *signifying* character of a *sign*, whenever such a character has not been immediately perceived by him.

tic and a logical moment—a distinction that cannot be upheld in romantic bourgeois language, however well-founded it may be), but rather (and romantic-bourgeois culture of the imperialist era knows this quite well) in the categorical antinomy between the contemplative and the practical (the disinterested and interested) in relation to mythopoesis. In fact, once one has realized, in a maturely dialectical conception, the ideologically active (practical) character implicit in every superstructural product, and equally in any other product of mythical mystification, one must affirm that the aesthetic judgment is defined exclusively *in relation to* praxis, or rather, in the sense in which praxis is the sole measure of ideology, directly *in* praxis. The critical paraphrase that characterizes judgment truly dwells in the historical verification of the practical efficacy of the mythic product, and nowhere else: the critical paraphrase is the ideological expression of the practical verification of myth: it is born out of the attempt to gain consciousness of the myth's practicabilty, by a chain of mediations which, beginning with the experience and consumption of the myth in the act itself of reading, brings us to mythopoesis as the ideological expression of a structure, and thus to the understanding of the product in the superstructural context in general into which it is inserted, hence ultimately to structure and praxis.

The superstructural concept would remain completely empty if the series of mediations we have referred to were to remain inactive and not lead to a continual baring — in paraphrasis, in reflection on mythopoeia, in judgment, in poetics, in aesthetics—the scientific foundation of the dialectic of poiesis and praxis; if necessarily the dialectical autonomy of poiesis were to be misunderstood again, ending up in sociology, perhaps, yet concretely halted once more at the "innocent" level of the superstructure; or if, on the contrary, with the collapse of the conceptual bulkhead that defines the dialectical re-

Alfredo Giuliani

I. When the fourth-century master rhetorician Marius Victorinus realized that quantitative metrics had been superseded by new linguistic conditions, he decided that poetry should be composed "ad iudicium aurium." Dag Norberg[1] has shown that the authors of the rhythmic hymns of the fifth and sixth centuries read their Latin models—that is, quantitative verses—like prose, respecting the ordinary accents of the words. They imitated the way their models distributed the verse *cola*, that is, the pauses. Translating quantitative rhythm into syllabic number, they were in reality opening the way to a new type of versification. The Greco-Roman ear would have heard medieval liturgical poetry as simple sung prose.

We moderns have just the opposite experience when we encounter the hymn such as *In te Domine speravi* translated into prose by Savonarola, which we read as though it were poetry, or the *Songs of the Greek People*, which Tommaseo considered he had translated into prose line by line. "Ad iudicium aurium" indeed, and, one might add, "metrica ratione"; because metrics, which is the art of measuring the beat of the verse line by devising and varying rhythms and phonic values, changes with the changes in language and in our disposition to hear one way or another the relations between discourse and song. Today we have available: the old "syllabic" verse (with its favored arsis and its subdued rhythms); "accentual" verse (to which, in our interpretation, we include the preceding; thus, we do not read, for example, "Dolce e chiara è la notte e senza vento" as a

---

1. *Introduction à l'étude de la versification latine médiévale Stockholm, 1958.*

hendecasyllable, or if it is, that is irrelevant); and of a "dynamic" or "open" verse dominated by semantic-structural thrust, bound neither by the number of syllables nor the isochronism of the stresses: a verse we can call "atonal," meaning one where the stress *serves* the modules we form each time with phrases; where the "weak" (or *silent*) syllables do not gain their rhythmic vitality from the relapse of the "strong," since both are only junctures, meshes of the discourse.

This last verse-line, which in all its varied expressions we have made our own, has nothing to do with Greco-Latin metrics; nonetheless, by the mere fact of its being freed from the traditional syllabic measure, it may give the impression of having regained that sensitivity to *quantity* that was so important to Pound when, forty or fifty years ago, he was hunting for some criterion to legitimate "vers libre." Eliot faced the same problem in 1908 or 1909. Since there was no new formal path left after Swinburne (the author of his youth), Eliot intuitively found the solution in grafting the lesson of Laforgue's "vers libre" onto that offered him by the late Elizabethans, who had variously lengthened or contracted or bent "blank verse" much the way Laforgue had the alexandrine. Eliot went on to theorize upon his solution in his "Reflections on 'vers libre'" of 1917: "No *vers* is *libre* for the man who wants to do a good job"; "the ghost of some simple metre should lurk behind the arras in even the 'freest' verse; to advance menacingly as we doze, and withdraw as we rouse."

Pound's attitude was more experimental: he assayed not only the modern French poets and the Elizabethans (whose translations from the Greeks and Latins he unearthed), but also Browning, Propertius, the Provençal masters, the *stilnovisti* and Dante, Villon, the ancient Anglo-Saxons and the Chinese. How to solidify "vers libre"? Pound thought that the law of the new verse resided in *quantity*. But what exactly can quantity mean for us moderns? Is it bound up with the music of verse or the music of language? Was its loss inevitable or is that simply an illusion? In the well-known "Re Vers Libre" (the pendant to Eliot's "Reflections," and published the same year) Pound concluded his remarks on his metrical experiments thus:

I think the desire for vers libre is due to the sense of quantity reasserting itself after years of starvation. But I doubt if we can take over, for English, the rules of quantity laid down for Greek and Latin, mostly by Latin grammarians... I think progress lies rather in an attempt to approximate classical quantitative metres (NOT to copy them) than in a carelessness regarding such things.

And again in "The Tradition":

As to quantity, it is foolish to suppose that we are incapable of distinguishing a long vowel from a short one, or that we are mentally debarred from ascertaining how many consonants intervene between one vowel and the next... The movement of poetry is limited only by the nature of syllables and of articulate sound, and by the laws of music or melodic rhythm.

Ultimately, the quantity of which Pound speaks is but one element of qualities, an "ear" giving form to the tendency of modern verse to sum up in itself, fusing them into a new measure, all prior systems. The true inner law is the one Pound states in *The ABC of Reading*: "Rhythm is a form cut into TIME"; a principle girded with the following corollaries: poetry atrophies when it gets too far from music; articulate sounds have different weights and lengths; the qualities of sound (pitch and length) may be natural or modified by the interdependence of sounds; the quality of sound is inseparable from speech.

Obviously the quantity of neo-classical meters is of no interest to us; but it is worth recalling that, apart from Carducci's 'restoration' (which, by the way, was preceded by the German romantics), as early as 1903, D'Ovidio, in his "Versificazione delle *Odi Barbare*," remarked that the romance languages can have their own quantity "of a wholly physiological and euphonic character, free of any historical link to Latin quantity." It is significant then that, in discussing philologists' hypotheses about the transformation of metrics from the quantitative to the accentual (which is the critical moment of the medieval phase), D'Ovidio bluntly asserts:

...the true cause, the sole or at any rate paramount cause, of the new versification, was the new structure of spoken Latin and the Romance tongues, which is to say, the mutation of verse was the natural effect of a language transformation.

Likewise T. S. Eliot, in "The Music of Poetry":

...the task of the poet will differ, not only according to his personal constitution, but according to the period in which he finds himself. At some periods, the task is to explore the musical possibilities of an established convention of the relation of the idiom of verse to that of speech; at other periods, the task is to catch up with the changes in colloquial speech, which are fundamentally changes in thought and sensibility. This cyclical movement also has a very great influence upon our critical judgement.

D'Ovidio's point of view concerns the radical transformation of one language into another; Eliot's the periodical shifts poetic language undergoes in its internal dynamic (Must I draw on my own resources or resort to the common language?). Our situation is one of a profound transformation in the common language from the nineteenth century to the present day, and thus it includes, indeed exacerbates, the necessity of adapting to shifts in thought and sensibility.

406

II. A history of the *metrical restlessness* experienced by the most recent tradition would probably offer, if not great surprises, at any rate useful indications for viewing the question of verse in terms of a redemptive formula and of neurosis, that is, of ritual. Metrical restlessness is a symptom revealing the poet's anxiety about reality.

The first modern given was the rebellion—symbolic—against the hendecasyllable: "Scarso, o nipote di Rea, ha l'endecasillabo il passo." ("Faint, o descendent of Rhea, is the footfall of hendecasyllables.") And since every era finds what it is looking for, Carducci discovered the "poses" of the blank verse hexameter of Parini's *"Giorno"*; while Thovez, toward the end of the century, sought to revitalize metrics with the "dactylic pulse," *"l'onda dattilica."* But meanwhile, the obsession with quickening the pace of the traditional line has broken its measure. As long as we treat hendecasyllables (or *quinary* and *septenary*, which amount to the same thing), we are dealing with a rhythmic convention that reduces sound kernels to the uniform time of the syllable (for this and this alone is "syllabic" verse: not a verse with a certain number of syllables, but with a certain number of preestablished sonorities wrapped in the syllabic beat). If, instead, we change "beat," while continuing to count syllables or feet, then the new caesuras, the different intonation and unexpected structural requirements, will lead us to ponder the nature (or naturalness) of this new "beat."

We have spoken of Thovez—a poet who clearly reveals the natural interweaving of metrics and linguistics. "Il poema dell'adolescenza," published in 1901 but written between 1890 and 1895, metrically speaking, comes out of an admiration for the Greeks, the example of the German lyric, the shock of Whitman's free verse, and reflections for and against Carducci. The result is not merely gray and earnest: it is also totally free of archaeological impediments. Not only is it monotonous: it is precise. Juxtaposed with Gozzano, Thovez is a bit heart-wrenching. He is an austere and elegiac, dejected narcissist, a poetic soul no object on earth can help embody; even his sensations are idealized. The tragic emotion he possesses is choked by moralism. Without a grain of wit, without the palest hint of play or ironic dividedness, he anticipates all the non-vitality of the Crepuscular poets, and seems to fall permanently short of invention. Despite this, he has a distinct epic vein and his diction is clean-cut; and his monomaniacal metrics (a hexameter composed of two octosyllables in consistently dactylic rhythm) reflects with great dignity, and with a syntactical neatness that is itself revolutionary, the purpose of opposing D'Annunzian artifice with a modern *sermo humilis*:

> *Dark, misted hills beneath a sluggish sky,*
> *green sea of woods, of pale knolls receding,*
> *and briefly glimpsed, fast-guttering sun: autumn.*
> *Bluish smoke rising from red roofs amid the green,*
> *and the trees' heavy sleep; then, in a flash,*
> *faint uproar, laughter, in the parched corn fields.*

("Outburst")

Were Thovez to gaze on objects with greater "anxiety," more edgily, we would already be at Pavese. He already has the latter's intonation, in fact; it takes one look at "Grappa a settembre" to prove it:

> *The mornings run their course, bright and deserted*
> *along the river's banks, which at dawn turn foggy,*
> *darkening their green, while they wait for the sun.*
> *In the last house, still damp, at the field's edge,*
> *they sell tobacco, which is blackish in color*
> *and tastes of sugar: it gives off a bluish haze.*
> *They have grappa there too, the color of water.*

(tr. William Arrowsmith)

408

It is interesting to note that, to make his verse gel—after the initial "rigmarole," "an emphatic cadence," semi-instinctual—Pavese enlisted the aid of the Elizabethans. The greater "form" and nervous energy of Pavese's verse in respect to Thovez seems self-evident and cannot quell our desire to compare the two: for both share (beyond Whitman and their Turinese background) that "emphatic cadence" constantly kept in the low registers, and a narrative relaxation, a basic "prosiness" conceived as a moral obligation to truthfulness, and also, shall we say, an ideological naturalism they secretly reject (we are thinking of Thovez's very Pavesian cry: "Make me live! Give me a body that is not base!"). There are other similarities, too, but let us keep to metrics. The accentual verse of *Lavorare stanca* ("Hard Work"), which generally varies from four to six beats, consists mostly of a thirteen-syllable line that in its very regularity evinces a strongly abiding rhythmic allegiance to tradition.

Similar in style, and falling chronologically between Thovez and Pavese, is the Bacchelli of the *Poemi lirici* (1914). Bacchelli too has forged a line to suit his needs, "a measure in four beats scanned on four stresses," which, perhaps because it is the least "competitive," seems rather independent from the old established way of hearing verse:

> *Spring/ in the gardens./ Behind the clouds/ desire*
> *changes clime,/ they move on/ and I stay,/ the air*
> *promises/ now rain/ now incredible/ clarity,*
> *I stay here/ seated/ in line with a row/ of wallflowers.*
> ("Appassionata," 7)

We have divided the "beats" with bars to show the fluidity of the movements. Bacchelli seems the most natural, perhaps because he confines himself to recording his own moods, to moralizing them with that intrusive "incapacity for introspection" Malaparte once noted (in an essay well worth remembering, which appeared in issue 38–39 of "Prospettive").

But let's come away from this digression with at least a hypothesis. In the "arguments" included in the 1930 edition, Bacchelli called his *Poemi lirici* an "adventure of adolescence, in a metrical, grammatical and syntactic sense as well." The influences are all too evident. Thovez's *Poema* was also an instance of metrical adolescence, compared to the mature forms of the turn of the century. And Pavese, in turn, in the second edition of his *Lavorare stanca*, calls his book "an adolescent's adventure," treating it as a venture put behind him, in a technical sense as well, after that naturally experimental period of life. We can ask ourselves then if what we are viewing here is not the adolescence of a line of modern poetry that seeks as best it can to mold a meter directly onto things or onto biography; if what he have here is not ultimately an anticipatory, organic intention: the recurrent ambition to create a formula that can compensate for the youthful, obviously traumatic, refusal of traditional poetic means—basically an antidote to the toxins the privileged rhythmical structures produced.

III. The hypothesis and the choice of examples in the preceding paragraph are meant to have a primarily allegorical weight. A complete sketch would have to take into account other more peripheral experiments in twentieth-century style (Jahier, Borgese...) and apply a present-day perspective to the metrical restlessness of the Novecento itself, its substantial insecurity, its compromise between modernity and classicism. Apparently the simple task has fallen to us of drawing attention back to the basic metrical crisis that from roughly the mid-nineteenth century gives way both to the semi-aware exercise of new meters, and to deliberate periodic experiments. The question of metrics is forever being posed in terms of the forward thrust of language—as we have seen in the least sensational of examples. But we might now see it more calmly on the opposite side: in the awkward scandal, the flagrant crudeness of the futurist rebels. The symptomatic significance of their "verso libero" is too well known for us to dwell on here. Yet it is worthwhile to reiterate that some of the motivations behind Marinetti's poetics have, far from vanishing in the whirlpools, followed the historical current, which was considerably more impetuous, astounding and rapid than anything the futurists could ever have expected. Why haven't these motivations died away? Because, as rhetoric, they still serve to illuminate the vital connection between metrics, grammar, and syntax. Marinetti's famous "simultaneity" and *objectivism*, his brutal assault (no doubt mirroring brutality in general) against poetical legitimism, filter out certain necessary, no longer adolescent experiments in our world, which is reified yet brimming with projective energies. Thus *at the present moment* we have no trouble understanding and adding among our tools the American type (as Charles Olson presents it) of "dynamic" or "open" or "atonal" verse we have already experimented with over the last few years, as the following paradigmatic excerpts should bear out:

consistent tail! frigid whip! oh muscle! oh fist! penetrating:
you've drunk enough (such was the warning); you gambled,
　　　[you sweated (such
a game you played, animal!); (such a game, beast!); chew
　　　[your hay! trample your
straw! and find me, now, animal!
　　　　　　(and I was taking him back to the silent stable);

　　　　　　　　　　　　　　　　(Sanguineti)

But me-here-now, sorrowful suspension, I know
it's not enough, I cannot accept the conclusion,
I do not indulge, it's the same, neglect
knits its brows. Over the years all becomes
symbolic, understanding is hearsay, poetry
no more than paralogia of the same old story.

(Giuliani)

His face expresses great suffering,
they are drawn out one after another in a hurry;
              biologically the same
(the bewilderment of the landscapes, the melancholy of the ships)
point of view   a constant effort, let them think
                what they want. In the wake of tradition
    comédie à tiroir,
    entirely different:

(Balestrini)

Over there, he squeezes the knob, towards,
there's none, neither certainty, nor exit, on the wall,
the ear, then to open, an uncertainty, doesn't open,
answer, the keys between the fingers, the belly open,
hand on the belly, trembles on the leaves,
rushing, across the sand, the point of the blade,
the son, under the desk, sleeps in the room.

(Porta)

(Another way would be "I love you"/tell her, insist you love her very much if
you've really decided to lose her/you'll see how she leaves pacified.)
If instead you're faking and you want her/to think "how generous (or proud)
he is and his heart, he expects in reply/that I'd surprise him and throw
all my limbs around his neck"/it's a matter of shabbiness.

(Pagliarani)

412

Important here—more so than it would seem—is Olson's helpful observation (from "Projective Verse," 1950) that the new verse is written in the meter of breath, and not for the eye but according to the ear.[2] Despite everything, we still risk writing for the eye, compromising the "projective" qualities of the meter which we have managed to master. We do not wish, however, to relapse (and here is why we are a bit apprehensive) into some historically more aware form of *paroliberismo* [trans. note—futurist "words in freedom"]. Our metrical evolution, precisely because it has been delayed and thwarted by the all-powerful courtliness of our classical language, precisely because it occurred under difficult conditions, gradually, in an absence of great masters, with innumerable relapses, is finally adult, and in no further need of manifestos. What it does need, on the other hand, is a good deal of passion and clarity—and poets who know the pleasure of writing verse.

2. Charles Olson: *Projective Verse,* in "Poetry New York" n. 3, 1950; and now translated in "Verri" n. 1, 1961.

NANNI BALESTRINI was born in Milan in 1935, and lived between there and Rome until relocating in Paris some ten years ago. He has been one of the editors of the seminal magazine *Il Verri*, and, with Alfredo Giuliani, was co-director of the remarkable bimonthly, *Quindici*, between 1967–1969. Besides his editorial work for publishers such as Cooperativa Scrittori and Feltrinelli, he was one of the driving forces and organizers behind "Gruppo 63", the experimental movement that followed close on the heels of the *Novissimi*'s appearance. Among his own publications are: *Il sasso appeso* (1961), *Come si agisce* (1963), *Tristano* (1966), *Ma noi facciamone un'altra* (1968), *Vogliamo tutto* (1971), *Le ballate della Signora Richmond* (1977), *Ipocalisse* (1986), *Il ritorno della Signora Richmond* (1987) and *L'editore* (1988).

ALFREDO GIULIANI was born in Pesaro in 1924 and lives in Rome. He holds a degree in philosophy from the University of Rome and currently teaches Italian literature at the University of Chieti. In addition to being the poetry editor of *Il Verri* between 1957–1961 and the director of the bimonthly *Quindici* from 1967–1969, he is a regular contributor to the literary pages of the daily *La Republica*. Among his published volumes are: *Il cuore zoppo* (1955), *Povera Juliet e altre poesie* (1965), *Il tautofono* (1969), *Il giovane Max* (1972), *Chi l'avrebbe mai detto* (1973), *Autunno del novecento* (1984), *Versi e non versi* (1986) and *Ebbrezza di placamenti* (1993), and two collections of critical essays, *Immagini e maniere* (1965) and *Le droghe di Marsiglia* (1977). Giuliani has translated work by such modern writers as Dylan Thomas, T.S. Eliot, William Empson and James Joyce, as well as Ben Jonson and Shakespeare.

ELIO PAGLIARANI was born in Viserba (Rimini) in 1927. He moved to Milan in 1945 where he worked in an office and later received a degree in political science from the University of

Padua. He worked for years in Milan teaching in trade and high schools and was an editor for the daily *Avanti*, until his move to Rome in 1960. He has been a regular contributor to and on the editorial board of numerous magazines, including *Nuovi argomenti*, *Rendiconti*, *Nuova corrente*, *Il menabò*, *Officina*, *Il Verri* and *Quindici*. After the publication of the *Novissimi* Pagliarani took part in "Gruppo 63" and, with Guido Guglielmi, edited the anthology of contemporary poetry, *Manuale di poesia sperimentale*, in 1966. He has been the theater critic for the daily *Paese Sera* and in the 70s founded and edited the literary magazine *Periodo ipotetico*. Among his publications as a poet are: *Cronache e eltre poesie* (1954), *Inventario privato* (1959), *La ragazza Carla e altre poesie* (1962), *Lezione di fisica e Fecaloro* (1968), *Esercizi platonici* (1985) and *Epigrammi Ferraresi* (1987). His forthcoming book is a collection of all the fragments of his long poem *La ballata di Rudy* which have appeared to date.

ANTONIO PORTA (Leo Paolazzi) was born in Vicenza in 1935, lived most of his life in Milan and died on a business trip to Rome in 1989. In the early 60s he was one of the youngest members of the editorial staff of *Il Verri* and, with Corrado Costa and Adriano Spatola, also edited the poetry magazine *Malebolge* from 1964–1966. He participated in the various manifestations of "Gruppo 63", as a linear and visual poet, and was one of the founding editors of *Quindici* in 1967. For many years he worked as an editor in the publishing industry, with such houses as Bompiani, Sonzogno and Feltrinelli, and was also the literary critic for the daily *Il Corriere della Sera* and a regular contributor to the weekly book review *Tuttolibri*. In 1979 he edited the well-known anthology *Poesia degli anni settanta*, and, from its inception, was on the editorial board of the influential cultural tabloid *Alfabeta*. Among his publications as a poet are: *La palpebra rovesciata* (1960), *Aprire* (1963), *Cara* (1969), *Metropolis* (1971), *Week-*

end (1974), *Quanto ho da dirvi* (1977), *Passi passagi* (1980), *Melusina* (1987) and *Il giardiniere contro il becchino* (1988). As a novelist his published work includes *Partita* (1967), *Il re del magazzino* (1978) and *Se fosse tutto un tradimento* (1981), while as a playwright he published *La presa di potere di Ivan lo sciocco* (1975) and *La stangata persiana* (1985).

EDOARDO SANGUINETI was born in Genoa in 1930, where he teaches Italian literature at the University. He was a vital participant in "Gruppo 63" and perhaps one of its most important theorists. His books of poetry include: *Laborintus* (1956), *Opus metricum* (1960), *Triperuno* (1964), *Wirrwarr* (1972), *Postkarten* (1978), *Segnalibro* (1982), *Nivissimum testamentum* (1986) and *Bisbidis* (1987). He has published two novels *Capriccio italiano* (1963) and *Il giuoco dell'oca* (1967), as well as numerous volumes of critical essays including: *Tre studi danteschi* (1961), *Tra liberty e crepuscolarismo* (1961), *Interpretazione di Malebolge* (1961), *Alberto Moravia* (1962), *Ideologia e linguaggio* (1965), *Guido Gozzano* (1966), *Il realismo di Dante* (1966), *La missione del critico* (1987) and *Letteratura del Decameron* (1989). In 1969 Sanguineti edited the seminal two-volume anthology, *Poesia italiana del novecento*. For the theater, he has translated texts from Aeschylus, Euripides, Sophocles and Seneca, as well as an adaptation of Ariosto's *Orlando Furioso*, and collaborated, writing texts and libretti, with the noted composer Luciano Berio. Sanguineti has also served as an elected official in the Genoa City Council and as a member of the Italian Parliament.

SUN & MOON CLASSICS

This publication was made possible, in part, through an operational grant from the Andrew W. Mellon Foundation and through contributions from the following individuals and organizations:

Tom Ahern (Foster, Rhode Island)
Charles Altieri (Seattle, Washington)
John Arden (Galway, Ireland)
Paul Auster (Brooklyn, New York)
Jesse Huntley Ausubel (New York, New York)
Luigi Ballerini (Los Angeles, California)
Dennis Barone (West Hartford, Connecticut)
Jonathan Baumbach (Brooklyn, New York)
Roberto Bedoya (Los Angeles, California)
Guy Bennett (Los Angeles, California)
Bill Berkson (Bolinas, California)
Steve Benson (Berkeley, California)
Charles Bernstein and Susan Bee (New York, New York)
Dorothy Bilik (Silver Spring, Maryland)
Alain Bosquet (Paris, France)
In Memoriam: John Cage
In Memoriam: Camilo José Cela
Bill Corbett (Boston, Massachusetts)
Fielding Dawson (New York, New York)
Robert Crosson (Los Angeles, California)
Tina Darragh and P. Inman (Greenbelt, Maryland)
Christopher Dewdney (Toronto, Canada)
Arkadii Dragomoschenko (St. Petersburg, Russia)
George Economou (Norman, Oklahoma)
Richard Elman (Stony Brook, New York)
Kenward Elmslie (Calais, Vermont)
Elaine Equi and Jerome Sala (New York, New York)
Lawrence Ferlinghetti (San Francisco, California)
Richard Foreman (New York, New York)
Howard N. Fox (Los Angeles, California)
Jerry Fox (Aventura, Florida)
In Memoriam: Rose Fox
Melvyn Freilicher (San Diego, California)
Miro Gavran (Zagreb, Croatia)
Allen Ginsberg (New York, New York)
Peter Glassgold (Brooklyn, New York)

Barbara Guest (Berkeley, California)
Perla and Amiram V. Karney (Bel Air, California)
Václav Havel (Prague, The Czech Republic)
Lyn Hejinian (Berkeley, California)
Fanny Howe (La Jolla, California)
Harold Jaffe (San Diego, California)
Ira S. Jaffe (Albuquerque, New Mexico)
Ruth Prawer Jhabvala (New York, New York)
Pierre Joris (Albany, New York)
Alex Katz (New York, New York)
Tom LaFarge (New York, New York)
Mary Jane Lafferty (Los Angeles, California)
Michael Lally (Santa Monica, California)
Norman Lavers (Jonesboro, Arkansas)
Jerome Lawrence (Malibu, California)
Stacey Levine (Seattle, Washington)
Herbert Lust (Greenwich, Connecticut)
Norman MacAffee (New York, New York)
Rosemary Macchiavelli (Washington, DC)
In Memoriam: Mary McCarthy
Harry Mulisch (Amsterdam, The Netherlands)
Iris Murdoch (Oxford, England)
Martin Nakell (Los Angeles, California)
In Memoriam: bpNichol
NORLA (Norwegian Literature Abroad) (Oslo, Norway)
Claes Oldenburg (New York, New York)
Toby Olson (Philadelphia, Pennsylvania)
Maggie O'Sullivan (Hebden Bridge, England)
Rochelle Owens (Norman, Oklahoma)
Bart Parker (Providence, Rhode Island)
Marjorie and Joseph Perloff (Pacific Palisades, California)
Dennis Phillips (Los Angeles, California)
Carl Rakosi (San Francisco, California)
Tom Raworth (Cambridge, England)
David Reed (New York, New York)
Ishmael Reed (Oakland, California)
Tom Roberdeau (Los Angeles, California)
Janet Rodney (Santa Fe, New Mexico)
Joe Ross (Washington, DC)
Jerome and Diane Rothenberg (Encinitas, California)
Edward Ruscha (Los Angeles, California)
Dr. Marvin and Ruth Sackner (Miami Beach, Florida)

Floyd Salas (Berkeley, California)
Tom Savage (New York, New York)
Leslie Scalapino (Oakland, California)
James Sherry (New York, New York)
Aaron Shurin (San Francisco, California)
Charles Simic (Strafford, New Hampshire)
Gilbert Sorrentino (Stanford, California)
Catharine R. Stimpson (Staten Island, New York)
John Taggart (Newburg, Pennsylvania)
Nathaniel Tarn (Tesuque, New Mexico)
Fiona Templeton (New York, New York)
Mitch Tuchman (Los Angeles, California)
Paul Vangelisti (Los Angeles, California)
Vita Brevis Foundation (Antwerp, Belgium)
Hannah Walker and Ceacil Eisner (Orlando, Florida)
Wendy Walker (New York, New York)
Anne Walter (Carnac, France)
Jeffery Weinstein (New York, New York)
Mac Wellman (Brooklyn, New York)
Arnold Wesker (Hay on Wye, England)

If you would like to be a contributor to this series, please send your tax-deductible contribution to The Contemporary Arts Educational Project, Inc., a non-profit corporation, 6026 Wilshire Boulevard, Los Angeles, California 90036.

SUN & MOON CLASSICS